THE FIRST PHARAOHS

THEIR LIVES AND AFTERLIVES

THE FIRST PHARAOHS

THEIR LIVES AND AFTERLIVES

AIDAN DODSON

The American University in Cairo Press
Cairo   New York

First published in 2021 by
The American University in Cairo Press
113 Sharia Kasr el Aini, Cairo, Egypt
One Rockefeller Plaza, 10th Floor, New York, NY 10020
www.aucpress.com

ISBN 978 1 649 03093 1

Names: Dodson, Aidan, 1962- author.
Title: The first pharaohs : their lives and afterlives / Aidan Dodson.
Identifiers: LCCN 2021010557 | ISBN 9781649030931 (hardback)
Subjects: LCSH: Tombs--Egypt. | Egypt--Kings and rulers. |
   Egypt--History--Early Dynastic Period, ca. 3100-ca. 2686 B.C. |
   Egypt--History--Third dynasty, ca. 2649-2575 B.C. | Egypt--Antiquities.
Classification: LCC DT85 .D63 2021 | DDC 932/.0120922--dc23

1 2 3 4 5   25 24 23 22 21

Designed by Sally Boylan
Printed in China

To Big Sister Anne

CONTENTS

PREFACE

This book marks a return to an old love: after many years of an academic center of gravity resting in the late second and early first millennia BC, I have now shifted back over 1,500 years to the formative phases of pharaonic civilization, which had fascinated me in my earliest days as a young enthusiast. It also marks a shift in the Life and Afterlife series from dealing with a single individual and a few decades, to a book that covers not only a series of rulers, but also a span of some five centuries, embracing the period from the unification of Egypt down to the historical and archaeological watershed represented by the foundation of the Fourth Dynasty by King Seneferu. However, the underlying approach remains the same: to give accessible accounts of what we know of the lives and monuments of the protagonists, how they were remembered by their own posterity, and how that detail has been ascertained in modern times.

In the present case, the latter two aspects comprise a significantly greater part of the book than in earlier volumes in the series. Thus, chapter 4 follows the posthumous story of the kings during the millennia following their demise, and brings into play the way in which the ancient Egyptians themselves received and made use of the historical and material culture that survived from their own remote past. One fascinating aspect is how one of the earliest royal tombs was appropriated as that of the god Osiris, giving a whole new purpose for the funerary landscape that had been created a millennium earlier for the kings of the first two dynasties.

Moving forward to modern times, chapter 5 is in many ways a case study in the way that history is written for periods at the very dawn of literacy, where there is a dearth of contemporary standing monuments, and archaeology forms a crucial part of the available data. This includes how the first modern Egyptologists assimilated data that had been transmitted through the lens of material produced during later periods of ancient Egyptian history. The chapter also shows the way in which knowledge can be utterly transformed by a handful of archaeological discoveries from, in the case of the First Dynasty, a list of second-and third-hand names lacking any material verification, to a solid sequence of kings, all of them attested by significant archaeological and contemporary epigraphic remains.

On the other hand, although nearer to us in time, the sequence of Second and Third Dynasty monarchs remains obscure to a greater or lesser degree, a circumstance that allows light to be shed on the methodologies that may be applied to producing at least a credible working hypothesis. Attribution of known monuments remains problematic, not to mention the identification of new ones, such as the likely pyramid of Huni, which was "hidden in plain sight" for well over a century before being reidentified in the 1980s (page 144). On the debit side, the Unfinished Pyramid of Zawiyet el-Aryan, long held to be a Third Dynasty monument, is now recognized as being of mid-Fourth Dynasty date.[1] Accordingly, this book can in no way claim to present anything approaching a definitive picture of the history of the first three dynasties, but nevertheless aims to give the reader an overview of the material and its interpretation in a historical sense in the light of current understandings.

To forestall comments by readers, I acknowledge that the application of the term "pharaoh" (itself the biblical version of the Egyptian *pr-ʿ3*) to refer to the individuals covered in this book is wholly anachronistic: it is not found as a designation of the king of Egypt until the New Kingdom, and its widespread use is even later. However, it has long since passed into the modern English language as a unique manner of describing an Egyptian king, and I am using it in this sense here.

As always, thanks are owed to various friends and colleagues (often one and the same!) for sharing their knowledge and offprints, welcoming me to their sites, and providing images, in particular Sarah Austin, Mirek Bárta, Hussein Bassir, Laurel Bestock, Reg Clark, Janice Kamrin, Geoffrey Lenox-Smith, Peter Lundström (aka pharaoh.com), David Moyer, Chris Naunton, Hana Navratilova, Adela Oppenheim, Joanne Rowland, the late Nabil Swelim, and Tarek Swelim. For proofreading, my gratitude goes as always to my wife, Dyan Hilton, and also to Alison Ball, Victoria Baylis-Jones, Reg Clark, Vanessa Foott, Claire Gilmour, Anne Hilton, and Paula Terrey. Residual errors of course remain my sole responsibility.

ABBREVIATIONS AND CONVENTIONS

Ashmolean	Ashmolean Museum, Oxford, UK.
Berlin	Ägyptisches Museum, Berlin, Germany.
BM	British Museum, London, UK.
BP	Before Present (i.e., before AD 1950, used for some scientifically derived dates, especially prior to the fourth millennium BC).
Brussels	Musée Art & Histoire/Museum Kunst & Geschiedenis, Brussels, Belgium.
Cairo	Egyptian Museum/Grand Egyptian Museum, Cairo, Egypt.
Garstang	Garstang Museum, University of Liverpool, UK.
Liverpool	World Museum, National Museums Liverpool, UK.
Louvre	Musée du Louvre, Paris, France.
Milan	Civiche Raccolte Archeologiche, Milan, Italy.
MMA	Metropolitan Museum of Art, New York, USA.
NMS	National Museums Scotland, Edinburgh, UK.
RMO	Rijksmuseum van Oedheden, Leiden, Netherlands.
Turin	Museo Egizio, Turin, Italy.
*	biography of individual available in Bierbrier 2019.

Adopting a uniform means of referring to the earliest kings of Egypt is somewhat problematic since, as discussed on pages 111–12, cartouche-enclosed names appear definitively only at the beginning of the Fourth Dynasty, and the "standard" five-fold Egyptian royal titulary was not universally adopted until the Sixth. During the first three dynasties the only name form we have for—almost—all kings is the Horus-name, which is accordingly used in this book as the standard way of referring to a given monarch.

The principal exception is the use of "Djoser" for the Horus Netjerkhet, for which there is no evidence of contemporary usage. However, it has become so ubiquitous as his modern designation that to insist on using the Horus-name for full consistency would seem to be gratuitously obscurist.

INTRODUCTION

Human occupation in Egypt goes back until at least around 300,000 BP, as attested by tools of the Acheulian lithic culture along most of the Nile Valley, implying the presence of *Homo erectus*–type early hominids.[1] However, the earliest actual human remains recovered from Egypt are of the anatomically modern human type, found at Taramsa Hill, 2.5 kilometers southwest of Dendara, in what may be a formal burial.[2] They date to around 50,000 BP, a time at which Neanderthals were still present in Europe. The next oldest Egyptian remains, from Nazlet Khater, come from some 20,000 years later.

These people lived during a period of hyper-aridity that lasted from around 100,000 BP until around 22,000 BP. A more humid environment then returned, before super-dry conditions returned around 20,000 BP. Thus, during these earliest times, habitation was periodically possible deep in what is now the Sahara desert. This would remain the case for some time. The humid interval, which would persist into the fifth millennium BC, coincided with the first Egyptian Epipaleolithic cultures, which were based on hunting and fishing. Subsequently, however, there was a move to the harvesting of wild grain, coinciding with a climatic shift that gave a degree of rainfall for a millennium. Aridity reasserted itself around 7000 BP,[3] and it is from around this time that we have the first monumental structures in the Nile Valley, at Nabta Playa, west of Abu Simbel (fig. 1).[4]

However, dryer conditions had already begun to intrude during the sixth millennium—around Farafra Oasis the density of the settlements rapidly drops after 5300 BC.[5] This renewed desertification had the effect of making life outside the Nile Valley increasingly untenable. There was thus an increasing shift of regional populations to the river-irrigated fertile margins of the Nile and its Delta. The cultures that developed here comprised a mixture of elements from the now-desert areas to the west and some coming in from the east, including Palestine, the latter seemingly including cultivated wheat and sheep/goats, although these creatures had previously been seen at Farafra.[6]

FIGURE 1 The Nabta Playa stone circle as displayed at the Nubian Museum, Aswan.

These cultures included the Qarunian (Fayyum B) and Neolithic Fayyumian (Fayyum A) (c. 5500–3800 BC), together with that of Merimde Beni Salama (c. 5000–4100 BC) in Lower Egypt. In the Nile Valley, the Badarian culture appears around 4400 BC, and interfaces with the Naqada I culture[7] around 3800 BC, marking what is generally seen as the beginning of the Predynastic Period.[8] Material from Naqada itself suggests that settlements were relatively small, and characterized by features such as enclosures for domestic animals, and human graves of ovoid form in which the body was placed in a fetal position, facing east. In the north, the Maadi-Buto culture appears around the same time as the Naqada I in the south.

The subsequent Naqada II series of southern cultures begin around 3700 BC,[9] followed around 3350 BC by those of Naqada III, which merge into the Early Dynastic Period.[10] Naqada II saw the introduction of a more figurative decoration of pottery, while siltstone cosmetic palettes became an important feature of grave equipment. The latter became vehicles for increasingly sophisticated artistic productions around the time of the transition to Naqada III toward the end of the fourth millennium (fig. 10). Other items of material culture included pear-shaped maceheads, replacing the earlier conical form; these would become vehicles for artistic effort in support of expressions of the power of their owners. Some graves become more regular in form, heralding the introduction of brick linings in elite interments later in the period.

Thus, as the Naqada II material culture evolves, an increasingly stratified society becomes apparent, especially in the south, with the development of what would ultimately become an Upper Egyptian kingdom. The center of this would appear to have been Hierakonpolis (Nekhen),[11] whose settlement goes back to Badarian times. It appears to have reached its first peak about 3700–3500 BC, when the settlement extended from its later center in the cultivation back into an area of low desert some three kilometers wide, and with elements up to 2.5 kilometers into the desert. The latter included tombs of great size, including HK6/T23, dating to Naqada IIC (fig. 3), accompanied by fragments of the earliest known life-sized statue. These sepulchers are rather different in form and furnishings from elite burials elsewhere in the south of Egypt (cf. pages 6–7), suggesting an exceptional status for those buried there.

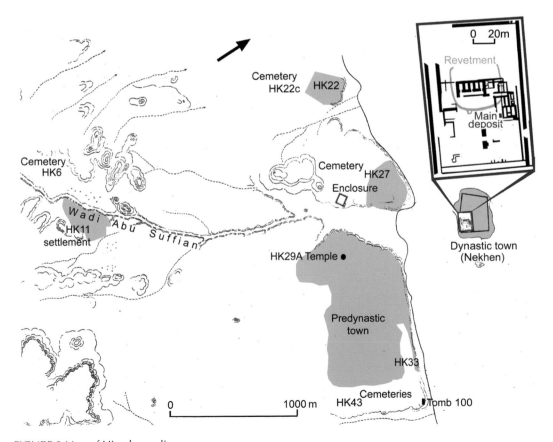

FIGURE 2 Map of Hierakonpolis.

FIGURE 3 Tomb 23 at the Hierakonpolis HK6 cemetery.

Close to the edge of the cultivation at Hierakonpolis, another cemetery includes a tomb of similar date, with the first example of painted decoration (fig. 4). These monuments are likely to be those of the proto-kings who would be among the ancestors of the later kings of all of Egypt. Tombs of very similar design to Hierakonpolis tomb 100—a brick-lined cutting divided in two by a partition wall—were constructed in Naqada cemetery T, and together are architectural ancestors of the early royal tombs at Abydos (see next chapter).[12]

What broader political organization existed during this time is unclear, but a credible model would be that regional polities were now coming into existence along the Nile Valley during the second half of Naqada II, including two centered on Hierakonpolis and Naqada repectively. Doubtless part of the latter will have been the site of Koptos, from which have been recovered what have generally been regarded as the earliest colossal statues in Egypt, depicting the local deity Min (fig. 5).

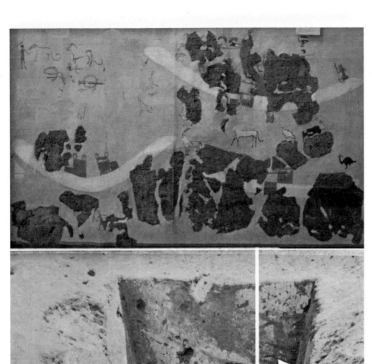

FIGURE 4 Section of the
paintings in Hierakonpolis
tomb 100 (Cairo), and view of
the tomb as discovered.

Another polity may have been centered on Thinis, as in its cemetery, Abydos, we find
some tombs of exceptional size. Burials at the site cover the whole of the Predynastic Period,
and while most were spread, over a kilometer deep, along the edge of the desert, cemetery
U lies along a wadi (much as was the case with HK6 at Hierakonpolis), on the eastern
extremity of the area now known as Umm el-Qaab (figs. 9, 15).[13] Cemetery U contains
some six hundred burials going back in time to Naqada I, and culminates in a number of
brick-lined tombs, some of exceptional size, from the very end of the fourth millennium.

FIGURE 5 Colossal figures of Min, from Koptos (Ashmolean AN1894-105c-e; CM JE30770).

Surviving contents and the size of some tombs indicate that cemetery U was a burial place of an elite throughout its existence. Interestingly, however, there is a dearth of particularly large graves at Umm el-Qaab during Naqada IIC—just the period when cemetery T at Naqada begins to include big tombs, and when tomb 100 was constructed at Hierakonpolis. Large tombs resume at Umm el-Qaab in Naqada IID. This could imply the absorption of the Thinite polity into the Hierakonpolitan one during Naqada IIC, with its center and elite cemetery being moved to the Thinite area (at Umm el-Qaab) during Naqada IID. Such a process would have included the assimilation of Naqada itself into the new political unit, lying as it did between Hierakonpolis and Thinis.[14]

If so, this will have been the final stage of a progressive merging of Upper Egyptian polities during the last centuries of the fourth millennium into a kingdom that probably embraced much of the Egyptian portion of the Nile Valley, with its center at Thinis. Nevertheless, Hierakonpolis remained important, perhaps supporting the idea that the Thinite kings were actually of the line that had previously ruled in Hierakonpolis,[15] now shifted to a location better situated for a final push into the north.

As for what lay in the north, a range of Delta sites have been investigated, including Buto in the west, and Minshat Abu Omar, Kafr Hassan Dowud, and Tell el-Farkha in the east. The latter[16] preserves ample evidence of a highly stratified society, including gold-covered statuettes of presumably the local ruler and his son (fig. 6). Although they indicate that elements of southern culture were increasingly present alongside local ones, and those deriving from Palestine, from Naqada IIB times onward,[17] the diversity of the local elements suggest that the kind of cultural cohesion apparent in the south during the late Predynastic was not present in the north.

This would argue against there ever having been the unified Lower Egyptian kingdom hinted at by later iconography. For example, names determined by kings wearing the Red Crown, generally associated with Lower Egypt, appear on the Palermo fragment (fig. 124) of the Fifth Dynasty Annals Stone(s) (see pages 112–15, fig. 98),[18] and were presumably intended to represent Predynastic kings of the north. In this, we may see a retrospective attempt to underpin the geographical component of the traditional duality of the Egyptian monarchy.[19] It would reflect a fictionalization of the past that is not uncommon in myths of state origins around the world.

FIGURE 6 Gilded wood male figure from Tell el-Farkha (Cairo R-486).

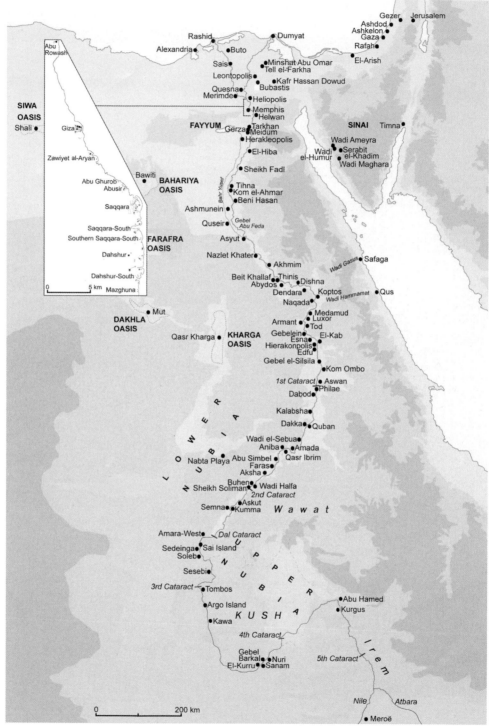

FIGURE 7 Map of Egypt and Nubia.

1 THE FIRST DYNASTY

Protodynastic Times

Among the final kings of the south must have been the owner of the huge tomb U-j at Umm el-Qaab (figs. 8, 9, 15).[1] It originally comprised six chambers surrounding a central burial room, in a configuration that has been interpreted as representing a subterranean palace for the dead king; this was later extended to the west and south. It was originally roofed with wood beams with one or more layers of mud brick and matting above the ceiling, but the form of any superstructure remains unclear. This is because of the almost total lack of preservation above the level of the substructure walls, not only in U-j, but also in almost all other tombs at the site. However, a few traces may suggest a concealed sand tumulus directly above the wooden roofs of the substructure in at least some later tombs. The whole structure may have been covered by a mound of gravel, perhaps defined by brick retaining walls, although no actual remains of such a mound have been identified at Umm el-Qaab.[2]

The tomb contained a considerable number of imported wine jars of so-called "Abydos wares," indicating the degree of interaction between Egypt and the Levant at the end of the fourth millennium. Such imports are found throughout Egypt during the First Dynasty, but the distribution of the two variants of the ware is somewhat different, with the finer of them found predominantly in the royal tombs at Umm el-Qaab, and the other mainly found in private burials elsewhere in Egypt, including the large tombs of the dynasty at Saqqara (page 22).[3]

The international links evidenced by the pottery can also be seen in elaborately decorated "slate" (more correctly siltstone) palettes that are a feature of the turn of the fourth and third millennia. Originating from a functional item that had been in use since late Naqada I times, these palettes now became high-status display items, with scenes of animals, hunting, and warfare (fig. 10a–c); similar scenes appear on knife handles (e.g., fig. 10d) and maceheads (see pages 10, 18, below).[4] Some decorative elements can be derived

FIGURE 8 The Umm el-Qaab cemetery at Abydos, viewed from the east.

from earlier Egyptian sources, such as painted pottery and the paintings in Hierakonpolis tomb 100. However, the palettes and knife handles, in particular, also incorporate significant material paralleled in Mesopotamian art, such as long-necked fantastic beasts and images of a "beast-master," who is also found on cylinder seals of the time. Accordingly, even at this early period there were clearly long-standing, and quite elaborate, exchange[5] and cultural links across the Near East, just as much as in later periods.

On the other hand, this period also saw the production of material that introduced what would soon be the classic Egyptian style of art. This included a limestone macehead from Hierakonpolis (page 155, below) with a depiction of a king apparently cutting the first element of an irrigation channel. The king wears the White Crown, later associated with Upper Egypt, and is labeled with the image of a scorpion, presumably his name (fig. 11). Pottery vessels from tomb U-j also bear images of a scorpion, which has been regarded as giving the name of the tomb owner. A short text found in the Wadi el-Malik, east of Aswan, has also been interpreted as naming a domain of a king of that name.[6] If so, it seems likely that all these items belong to the same monarch, who must have been one of the very last kings of Upper Egypt.[7]

FIGURE 9 Abydos, Umm el-Qaab tomb U-j from the east.

The southwestern part of cemetery U merges into cemetery B, two tombs at their juncture, B0/1/2 and B7/9,[8] having been attributed to Kings Irihor and Ka, respectively. The kings' independent existence has been questioned,[9] but the former's name has been found in the Wadi Ameyra in the Sinai, along with the slightly later Narmer.[10] In any case, given the location of their tombs, they would be the immediate predecessors of the first kings of the First Dynasty, whose tombs lay immediately beyond B0/1/2 and B7/9.

The Unification of Egypt

The presence of the name of Irihor in the Sinai would seem to indicate that the kings of the south had access through the eastern Delta to that region. Whether this indicates that the area was already under some degree of southern control is a moot point, although the previous appearance of southern material culture at east Delta sites may point in this direction. In this case, it may be that the "unification" was primarily concerned with the accretion of the western part of the Delta into the incipient pan-Egyptian monarchy.

Tradition, as enshrined in a number of New Kingdom sources (pages 122–28) and in the works of Manetho and other Classical writers (pages 131–33), placed a certain "Meni"

FIGURE 10 a. Dog Palette, from Hierakonpolis (Ashmolean AN1896-1908 E.3924); b. Bull Palette (Louvre E.11255); c. Hunter Palette (Louvre E.11254); d. handle of Gebel el-Arak knife (Louvre E.11517).

FIGURE 11 Top: the "Scorpion" macehead, from Hierakonpolis (Ashmolean AN1896-1908 E.3632); bottom: visualization of the scene on the macehead by Cyril Aldred (NMS).

or, in Greek, "Men(es)" at the head of the list of kings of Egypt. Herodotus also attributed to him the establishment of a new national capital at Memphis, although Manetho places the building of a royal palace there under his successor. The various editions of Manetho (appendix 4) give "Menes" a reign of either 62, 60, or 30 years, and note that he "made a foreign expedition and won renown" and was "carried off by a hippopotamus."

The question as to which among the monarchs known from contemporary monuments might have been "Menes" has been the subject of long-running debate.[11] An influential source has been the so-called "Menes Tablets"[12] from the "Royal Tomb" at Naqada (for which see pages 21, 151, below). These are a duplicate set of ivory tablets which pair the *serekh* of King Hor-Aha with a pointed-topped enclosure containing signs reading "*nbty mn*" (fig. 12). At first sight they might suggest that the Nebty-name of Hor-Aha was "Men(es)"[13]—tying in with other cases where names used for early kings in later sources (cf. pages 33, 36, 111–12, 152, below) were originally Nebty-names. On the other hand, the shape surrounding "*nbty mn*" is not otherwise known as the enclosure of a Nebty-name. Rather, it has been argued to actually represent some kind of funerary pavilion, in which case "Menes" would be a predecessor of Hor-Aha. An additional objection is that the "*nbty mn*" is found in no other context alongside the *serekh* of Hor-Aha.[14]

Two of the king lists produced in the early Rameside Period (for which see pages 122–28, below) include the beginning of the First Dynasty, but are inconsistent with the number of kings between "Meni" and "Mer(bia)p(en)." The latter is certainly to be equated with Anedjib, who ruled three reigns before the end of the First Dynasty:

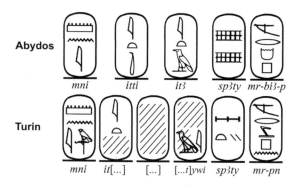

The list from Abydos thus gives seven names for that dynasty, starting with "Meni." A sealing of the reign of Qaa, which places the First Dynasty kings buried at Umm el-Qaab in chronological order,[15] combined with the archaeological evidence from that cemetery, makes it clear that seven kings ruled from Hor-Aha to Qaa at the end of the dynasty; this

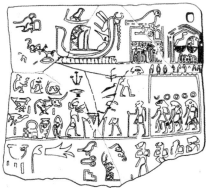

FIGURE 12 The two "Menes Tablets," from the Royal Tomb at Naqada (Cairo CG14142, Garstang E.5116), with composite drawing.

would support the equation of Hor-Aha with "Men(es)." However, the Turin Canon gives *eight* names for the dynasty, with the additional name (T3.13 or T3.15)[16] close to the beginning of the sequence, supporting Meni being identified with the predecessor of Hor-Aha. That this was Narmer is clear from the aforementioned sealing of Qaa, which places him directly before Hor-Aha—as does an earlier sealing of the reign of Den.[17]

The Ptolemaic list of Manetho (pages 133, 173) also gives eight names for the dynasty. It is possible that the omission of the additional name in the Abydos list was simply an error (it is also omitted from the late Second Dynasty names found in other lists)—or it may indicate that even in ancient times there was historiographic confusion over which historical king should be equated with the traditional founder of the united Egyptian monarchy.

Another issue regarding "Menes" is his date. The Turin Canon states that 955 years and 15 days elapsed between him and the end of the Memphite line (Seventh/Eighth Dynasty) during the early First Intermediate Period (probably the reign of the Neferirkare II who seems to fill this position in the Abydos list). However, the chronology of the First Intermediate Period is distinctly problematic, as there is little clarity on the time span that separated the end of the Memphite line from the Eleventh Dynasty, which can be estimated (on the basis of an astronomical observation under Senwosret III of the Twelfth Dynasty)[18] to have begun around 2080 BC. Estimates for this gap have varied from a few decades (if that), through to a century or more, thus probably placing "Menes" somewhere between 3150 and 2950 BC, depending on the assumptions made. A disputed astronomical calculation[19] has placed the foundation of the pyramid of Khufu around 2478 BC, which would support a "Menes" date no earlier than 3000 BC, if not up to a century later. In this case, the problem is not only with the correctness of the astronomical calculation, but also the lack of certainty regarding the lengths of reigns throughout the period in question.

Radiocarbon dates from the Early Dynastic Period and Old Kingdom are rather unhelpful.[20] For example, while two samples from the reign of Djer produced a calibrated date range of 3023–2891 BC—fully compatible with a start of the First Dynasty during 3100/3000 BC—ones from the time of his predecessor Hor-Aha yielded a date span of 3640–3104 BC, and two from that of Narmer 3650–3370 BC. Accordingly, radiocarbon can play little role in determining the true date of the beginning of Egyptian history.[21]

Narmer

That at least part of the final absorption of the north was the work of the king who preceded Hor-Aha has long been suggested by a large ceremonial palette from Hierakonpolis (fig. 13). On one side, King Narmer is shown wearing the White Crown and smiting an enemy—an icon that would endure as a mode of royal representation until Roman times. The victim is identified by the rebus above his head as an inhabitant of the "papyrus country"—clearly the Nile Delta—tethered by a raptor—doubtless Horus, the historic patron of the Egyptian monarchy. On the other side of the palette, Narmer wears the Red Crown in the presence of the decapitated corpses of his enemies, while his servants tether a fantastic beast. Below this, a bull—long an incarnation of royal physical might—demolishes the wall of an enemy town. The palette is usually interpreted as a record of the unification of Egypt and the foundation of the First Dynasty, although as noted above, this "event" is more likely to have been incremental.[22] Indeed, Cairo Fragment 1 (CF1) of the Annals appears to show Double-Crowned figures determining the now-lost names of some Predynastic kings.

The palette is interesting in the way that it combines art that conforms to what would be traditional modes of Egyptian representation until Roman times, with the elements of the "Predynastic" and "Mesopotamian" styles seen on the earlier ceremonial palettes, including the long-necked fantastic beast. This underlines that, whether or not Narmer was "Menes," his reign constitutes a significant point of interface between Predynastic and Dynastic times. A similar mix of styles is to be seen on a ceremonial macehead (fig. 14), found with the palette. The decoration of the macehead has often been interpreted as a record of the arrival of a northern princess, to marry the king and thus cement the union of the country. However, all that can be said is that it represents some form of triumph, with a high-status individual placed before the king, accompanied by tribute alleged to number 400,000 cattle, 1,422,000 goats, and 120,000 captives. A second, fragmentary, macehead also seems to be related to this event, as do a number of other items, including an ivory cylinder (also from Hierakonpolis), bone inlays from a box, and an ivory tag naming a year after it (from Abydos).[23] Narmer's implied status as the dynastic founder is supported by his name being the first in the royal sequence found on sealings of Den[24] and Qaa.[25]

FIGURE 13 Narmer Palette, from Hierakonpolis (Cairo CG14716).

Well over fifty objects bearing Narmer's name are known, including from the northern Egyptian sites of Buto, Tura, Helwan, Tarkhan, and Zawiyet el-Aryan. In addition, at Koptos, one of the early Min statues (fig. 5 right) was inscribed with the king's name, perhaps following on from a sequence of Predynastic rulers.[26] His name also appears in the Wadi Ameyra in the Sinai.[27] A life-size statue of a baboon of unknown provenance[28] is inscribed with Narmer's name, suggesting a step change in the production of divine images during his reign. Wine-jar sealings of Narmer from the eastern part of the Delta (at Minshat Abu Omar and Tell Ibrahim Awad) and from Palestine (Arad, Tell Erani, Tell Gath, Nahal Tilal, and Raphia) indicate exchange links (if not more) between the two regions.

For his tomb, Narmer chose a spot close to the sepulchers of Ka and Irihor (figs. 15, 16, top). Now numbered B17/18, it originally comprised two contiguous chambers, but with a partition added following the partial collapse of the southern element (fig. 20a).[29] Narmer also seems to have constructed the first of what would become a long sequence

FIGURE 14 The better-preserved of the two Narmer maceheads, from Hierakonpolis (Ashmolean AN1896-1908 E.3631).

of mud-brick enclosures some two kilometers to the northeast, of which only the late Second Dynasty example of Khasekhemwy remains standing (fig. 48). Only a small part of Narmer's putative structure has yet been examined (fig. 16 bottom).[30]

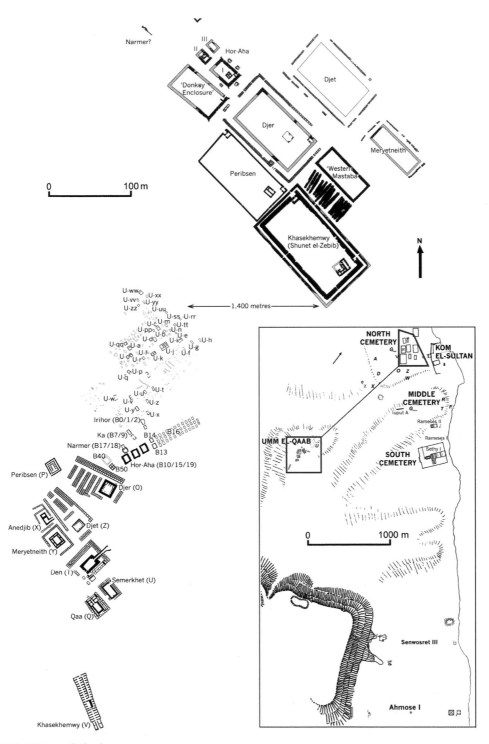

FIGURE 15 Map of Abydos.

FIGURE 16 Top: the tomb of
Narmer (B17/18) at Umm
el-Qaab; bottom: remains of
the south wall of the possible
funerary enclosure of the king.

These enclosures were clearly linked conceptually to the royal tombs at Umm el-
Qaab, with most of the latter having a corresponding enclosure. However, their precise
purpose remains a matter of debate.[31] Although at least some contained single small
buildings (pages 50, 60, below), most of their interior space seems devoid of significant
archaeological features (indicating no long-term structures), while all but the last one to

be built (pages 60–61) seem to have been purposely dismantled before the next one was constructed. Accordingly, one possible hypothesis is that the enclosures were built for actual funerary ceremonies of the king, most of which were carried out in temporary structures of perishable materials (cf. page 70), but after this the ongoing cult was carried out at the tomb itself. Here, the cult space was (at least from the time of Djer) defined by a pair of stelae bearing the king's names (fig. 23). The enclosures will then have lain derelict until taken down to make way for the one intended for the funeral of the next king—possibly with a significant reuse of materials.

Hor-Aha

The complete succession following Narmer down to the end of the dynasty is set out on the aforementioned seal impression from the time of Qaa,[32] which makes it clear that Hor-Aha was indeed his direct successor. Whether or not he was the prototype for "Menes," Hor-Aha was certainly a key figure in the early years of the unified Egyptian monarchy, with a significantly larger tomb at Abydos than his immediate predecessors. He seems to have been the husband of a prominent lady named Neithhotep, who was apparently buried in the so-called Royal Tomb at Naqada (fig. 17),[33] which contained a number of sealings and labels bearing Hor-Aha's name—including the so-called Menes Tablets (pages 14–15, above).

FIGURE 17 The Naqada Royal Tomb, with De Morgan's original reconstructed sketch inset.

Although he is not as widely attested as Narmer, objects bearing the king's name have also been found in tombs at Zawiyet el-Aryan and Helwan, and also in the earliest known tomb in a new cemetery at Saqqara. The latter was concentrated at first on a prominent ridge overlooking not only the city of Memphis to the east, but also the broad wadi to the west that actually provided access to the tombs (figs. 18, 25, 73). This would soon become the gateway to the rapidly expanding southward extension of the Saqqara necropolis (cf. pages 41–47, 58, below). The principal sepulcher datable to Hor-Aha's time is S3357, an elaborate paneled mastaba, with a series of magazines within its superstructure (adorned with the so-called palace-façade paneling), and wood-roofed chambers cut into the desert surface below. An associated boat burial lay thirty-five meters to the north.[34]

FIGURE 18 Views of the Early Dynastic necropolis at Saqqara, from the west and south. The former shows, on the extreme right, the Sixth Dynasty pyramid of Teti and, at a lower level, the Late Period Sacred Animal Necropolis (fig. 130). In the latter, the Old Kingdom pyramids of Abusir and Giza may be seen in the distance.

FIGURE 19 The tomb of Hor-Aha (B10/B15/B19) at Umm el-Qaab.

Of Memphis itself, any remains of its earliest days lie well below the modern water table. However, coring work suggests that its first structures may have lain not far from the base of the escarpment upon which these earliest tombs were constructed.[35] Subsequently, however, the city expanded eastward, in the wake of the demonstrable gradual move of the Nile in that direction. This resulted in the New Kingdom phase of the city and the great temple of the local god Ptah lying some four kilometers to the southeast of the probable Early Dynastic core.

The last year and a half of Hor-Aha's reign is recorded on the Palermo fragment of the Annals, but details are limited to noting the ritual of the "Following of Horus"— which seems to have been some kind of regular royal progress, perhaps for tax-collection purposes[36]—and the manufacture of a figure of Anubis in the last full year. According to the Palermo fragment, the king died six months and seven days into his final regnal year. Of events earlier in the reign, two labels from Abydos may record a royal visit to the Delta.[37]

Three pits (B10/15/19), with brick linings between 1.5 and 2.1 meters thick, comprised the tomb of Hor-Aha at Umm el-Qaab (figs. 19, 20b),[38] with chamber B15 serving as the burial chamber. The three chambers covered an area of 12 by 9 meters, roofed with five to nine layers of mud brick, laid on matting and supported by wooden beams. It has been suggested that the whole of the substructure was topped by a single mound of sand and gravel, measuring 40 by 16 meters. A series of subsidiary graves lay northeast of the main tomb, those closest to the king's tomb probably belonging to members of his family and household.

Hor-Aha's complex at Umm el-Qaab was supplemented by a group of three brick remote enclosures, all dated to the reign by sealings;[39] they lie close to the putative example of Narmer. The largest of Hor-Aha's enclosures included key features that would recur in later examples. In particular, there was a complex entrance at the southern end of the east wall, with a brick-built multi-room structure just inside. There were at least four—probably originally six—subsidiary graves outside the enclosure, while on the northwest side were a pair of much smaller enclosures (perhaps attributable to his wives?). One of the wives of the king appears to have been Benerib, who was buried in tomb B14, adjacent to Hor-Aha's own tomb.

Djer

Djer was presumably a son of his predecessor Hor-Aha, the name of his mother being confirmed as Khenthap by Annals Stone CF1 (fig. 98). This also gives his personal name—at least as identified in the Fifth Dynasty—as Iti. This is also the name that appears in the Abydos list as the third king of Egypt. The Palermo fragment records the first ten years of the king's reign, with another nine appearing on Annals CF1, possibly out of a total reign of forty-one years. The record of his first regnal year is odd: it is noted as only lasting four months and 28 days—45 days less than the expected balance, given the recorded duration of Hor-Aha's final regnal year. This may indicate that at this period the interval between one king's death and his burial was formally regarded as an interregnum, with the new king only taking office when he had buried his predecessor.[40] Other suggestions have, however, been made.[41]

The annual Nile flood height is recorded in Djer's segment of this "shared" year, suggesting that he came to the throne in the summer: the first indications of the inundation generally appeared at Aswan in early June. The waters then continued to rise until early September, before stabilizing for some weeks and then rising to their maximum level in October. The height reached by the flood is the consistent piece of information provided for every year in the Annals Stones. Other data are of a more diverse nature, but in the earlier reigns tend to be restricted to records of Followings of Horus and the creation of divine images and other ritual acts—often couched in terms that are now distinctly obscure.

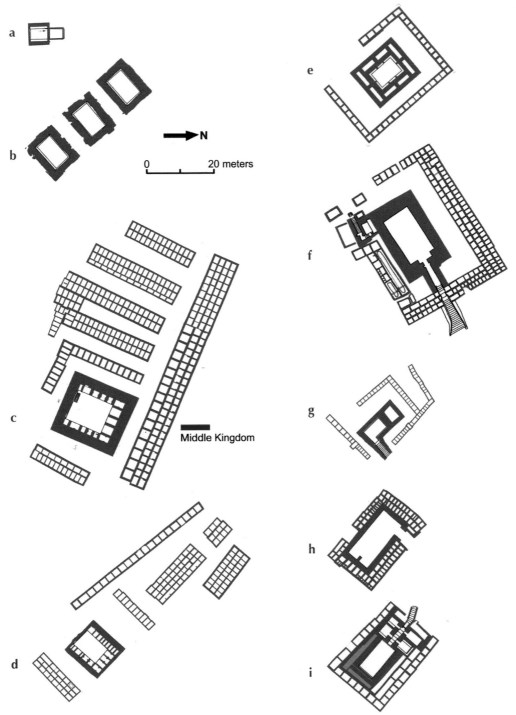

FIGURE 20 Plans of the royal tombs of the First Dynasty at Umm el-Qaab: a. Narmer (B17/18); b. Hor-Aha (B10/B15/B19); c. Djer (O); d. Djet (Z); e. Merneith (Y); f. Den (T); g. Anedjib (X); h. Semerkhet (U); i. Qaa (Q).

Thus, Djer's second year saw a Following of Horus and a "*dšr*-festival"—the latter of unknown nature. His third year included the "birth" of two "royal children"—but the determinates given to the latter suggest that they were actually some kind of divine images. A Following of Horus is recorded for the next year, suggesting that this was normally a biennial event. The same year also has an entry that is difficult to interpret, but may denote some kind of human sacrifice. The fifth year saw the building of a structure called *smr-nṯrw*, perhaps at Saqqara, to judge from the presence of vessels bearing its name in galleries under the Step Pyramid there (for which see page 81). A festival, perhaps to be read as that of the god Sokar, is also noted in the Annals.

Succeeding year-notes conform to the same pattern of a royal act (the Following of Horus in alternate years) or festival and the creation of divine images. The surviving Annals break off in Djer's tenth year (all details lost), resuming after a gap of uncertain length, on Annals CF1. This includes the king's titulary and name of his mother above its year-compartments, and would thus appear to represent the middle years of the reign. The first of the new set of years saw a Following of Horus and the creation of another image of Anubis,[42] with some other kind of royal progress, the otherwise unattested *pḥr-t3wy*, and a *dšr*-festival the following year. The pattern of the kinds of acts recorded continues on as before, with the fifth of this run of years including the first Annals mention of a military activity—a "smiting of the land of *Sṯt*," a term later referring to Syria-Palestine. That Djer was active in the southern Sinai is confirmed by a rock stela in the Wadi el-Humur[43] and a *serekh* in the nearby Wadi Ameyra.[44]

Whether Djer undertook any military activities in Nubia is not wholly clear. A relief at Gebel Sheikh Soliman, just above the Second Cataract,[45] showing captives and slain enemies (fig. 21), was long held to be dated to Djer's reign by a *serekh* at the extreme left. While this has subsequently been questioned,[46] the original dating has been reinstated in some recent works.[47]

If the modern reconstruction of the Annals Stones is anything like correct (pages 114–15), Djer's reign will have been some five decades long. Posterity regarded him as something of a scholar, Manetho stating him to be the author of an anatomy textbook, still extant in Greek times (cf. page 122, below). His tomb at Umm el-Qaab (O: figs. 20c, 22)[48] marks a major advance over the sepulchers of his predecessors, although in many ways reminiscent of the earlier U-j. Rather than the series of separate adjacent pits employed by Hor-Aha, a single large cavity was sunk in the desert gravel and lined with brick nearly three meters thick. Along all sides but the south, a series of stub walls was built, creating storerooms. The remaining area of the tomb was then lined with wooden partitions to define the burial chamber itself. Of its original occupants, a mummified arm survived until the beginning of the twentieth century AD (pages 154–56, below). The tomb was modified during the Middle

FIGURE 21 Relief from Gebel Sheikh Soliman, apparently commemorating a military operation of Djer into Nubia.

FIGURE 22 The tomb of Djer (O) at Umm el-Qaab.

Kingdom, when it was converted into the symbolic tomb of Osiris, an entrance stairway being added at the south end, together with a recumbent figure of the god, datable to the Thirteenth Dynasty (see pages 117, 119, 153).

The tomb is the first from which any trace of an offering place survives. Although nothing has been recorded in situ, a stela bearing the king's name, and closely resembling others from later reigns, survives, decorated with the king's *serekh* (fig. 23a). Later examples certainly came in pairs and seem to have regularly stood together on the eastern side of the tomb as a focus for the dead king's cult, down to at least the early Fourth Dynasty.[49]

FIGURE 23 Stelae from the offering places of the royal tombs at Umm el-Qaab: a. Djer (Cairo JE34992);
b. Djet (Louvre E.11007); c. Merneith (Cairo JE34550); d. Den (Brussels E.0562); e. Semerkhet (Cairo
CG14633); f. Qaa (Cairo CG14631).

While the tomb of Hor-Aha was accompanied by thirty-three minor subsidiary burials to the east (B16), these were in independent single graves, with no indication of relative dates of interment. However, the tomb of Djer had no fewer than 318, arranged in geometric blocks, principally to the north and west of the king's tomb itself. Unlike those of Hor-Aha's complex, the graves of Djer were formed by subdividing long trenches with brick cross-walls. This made it impossible for graves to be covered over on an individual basis. Thus, all those in a given group will have been closed simultaneously, showing that their occupants must have all been interred—and thus presumably died—at the same time. It seems difficult to question that this took place at the time of the king's interment, and that the occupants of the grave represent human sacrifices.[50] No conclusive signs of violence have been reported on the remains—although proper examinations have been rare—suggesting that death was owing to the voluntary taking of poison, although a suggestion has been made that dental evidence might suggest death by strangulation.[51]

At least a third of the graves held a small stela (fig. 24).[52] Eighty-five percent of known examples belonged to females; the occupants of the graves were most probably members of the royal household. The single remote enclosure of Djer—all later kings would have only one such structure—covered some six times the area of the largest of Hor-Aha's examples, and was surrounded by 269 further subsidiary graves. Such a large-scale sacrifice of retainers at the death of a king has parallels in the slightly later (c. 2600–2450 BC) royal tombs at Ur in southern Mesopotamia,[53] although the mode of death and treatment of the bodies were very different.[54] Further parallels in the Nile Valley are to be found in the eighteenth/seventeenth century BC Kerma tumuli in Upper Nubia,[55] and in those of the fourth/sixth century AD X-Group at Ballana and Qustul close to the Second Cataract.[56] However, in Egypt numbers of such burials decline after the time of Djer, and are unknown after the end of the Second Dynasty (see pages 32, 36, 37, 59).

The number of noble tombs built at Saqqara seems to have expanded during the reign of Djer, with at least S2171H, S2185, and S3471 datable to his time.[57] Of these, the burial chamber of the last-mentioned had been set alight in antiquity—a situation found in other tombs of the First Dynasty in the same cemetery, and also at Umm el-Qaab. Nevertheless, a huge amount of material survived, including a stone palette showing the king smiting an enemy before a lion, as well as wine jars sealed with the name of the king. Material bearing the king's name has also come to light at Tura and Helwan, while a possible statuette of the king has been found at Elephantine.[58]

Djet

Djet was presumably the son of his predecessor Djer. His personal name may have been Ita, to judge from the Abydos list. None of the year-records of Djet's reign are preserved

FIGURE 24 Stela of a
woman named Sesherka,
from one of the subsidiary
graves around the tomb of
Djer (BM EA35613).

on any of the Annals Stones, while nothing of historical import survived in his tomb. It is likely that the reign was relatively short, as Djet's successor Den had a long reign and at least one official's career that had begun under Djer was still continuing under Djet's successor Den. The reconstructed Annals Stones seem to point in the same direction, as Djer's reign occupies all of the surviving left-hand part of Register rII, and that of Den all of the right-hand part of Register rIII, meaning that Djet's reign would be restricted to the far left of Register rII or the very beginning of Register rIII.

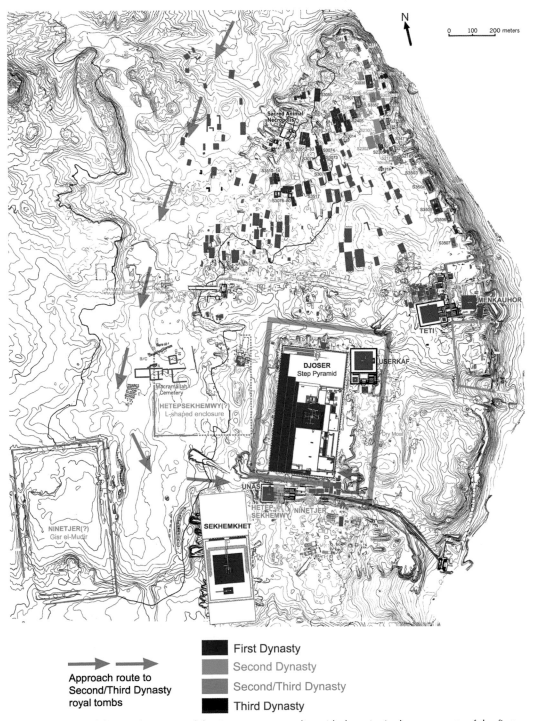

First Dynasty

Second Dynasty

Second/Third Dynasty

Third Dynasty

Approach route to
Second/Third Dynasty
royal tombs

FIGURE 25 Map of the northern part of the Saqqara necropolis, with the principal monuments of the first three dynasties marked.

In addition, the rule of Egypt directly after Djet's death was in the hands of a woman, Merneith, presumably a wife of Djet and mother of Den, ruling during her son's minority (see below). The latter relationship may be confirmed by the Palermo fragment, where the end of the name of Den's mother is potentially restorable as [Me]ret[neith] (see below). A short reign may also be indicated by the fact that only two nobles' tombs can be dated to the time of Djet: Saqqara S3504, probably belonging to one Sekhemkasedj,[59] and most likely the anonymous tomb V at Giza.[60]

Djet's tomb, Umm el-Qaab Z (fig. 20d),[61] was very similar to that of Djer, but slightly smaller, as was also the case with the funerary enclosure. As compared with the complex of Djer, the number of subsidiary graves around the tomb dropped to 175, while those at the enclosure fell to only 154. Traces survive to indicate that the tomb's substructure had been topped by a sandy mound that lay entirely below the surface of the ground: this was perhaps a representation of the primeval mound upon which creation was believed to have occurred. It seems likely that this was a feature of other First Dynasty royal tombs as well,[62] and was certainly to be found in some contemporary private tombs at Saqqara, such as S3471, albeit in mud brick.[63] The surviving example of the two limestone stelae that once marked the offering place of Djet's tomb is of much higher quality than that of Djer (fig. 23b).[64]

Merneith

The evidence for the status of Merneith[65] as the first ruling woman in Egypt's history derives entirely from the presence of her tomb among those of the kings of the First Dynasty at Abydos. Merneith's attested titles comprise "Foremost (of Women)" and "King's Mother," the latter accompanying her name in the "necropolis seal" of Den, which lists her alongside the kings buried at Umm el-Qaab from Narmer onward.[66] This supports the idea that Merneith was Den's mother, her burial among the kings being derived from her serving as regent during Den's minority. That the latter came to the throne while yet a young child is suggested by Djet's apparently short reign and Den's own subsequent long reign (see below). Apart from her Abydene funerary monuments, Merneith is known from sealings in tomb S3503 Saqqara.[67]

Her tomb at Umm el-Qaab is of the same general size and type as those of Djer and Djet, although with storerooms arranged outside the brick walls of the burial chamber, rather than as partitioned compartments within it (fig. 20e).[68] Like those of the male rulers, the tomb's offering place on the east side was equipped with stelae bearing the tomb owner's name, the principal difference between those of Merneith and those of the kings being that her name was not enclosed in a *serekh* (fig. 23c). The tomb also had only a single line of subsidiary graves on each side, totaling forty-one; the remote enclosure followed the usual pattern, but again with a greatly reduced number of graves (seventy-nine).

Den

Den is the first monarch for whom we have clear contemporary evidence of his Nebty-name, which was written with two land signs—perhaps reading "Khenty." This was clearly the origin of the cartouche names assigned to him in later documents (cf. pages 111–12), although the signs in the latter seem to read "*Sp3ty*," or perhaps "*Ḥ3sty*." This form is found (as is a corruption, "*Qnty*") in some copies of the Book of the Dead, as a gloss to Chapter 64 attributes it to his reign (cf. page 122).

Six years of Den's long reign are included on Annals CF5, although only five are readable in whole or part, with another fourteen almost certainly belonging to his later years on the Palermo fragment.[69] The events mentioned are generally akin to those found in previous reigns although, curiously, the Following of Horus is not to be found anywhere, suggesting either that the practice was dropped under Den or that it was not recorded for some other reason during his time: it was certainly once again being practiced by the reign of Semerkhet (page 37, below).

The middle years of the reign as covered on Annals CF5 include the remains of the beginning of the overall heading for Den, with the *serekh* of the king. However, the first year is only partly preserved, with what may be part of the writing of Hedjwer, the "Great White Baboon," surviving—presumably from a note of the manufacture of a divine image. The next year, however, contains a record of smiting the "*stti(w)*," another designation of those living to the northeast of Egypt, and perhaps the event depicted on an ivory label from the king's tomb (fig. 26 top left).[70] The next entry records the making of an Imywet fetish, followed by a smiting of the otherwise unknown "*iwti(w)*"—whose reading is in any case uncertain. The last preserved annal for Den records the planning of a building and a Sokar festival.

The Palermo fragment of the Annals preserves the end of the heading for the reign, including the end of the name of the king's mother, which, as noted already, is consistent with it having given the name of Merneith. On the basis of the likely length of the complete reign heading, it has been estimated that six years may have separated the last one of Annals CF5 from the first of those on the Palermo piece. This seems to record an "Appearance" (a formal ritual act) of the king at a temple, but the next year-record is of the smiting of the "*iwntiw*"—a term meaning "bowmen," which was later applied to the inhabitants of territory to the northeast of Egypt. This is another candidate for the prototype of the event depicted on the aforementioned label from the king's tomb. The next year features an Appearance of the king and a *sd*-festival jubilee—another event also found on a label from the royal tomb (fig. 26 top right). Den appears to be the first king for whom a *sd*-festival is recorded. Later in Egyptian history, this jubilee was usually first held in a king's thirtieth regnal year. However, this was by no means universal, and its appearance at this point in the Annals does not allow us to assume that this indeed marks Year 30. A second occurrence of the jubilee is

FIGURE 26 Top: labels of Den from his tomb at Umm el-Qaab, commemorating an eastern military campaign and his *ḥb-sd* jubilee (BM EA55586; EA32650); bottom: seal impression from the tomb of Hemaka (S3035), showing (left) Den running with the Apis bull.

recorded on a limestone vessel from the royal tomb.[71] The Annals indicate that the jubilee year also marked an exceptionally high inundation. This may tie in with the next year's record, which is difficult to interpret, but which might refer to exceptional flooding in the Delta. With the height of flood recorded in one year, but its possible effects in the next, this might suggest that Den came to the throne in the early autumn (cf. page 24, above).

The next four years saw a "second occurrence of the *ḏt*-festival," the planning of a temple, its foundation, and the inauguration of its sacred lake. The fourth year also featured a "spearing of the hippopotamus" ceremony. Next year, the king is noted as making a visit to Herakleopolis, at the mouth of the Fayyum, including the sacred lake of the temple of the god Arsaphes there. More royal travel is recorded in the following year, downstream from an unknown location to two towns whose locations are also not known. Of the last four years of Den's reign that survive in the Palermo fragment, the first was only notable for the making of an image of the obscure god Sed. However, the next one records not only a ceremonial Appearance of the king, but also a "first occasion of the running of the Apis bull." This ties in with a depiction of the bull and Den himself taking part in that very ritual on a sealing from tomb S3035 (of Hemaka) at Saqqara (fig. 26 bottom).[72] The final pair of years saw respectively the creation of a divine image, and a royal Appearance.

On the basis of extrapolation from the preserved portions of the Annals, Den's reign will have lasted at least into its mid-thirties, and if the jubilee mentioned on the Palermo fragment indeed took place in Year 30, its length would be raised to around fifty years. It has been proposed that not only was Den's reign long, it was also extremely significant for the development of the Egyptian state, including a fundamental administrative transformation of the country, and instigating an aggressive foreign policy toward Nubia and Palestine.[73]

In the fullness of time, however, Den was buried in tomb T at Umm el-Qaab.[74] This sepulcher was of innovative design, being the first royal tomb with a stairway entrance (figs. 20f, 27). Previous royal tombs had had no means of access to their substructures except through their roofs: final structural completion, including the emplacement of a superstructure, was therefore not possible until after the burial. However, the tomb of Den incorporated a twenty-nine-meter-long stairway, running under the northeastern range of the tomb's subsidiary graves and (lost) superstructure. This gave access to the burial chamber via a door closed after the burial with brick blocking and a wooden portcullis.[75]

FIGURE 27 The tomb of Den (T) at Umm el-Qaab, with modern restoration.

The internal layout of the tomb also diverged from earlier examples, storerooms being placed entirely outside the burial chamber structure to the south, and apparently only accessible from above, while a stair-accessed complex in the southeast corner of the tomb was possibly a shrine. The brick walls of the wood-lined burial chamber were four meters thick. The room was paved with rough-dressed granite—the first use of stone in the structure of a royal tomb, although a limestone chamber lining had been used in a private tomb of the previous reign.[76] The tomb featured significantly fewer subsidiary graves than those of the preceding kings' tombs—around 130—reflecting a downward trend that continued until the end of the dynasty.

A fragment generally interpreted as from one of Den's funerary stelae is known (fig. 23d),[77] but the king's remote enclosure has not been positively identified. It may be one of two anonymous examples: the so-called Donkey Enclosure (named after the burials made in front of it at the time of construction), directly behind those of Hor-Aha, or the Western Mastaba, directly south of the enclosure of Djer. Directly adjacent to the western face of the Western Mastaba is a series of fourteen wooden boats, placed within individual brick "tombs."[78] Boats were also associated with certain other tombs of the Early Dynastic Period,[79] and would later form parts of royal tomb complexes from the Fourth Dynasty onward, but their purpose remains moot, and they appear to be absent from all royal funerary monuments down to the time of Khufu. A possible point in favor of Den's ownership of the Western Mastaba is the fact that it lacks any subsidiary graves, human or animal, paralleling the reduction in numbers of the former at the king's Umm el-Qaab monument.

At Saqqara, five major private tombs (S3035, S3036, S3111, S3506, and S3507) have revealed sealings naming Den, as has the so-called Macramallah Cemetery, a kilometer to the southwest of the main First Dynasty necropolis.[80] This comprises six groups of graves very similar to the subsidiary burials around the earlier tombs at Umm el-Qaab. They appear to be oriented toward a north–south rectangular space, but its original southward extent is obscured by the probably Second Dynasty "L-shaped Enclosure" (page 43); Late Period ritual structures were also built in the area, causing further disturbance. It has been suggested that the space might have been analogous to the Abydos enclosures—or might even represent the actual enclosure of Den, given the lack of a definite one belonging to him at Abydos.[81] On the other hand, it may simply be a cemetery of middle-ranking individuals, without any particular wider significance.[82]

Anedjib

Anedjib seems to have employed a new royal title, comprising a pair of raptors on a standard. This preceded the name "Merpabia," also attested as a Nebty-name, and which provided the prototype for the cartouche names later used for him in the Abydos, Saqqara, and Turin lists. The foundation of a fortress and palace are recorded on seal impressions,[83] while texts on stone vessels record the production of a considerable number of divine images, plus at least six of the king himself.[84] Unfortunately, nothing of Anedjib's records is preserved in any fragments of the Annals, except for the inundation level of his final year on Annals CF1. Given the likely gap between this and the last year of Djer preserved on the Palermo fragment, it would seem that Anedjib's reign lasted around a decade.

This, however, seemingly contradicts jubilees mentioned on two vessel fragments, found in the king's own tomb and in S2446 at Saqqara.[85] On the other hand, neither fragment actually bears Anedjib's name, and may in reality come from items made under Den. Supportive of a shorter reign is the fact that the tomb of Anedjib (X; fig. 20g)[86] is far less elaborate than that of Den, with a much shorter stairway, which like that of the latter terminates at a wooden portcullis. Anedjib's burial chamber was half the size of Den's, with a wooden lining built directly on the desert surface, rather than any stone paving, and had a separate storeroom to the west, apparently accessible only from above. The number of subsidiary graves continued the downward curve, falling to sixty-four. Anedjib's remote funerary enclosure has yet to be identified.

Semerkhet

The personal/Nebty-name of Semerkhet seems to have been written with the image of a standing figure that was ultimately used as his cartouche in Annals CF1 and the Abydos list, and interpreted phonetically as "Semsem" in the Turin Canon (fig. 28). Annals CF1 preserves the whole of the king's nine-year reign, including the heading giving his mother's name. There has been debate as to the latter's actual reading, although "Batirset" is perhaps the most generally accepted rendering.

The events recorded in the Annals begin in Year 1 with Semerkhet's "Appearance as Dual King," "uniting Upper and Lower Egypt," and "circumambulating the wall"—all ceremonies regularly associated with a king's accession, and found throughout the Annals. The biennial Following of Horus was now once again noted, after its omission from those of the reign of Den: as remarked above, we have no Annals data from the reign of Anedjib. Year 2 also saw a Running of the Apis. The remaining non-Following years feature little more than royal Appearances, religious festivals, and the manufacture of divine images; curiously, in view of his short reign of only eight years, Semerkhet seems to have celebrated a jubilee, attested by a seal impression from his tomb at Umm el-Qaab.[87] A short reign is also supported by the lack of any Saqqara tombs datable to his reign.

The king's sepulcher at Abydos, tomb U (figs. 20h, 29), is of the now usual construction, with the burial chamber accessible via a ramp, and containing a wooden shrine. The upper parts of the mud-brick walls appear less well built than the lower

FIGURE 28 Fragment of rock-crystal vessel with the names of Semerkhet, from his tomb at Umm el-Qaab (BM EA49278).

elements, suggesting hurried completion.[88] Unusually, the tomb's sixty-nine subsidiary burials, rather than being separate from the main tomb structure, as previously, directly abutted the mud-brick walls of the main burial chamber and its storerooms. The offering place was marked in the usual manner by stelae, of which one fragment survives.

Qaa

As with most of the other kings of the time, nothing is known of the background of Qaa, the last king of the First Dynasty. In later documents, he is given the cartouche name "Qebeh." Of his reign, the only surviving Annals record is of his first year (on Annals CF1), which merely gives the usual events of a king's accession. On the other hand, labels from the king's tomb include certain events of the kind found in the Annals, including Followings of Horus, the foundation of ritual structures, and religious festivals. Rock inscriptions survive in two locations near El-Kab, suggesting some activity in the region, and also in the Western Desert.[89] The length of the reign is uncertain, but a fragment of bowl from below the Step Pyramid at Saqqara mentions a second jubilee,[90] implying a potential reign of over three decades.

FIGURE 29 The tomb of Semerkhet (U) at Umm el-Qaab.

Qaa's Umm el-Qaab tomb (Q: figs. 20i, 30)[91] was a much more elaborate structure than those of his immediate predecessors, including two pairs of storerooms opening off the descending stairway, which terminated in a limestone portcullis—the earliest example to be found in situ in a royal tomb. This combination of lateral chambers opening from the main access route into the tomb and stone portcullis blocks would be key elements of the following generations of royal tomb substructures. Only twenty-six subsidiary compartments surrounded the king's tomb, and like those of Semerkhet formed an integral part of the structure. While most were certainly graves of his entourage, a few may have actually been storerooms for the king's tomb itself. Both of Qaa's funerary stelae survive (fig. 23f), but his funerary enclosure remains unidentified.

At least four tombs belonging to officials of the reign of Qaa have been identified at Saqqara (S3120, S3121, S3500, and S3505). Of them, S3505, belonging to one Merka,[92] is of an elaborate design, with a large free-standing chapel to the north, of a plan that seems to foreshadow that of the mortuary temple of the Third Dynasty Step Pyramid (pages 78–80, below), which included wooden statuary. It also had a stela in a niche at the southern end of the mastaba's eastern façade, apparently the first example of such marking of a private offering place.

FIGURE 30 The tomb of Qaa (Q) at Umm el-Qaab.

Qaa's tomb was the last royal tomb to be built at Umm el-Qaab until the middle of the Second Dynasty. Since he was also the last king of the dynasty, it has been suggested that there had been an abrupt break after Qaa's death, and that the reign may have been followed by disorder. Indeed, extensive burning seen in First Dynasty tombs at both Abydos and Saqqara has on occasion been attributed to the interface between the First and Second Dynasties, with the ephemeral kings Ba and Seneferka possibly to be placed in an alleged interregnum.[93] On the other hand, sealings of Hetepsekhemwy, first king of the Second Dynasty, have been found in the tomb of Qaa, indicating the absence of any significant interregnum.[94] In addition, both the burning and Ba and Seneferka may perhaps be better placed later during the troubled times of the third quarter of the Second Dynasty (pages 48, 52, below).

2 THE SECOND DYNASTY

Hetepsekhemwy

Very little is known of the reign of Hetepsekhemwy, only a few scattered fragments bearing his name having been found in places other than his own tomb and that of his predecessor Qaa. That it nevertheless marked some real changes is suggested not only by his being regarded by posterity as beginning a new dynasty, but also that with him the royal cemetery shifted from its time-hallowed location of Abydos to Saqqara. This would hint at a significant move of the center of gravity of the state from the south to the north. Indeed, the new king himself could have been a northerner, breaking the chain of southern rulership that stretched back beyond Narmer.

The move of the royal cemetery to Saqqara is interesting in that the royal tomb was not built near the existing private tombs at the northern extremity of the site. Rather, Hetepsekhemwy chose a location nearly two kilometers to the southwest, in an area apparently without earlier mortuary occupation. In view of the fact that private tombs continued to be built in the old necropolis through the Second Dynasty and beyond, it would seem most likely that this move was intended to create an exclusively royal burial area, just as Umm el-Qaab had become at Abydos.

This exclusivity was seemingly enforced by the cutting of an east–west trench across the plateau, creating a kind of raised precinct, upon which the actual tomb was constructed (fig. 31a).[1] Nothing is known of the superstructure of the monument, as the whole precinct was appropriated for the pyramid complex of King Unas some five centuries later, at the end of the Fifth Dynasty, leaving no trace of any above-ground Second Dynasty constructions.

On the other hand, the substructure of Hetepsekhemwy's tomb, identified by seal impressions of both the king and his successor, Reneb, remains.[2] Unlike the royal tombs at Abydos—and the First Dynasty private tombs to the north at Saqqara—it was largely

FIGURE 31 The tomb of Hetepsekhemwy at Saqqara, the location of its entrance marked by the railings close to the edge of the east–west cutting that defined the location of the Second Dynasty royal necropolis. The lower images show (b) the entrance and (c) the beginning of the wholly rock-cut section of the tomb, with the location for the portcullis.

tunneled into the bedrock, with an axial corridor and flanking storerooms. This was a scheme also employed for some Saqqara private tombs of the Second Dynasty (fig. 32a).[3] In the king's case, the underground complex ultimately covered an area of some 122 by 48 meters (nearly two soccer pitches), but had originally been intended to be considerably smaller. The wholly rock-cut innermost part included apartments clearly imitating those of the living quarters of a house and possibly cult rooms, plus storerooms. This then saw internal modifications to increase the number of the latter.

The axial corridor was then extended northward as an open trench that was then roofed over with limestone blocks, and a number of further lateral rooms added (fig. 31b).[4] Finally, apparently in two phases, yet more chambers were added on either side of the outer part of the entrance corridor, the tomb ending up with at least 120 storerooms, all around two meters high. Security was entrusted to four successive vertical portcullises, the last of which blocked the doorway into the inner wholly rock-cut section of the tomb (fig. 31c).

At Abydos, the tombs at Umm el-Qaab had been accompanied to the east by monumental enclosures between the cultivation and the actual sepulchers. These overlooked the wadi that led from the edge of the desert up to Umm el-Qaab. Given that these enclosures would also be found associated with the later Second Dynasty tombs at Abydos (pages 50–51, 58–61), one would expect corresponding structures at Saqqara. The principal access to the site was from the north, via a wide wadi that ran from behind the First Dynasty necropolis to a point west of Hetepsekhemwy's tomb (see fig. 25).[5] It is thus in this area, rather than to the east of the royal tomb itself (where the terrain was in any case unsuitable), that Hetepsekhemwy's enclosure might be expected to have lain.

In just this spot is to be found the so-called L-shaped Enclosure—dubbed thus owing to only its southwest quadrant being tolerably preserved. In contrast to the brick enclosures of Abydos, this monument was defined by embankments of desert sand and gravel, although potential brick and limestone traces are also present. One hundred forty meters of the southern end of the west wall survives, together with probably two hundred meters of the south wall.[6] Its full extent remains unclear,[7] but the southern wall may have extended as far east as the point where a north–south extension of the aforementioned east–west rock cutting begins.

While no inscribed material has been found to link the enclosure with the tomb of Hetepsekhemwy, the "L-Shaped Enclosure" is, by its mode of construction, certainly a very early piece of work, and its location on the access route to the tomb of Hetepsekhemwy is highly suggestive. In addition, there is a second enclosure of somewhat more advanced constructional techniques to its southwest, which would neatly twin with the tomb of Hetepsekhemwy's second successor, Ninetjer, which lay a little to the south of that of Hetepsekhemwy (pages 46–47, below).

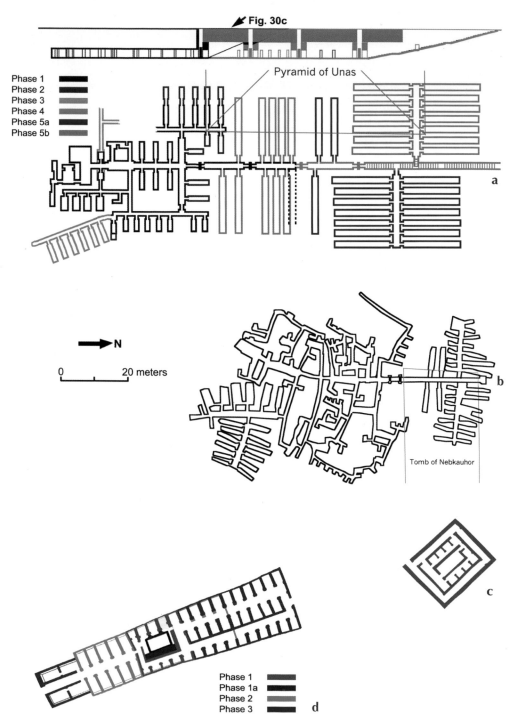

Fig. 30c

Phase 1
Phase 2
Phase 3
Phase 4
Phase 5a
Phase 5b

Pyramid of Unas

a

N

0   20 meters

Tomb of Nebkauhor

b

c

Phase 1
Phase 1a
Phase 2
Phase 3

d

FIGURE 32 The royal tombs of the Second Dynasty: a. Hetepsekhemwy; b. Ninetjer (both Saqqara);
c. Peribsen (Umm el-Qaab P); d. Khasekhemwy (Umm el-Qaab V).

Reneb

As noted above, Reneb buried Hetepsekhemwy, but beyond the sealings in Hetepsekhemwy's tomb and a few inscribed stone vessels, Reneb's reign is commemorated only by the presence of his name on a rock west of Armant and in the Wadi Ameyra in the Sinai[8]—and by the stela from his lost tomb (fig. 33).[9] The stela, of the same simple kind as employed at the royal tombs of Abydos, with just the king's *serekh*, was apparently found at Mit Rahina, part of the site of Memphis, suggesting that it was originally erected at Saqqara. However, only two Second Dynasty royal tombs (and two remote enclosures) have definitely been identified there, and nothing has ever come to light in the area between the tombs of Hetepsekhemwy and Ninetjer, where one might have expected to find the sepulcher of Reneb. One possibility is that Reneb usurped the tomb of Hetepsekhemwy, especially if he had a short reign, which may be implied by his poor attestation. Reneb's name has certainly been added next to that of Hetepsekhemwy on a stone vessel from under the Step Pyramid. It may also be noted that the mortuary cults of Hetepsekhemwy, Reneb, and Ninetjer were supported by the same priest in Third Dynasty times (fig. 34).

FIGURE 33 Stela of Reneb, from Memphis (MMA 60.144).

Ninetjer

Significantly more material survives from the time of the next king, Ninetjer, including the first complete three-dimensional image of a ruler of Egypt (fig. 35). At least five private tombs—S2171, S2302, and S2498 at Saqqara,[10] 505 H.4 at Helwan,[11] and one at Giza[12]—can be attributed to his reign, while large numbers of stone vessels bearing his name were found under the Step Pyramid, plus an ivory vessel from the area of Saqqara. A significant part of the first half of the king's reign is preserved on the Palermo fragment of the Annals. This includes the first part of the heading, giving his Horus-name and what may be a forerunner of the Golden Falcon-name. The first preserved year is called the "3rd occasion of the Census," which, assuming a biennial count, would probably have been his Year 6. Accordingly, the Annals data would give him a reign of thirty-nine to forty years.

FIGURE 34 Statuette of Hetepdief, with names of the first three kings of the Second Dynasty on its shoulder (Cairo CG1).

FIGURE 35 Statuette of King Ninetjer (RMO F2014/6.1).

Each census year also includes a Following of Horus, which may by then have been linked with the census process. The other years generally follow the usual pattern of being named for royal Appearances, building works, and ritual acts. The year after the 4th Census is interesting in that it includes a running of an otherwise unknown sacred bull, *S3-ʿnḫ*. Even more intriguing is the year after the 6th Census, where two places—*šmr-rʿ* and *ḥ3*—are recorded as being "hacked up." These would appear to be places in Egypt, and thus could be early manifestations of the civil war(s) that would wrack Egypt over the next few decades. No further such activities feature in the remaining preserved records, which include, however, a "second running" of the Apis bull (year after 7th Census).

The Palermo fragment cuts off in the year after the 10th Census, and it is not fully certain if Ninetjer's reign is resumed on Annals CF1. However, if the gap between the fragments has been correctly estimated, the king's last three or so years may be found there. In light of later events, it is intriguing that two of them featured building or other activity associated with the god Seth.

Manetho's chronicle alleges that under "Binôthris" (based on his position and similarity of name, clearly Ninetjer), "it was decided that women might hold the kingly office." However, as with most of his anecdotes (an exception being one attached to Djoser—see pages 84–85, below) it is unclear how this originated—and in any case no actual female pharaoh (Merneith was only queen regent) is known until Sobekneferu at the end of the Twelfth Dynasty.[13]

Ninetjer's tomb was cut 140 meters due east of that of Hetepsekhemwy. Its entrance was likewise close to the edge of the east–west cutting, and comprises a thirty-three-meter-long main corridor, blocked by two portcullises, flanked with storerooms (fig. 32b).[14] However, in contrast to the layout of the earlier tomb, Ninetjer's main corridor curves toward the west, and descends rapidly into the bedrock to reach the burial chamber. This is flanked by an intricate network of corridors and nearly two hundred chambers, some of which may belong to the original phase of construction, but which seem to have been further elaborated during a second phase of construction. The final form of the tomb covered an area of some 3,850 square meters, which, while extensive, was nevertheless around a third less than that of Hetepsekhemwy. Some parts of the tomb seem to have had, like elements of the tomb of Hetepsekhemwy, ritual significance, including cult places and even the streets and structures of a symbolic residence.[15]

The tomb's remote enclosure would seem likely to have been the one mentioned above as lying to the southwest of Hetepsekhemwy's putative example, and datable by pottery to the Second/Third Dynasty.[16] Known today as the Gisr el-Mudir, and covering an area of some twenty-five hectares, it used a rather more advanced mode of construction than the L-shaped Enclosure.[17] Its fifteen-meter-thick walls comprised a mixed filling within pairs of walls of limestone blocks, still standing in places to a height of over three meters, and still comprising perhaps the earliest known major stone construction in Egypt. No trace of any structure at the center has been identified, underlining its similarity to the Abydos enclosures.[18]

The Problems of the Mid-Second Dynasty

The succession of the first three kings of the Second Dynasty seems secure on the basis of the aforementioned priest's statue, while the various king lists are broadly consistent in the names they give to the first rulers of the line.[19] However, after Ninetjer ("Baennetjer"/"Banetjeru"/"[…] netjeren"/"Binôthris") the situation becomes more problematic:

Abydos	Saqqara	Turin	Manetho
Wadjnes	Wadjnes	[…]s; […] yrs	Tlas; 17 yrs
Senedi	Sened	Sened; […] yrs	Sethenês; 41 yrs
—	Neferkare	Aaka; […] yrs	Khairês; 17 yrs
—	Neferksokar	Neferkasokar; 8 yrs	Nepherkherês; 26 yrs
—	*ḥwḏf3*	*ḥwḏf3*; 11 yrs	Sesôkhris; 48 yrs
Djadjay	Beby	Bebty[…]; 27 yrs	Khenerês; 30 yrs

As may be seen, the Saqqara, Turin, and Manethonic lists give six further kings for the dynasty, while the Abydos has only three. They do, however agree (subject to orthographic variation) concerning the first two names after Ninetjer and the last king of the dynasty, focusing the problem clearly in the third quarter of the dynasty. This is underlined by the Saqqara and Turin lists including in this part of the dynasty a cartouche whose contents, "*ḥwḏf3*," seem not be a real name, but a word meaning "gap," although a full reign length (11 years, 8 months, and 4 days) and lifespan (34 years) are provided in the Turin Canon.[20]

These latter facts might suggest that the gap was based on the loss of a single name from one of the Canon's source documents. On the other hand, these may simply be the only details surviving from a gap in a source document that originally held a number of (possibly rival) kings. Perhaps belonging to this period is the Horus Ba, known from a piece of stone found at the Step Pyramid,[21] who has, however, also been proposed for placement at the beginning of the Second Dynasty[22] or during the latter part[23] of the Third Dynasty.

The "ḥwḏf3 Period" is preceded in both the Turin and Saqqara lists by a King "Neferkasokar." Before him the Saqqara list enumerates a King Neferkare, while the Turin Canon places here a King Aaka. It seems fairly clear that the '3-sign in the latter has been written in error for the *nfr*-sign, so that the name should actually be read as "Neferka." No Early Dynastic material survives that might provide a prototype for the name "Neferkasokar" (but see page 52, below, for a possible identification), but it has been suggested that there might be a connection between "Neferka(re)" and a king with the Horus-name Seneferka.[24]

Seneferka's name is known from a number of fragments of stone vessels. One came from under the Third Dynasty Step Pyramid, one from the area of tomb S3505 (datable to the reign of Qaa) at Saqqara, and one is of unknown origin. Others have come from an unpublished tomb at Saqqara, in the same general area as S3505. On the first two mentioned, the *serekh* is accompanied by texts that have exact parallels on similar fragments of Qaa, and on at least one of them the *serekh* of Seneferka has replaced an earlier royal name. Given the textual parallels and date of tomb S3503, Seneferka has generally been dated soon after Qaa, perhaps as his ephemeral successor—or even as an alternate Horus-name of Qaa. The latter lacks any external support, while there is no obvious reason to assume that the usurpation had to have taken place directly after Qaa's death. Accordingly, it is possible that the king lists' "Neferka(re)" could actually be a record of Seneferka, his absence from the Saqqara list perhaps reflecting ephemerality or doubtful legitimacy.

Going back to the succession following the end of the reign of Ninetjer, the Abydos and Saqqara lists agree in making the king who followed him "Wadjnes" (the Turin list is damaged at this point). Annals CF1 appears to cover the period at and following the end of Ninetjer's reign, ending in the beginning of the reign of a king Peribsen. It is not, however, clear whether the wholly effaced years directly before Peribsen's accession constitute the final years of Ninetjer, or one or more short reigns.

If the latter is indeed the case, "Wadjnes" might be the corruption of a Nebty-name, Weneg,[25] found in tomb S3014 at Saqqara,[26] as well as under the Step Pyramid. Whether this king may also be the "*nswt-bity* Nubnefer" named on two stone vessels from the Step Pyramid,[27] which have been dated to the period directly following Ninetjer,[28] is wholly unclear.[29]

All three king lists name the next king as "Sened/dj." A fragment of stone bowl was found in the Fourth Dynasty mortuary temple of Khaefre at Giza bearing the text "*nswt-bity* Sened,"[30] while it has been queried whether a stamped brick, found near the tomb of Ninetjer, with the cartouche Nefer*senedj*re[31] might refer to him. However, *if* this were a variant of the simple name "Senedj," it would almost certainly not be contemporary (cf. pages 94–95 on the question of the earliest cartouche); more likely it refers to an otherwise unknown king of the First or Second Intermediate Period. For the survival of Sened's name down to the latter period, see page 122, below.

Sened's funerary cult was, in any case, certainly still extant during the Fourth Dynasty, as evidenced by the Saqqara tomb (B3) of a certain Shery, who also served the cult of another Second Dynasty king, Peribsen (figs. 36, 95).[32] Peribsen was certainly buried at Umm el-Qaab (pages 50–51, below), but no trace of any potential sepulcher of Sened has ever been found there, and his tomb would seem most likely to have been at Saqqara, in which case Shery's responsibilities will have been widely spread geographically.

It has been suggested that a Second Dynasty king might have been responsible for the galleries (and possibly the mounds above them) that now form the western side of the Third Dynasty Step Pyramid complex (fig. 55a),[33] with Sened as a potential candidate. There are indeed similarities between these passages and rooms and those of the tombs of Hetepsekhemwy and Ninetjer, with the principal entrance at the north end of the long, rectangular superstructure. Their location is certainly not inconsistent with their being part of the same cemetery, the southern extremity of the structure being only fifty-five meters due north of the entrance to Hetepsekhemwy's tomb. Yet the galleries' resemblance to the tombs of Hetepsekhemwy and Ninetjer may be purely superficial, without any obvious burial chamber, and most probably belong to the Third Dynasty constructional program.[34] In any case, no trace of Sened's name has been

FIGURE 36 False door from the tomb chapel of Shery, from Saqqara (Cairo CG1384).

found anywhere in the area. If, as implied by the Annals, his reign was short, it seems unlikely that he could have been responsible for an enterprise of such magnitude.

Peribsen and Sekhemib

The second king whose cult was served by the aforementioned Shery, Peribsen, is, however, much better attested, but also presents major problems. He resumed the practice of kingly burial at Umm el-Qaab, his tomb there reverting back to the kind of structure employed by the kings of the First Dynasty, with brick chambers built in a cutting in the desert gravel (tomb P, fig. 37).[35] The remote enclosure (the so-called "Middle Fort") lay adjacent to the First Dynasty examples. Compared with them, it seems to have had a more elaborate north gate and—most importantly—lacked subsidiary burials.[36] Its walls had been dismantled in the same way as earlier ones, but enough survives to show that it had been decorated with the paneling that is typical of Early Dynastic private tombs, with gateways in the southeast and northeast corners and containing a small brick building. The lower parts of the enclosure's walls were painted red, as was a strip around the interior of the southeast gate.

FIGURE 37 The tomb of Peribsen (P) at Umm el-Qaab.

Back at Umm el-Qaab, Peribsen's burial chamber in tomb P (fig. 32c)[37] was surrounded by a series of storerooms, the whole structure having a corridor running between it and the outer retaining walls of the tomb. The two stelae that marked the offering place were of granite (fig. 38),[38] following the pattern seen with Reneb's surviving stela—with one important exception. This was the fact that the *serekh*s were topped, not by the Horus-falcon, but by the quadruped composite animal of Seth. This is also true in the sealings of Peribsen found in the tomb, at his remote enclosure, and elsewhere.[39] The tomb lacked subsidiary burials, as did its associated enclosure.

As retold by Plutarch, and supported by a whole range of pharaonic texts, Seth was the enemy of Horus, the murderer of the latter's father Osiris, over whose throne the two gods fought. Extensive texts in the great Ptolemaic temple of Horus at Edfu (fig. 39) give graphic accounts of the war that took place between the two gods and their followers,[40] and it has been suggested that these texts preserve a mythologized remote remembrance of the Second Dynasty civil war.[41] Others have denied any such connection, but it seems difficult to doubt that *some* real conflict provided the basis for parts of the account.[42] The "Myth of Horus" recounts that a rebellion occurred while the king (Horus) was en route back from a Nubian campaign, leading to a battle opposite Edfu. Further actions occurred as he pressed northward, at Dendara, Minya, and in the Fayyum, until the final defeat of the rebels in the northeast Delta, after which the survivors sought sanctuary in Nubia. While some attempts have been made to link the war (if real) to the reign of Ninetjer, in view of the possible mention of despoiling Egyptian towns in the Palermo fragment,[43] any echoes are more likely to refer to the period that begins with "the Seth" Peribsen.

That *something* had happened under (or just before) Peribsen is suggested by the resumption, after a fairly long gap, of royal burial in the south by that king. A breakdown in national unity may also be suggested by the presence of a brick enclosure akin to the remote enclosures at Abydos at

FIGURE 38 One of the two stelae from the offering place of the tomb of Peribsen (Cairo JE35261).

FIGURE 39 Part of the texts relating to the conflict between Horus and Seth; Ptolemaic Period, temple of Horus at Edfu.

Hierakonpolis (fig. 43),[44] possibly suggesting the presence of an Early Dynastic royal tomb there as well (see further below).[45] However, if the active "Sethian" protagonist in the civil war was Peribsen, it seems unlikely that he would have had an ongoing funerary cult that lasted into the Fourth Dynasty. Perhaps more likely is that Peribsen was merely the originator of a movement that only engendered full-scale civil conflict under a successor. The latter would most likely be the individual (or individuals) of the "*ḥwḏf3* Period" in the Saqqara and Turin lists. If so, and if Seneferka was indeed the origin of "Neferka(re)," Peribsen might lie behind "Neferkasokar," although nothing can be said as to how any of this latter name could have been derived.

A further complication is added by the fact that, as well as the sealings that name Peribsen, tomb P also contained sealings of a "Horus Sekhemib." The consensus has long been that this had been the original version of Peribsen's name, and that he had thus transitioned from being a Horus-king to a Seth-king—much as Amenhotep IV had become Akhenaten during the late Eighteenth Dynasty. However, an alternative is that Sekhemib had actually been Peribsen's successor. In this case the sealings would come from Sekhemib carrying out the funeral of his predecessor. This solution may be supported by the presence of a mass of Sekhemib sealings on what had been the contemporary desert surface just north of the tomb.[46] If this is the case, nothing else is known about Sekhemib, and he may thus be added to the list of potential owners of the late Second Dynasty cartouches of the Saqqara and Turin lists.

Of them, an unprovenanced cylinder seal exists bearing the cartouche of Neferkasokar,[47] but its style would strongly suggest that it was made some time after the Second Dynasty, tying in with the fact that the name was apparently still remembered as that of an early king as late as the second century AD (pages 135–36, below). Among these late mentions is a text that attributed to his time a seven-year famine (a trope also attributed in Greco-Roman times to Djoser—pages 137, 135–36): one wonders whether this represented some remote remembrance of an aspect of the crisis of the later Second Dynasty.

Khasekhem(wy)

While the beginning(s) of the troubles that seem to have enveloped the middle years of the Second Dynasty are obscure, their end is rather better defined. From Hierakonpolis come vessels naming a King Khasekhem, in each case with his name accompanied by a monogram showing the goddess Nekhbet standing on a hieroglyph for "rebel" and a label text reading "year of fighting the northern enemy" (fig. 40). In addition, the bases of a pair of statues of the king bear depictions of fallen enemies, with labels referring to "47,209 northern enemies" (fig. 41). Warfare to the south, into Nubia, may be indicated by a fragment of stela from the same site (fig. 42).

The same king is also associated with the aforementioned enclosure at Hierakonpolis (fig. 43),[48] and if correctly identified as a funerary monument, on the basis of its similarity to the remote enclosures at Abydos, it would suggest that Khasekhem ("Appearance-of-Power") intended to be buried there—presumably being excluded even from Abydos by his "northern enemies." However, the king would ultimately find rest in the ancient Umm el-Qaab cemetery, having seemingly overcome all foes and now the king of a reunited Egypt, the Hierakonpolis enclosure being apparently repurposed (see below). On the basis of sealings from the king's tomb which name her as "Mother of the King's Children," his principal wife was one Nimaathap, who would be the mother of his successor (page 64, below).

Having achieved victory, the king amended his *serekh* name, doubling its second element to make the name read "Appearance-of-*Two*-Powers," adding the epithet "The-Two-Lords-Are-Content-in-Him," and topping the *serekh* uniquely with both the Horus falcon and the Seth animal. The implications of this are clearly that not only was the

FIGURE 40 Granite vessel bearing the name of Khasekhem and text commemorating fighting against a northern foe; from Hierakonpolis (Cairo CG14724).

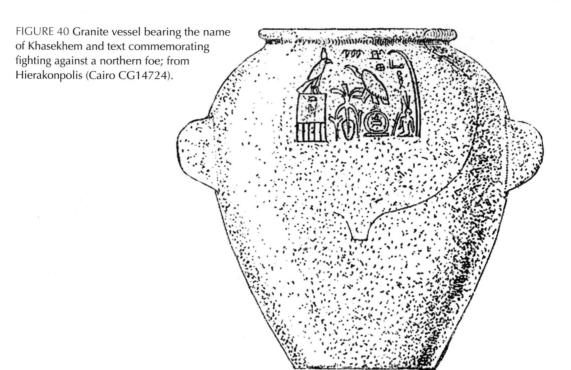

FIGURE 41 Two statuettes of Khasekhem, from Hierakonpolis (left: Cairo JE32161; right: Ashmolean AN1896-1908 E.517).

FIGURE 42 Fragment of stela of Khasekhem; from Hierakonpolis (Cairo JE33890).

now-Khasekhemwy victorious, but also that reconciliation was at least nominally the policy now being followed. That it was successful in renewing the country and building up its economy is strongly suggested by the availability of the resources required for his successor to build the extraordinary funerary monument that is now known as the Step

Pyramid (pages 67–83, below). The reunification is indicated archaeologically by tomb S3043 being the first sepulcher at Saqqara to contain a sealing of a king since the time of Ninetjer.[49] Nevertheless, Khasekhemwy's principal surviving non-funerary monuments are from the Hierakonpolis region, both at the city itself and across the river at El-Kab.[50] Elsewhere in Egypt, reliefs of Early Dynastic Period style from Gebelein[51] may date to Khasekhemwy's time.

At the Hierakonpolis enclosure,[52] a central brick structure was equipped with major granite elements. Surviving parts include a pink granite column base, originally one of a pair, a lintel featuring the king performing rituals and in the company of the gods. Since Khasekhemwy is shown at least once wearing jubilee dress, it is possible that the enclosure may have been repurposed as a jubilee monument once the king had decided to be buried elsewhere.

Within the temple area at Hierakonpolis (fig. 2, top right), a number of architectural fragments bearing the king's name have been found. They include a stela fragment near its entrance (fig. 42), and three granite blocks that lay close to a revetment that formed the facing of a sandy mound that served as the base of a temple, apparently founded back in the First Dynasty (fig. 44). These blocks included part of a monumental gateway, with the king's *serekh* on the doorjamb, and a scene on the interior (later erased) of the king carrying out a foundation ritual (fig. 45).[53] Clearly, Khasekhemwy had extended and adorned this ancient temple, the aforementioned statuettes also forming part of this program.

What seem to be records of the last part of Khasekhemwy's reign are preserved on the Palermo fragment of the Annals. The first surviving year features a Following of Horus and the 6th Census, the latter implying that this is the king's Year 12. The following year featured an Appearance of the king, and the construction of a stone building called "The

FIGURE 43 The enclosure of Khasekhemwy at Hierakonpolis.

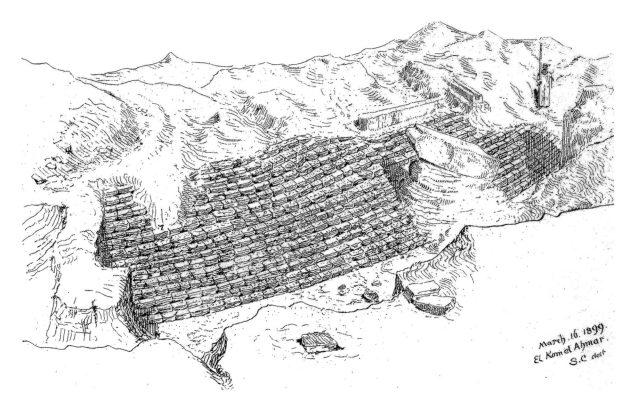

FIGURE 44 Revetment of the Early Dynastic foundation mound of the temple at Hierakonpolis, with fragments of a structure of Khasekhemwy in the foreground.

Goddess Endures." This was perhaps at Hierakonpolis or Gebelein, both of which were female cult centers (of Nekhbet and Hathor respectively) and preserve material of the period. The 7th Census (now qualified as "of gold and fields," as is the 8th Census) is then followed the next year by "creating a copper statue (named) 'High is Khasekhemwy.'" This is the first mention of such a genre of sculpture, the earliest surviving examples of which come from the Old Kingdom. The king's last full year (after the 8th Census) saw the fourth occasion of "reaching(?) the wall," an otherwise unknown ritual, and a shipbuilding enterprise in an unidentifiable location. In connection with this, a fragment of stone vessel bearing Khasekhemwy's name was found at Byblos on the Lebanese coast,[54] suggesting contacts with that region. A broader interest in overseas relations is indicated by a sealing from the reign that gives the earliest known mention of the title *imy-r ḫ3swt*, "Overseer of Foreign Countries."[55] The next year, however, saw the king's death, two months and twenty-three days into what would appear to have been (assuming biennial censuses) his Year 18.

FIGURE 45 Granite block from a doorway, with intact names of Khasekhemwy on its outer part. The interior was decorated with a scene of the king carrying out a foundation ceremony in the company of the goddess Sesheshet, but this was later erased; from Hierakonpolis (Cairo JE33896=CG57107).

With the reunification, the Saqqara necropolis will have become available again as a royal burial place. Certainly, before the end of the reign a new private necropolis had been established in a new area some two hundred meters south of the royal cemetery, with one burial dated by the presence of a sealing of Khasekhemwy.[56] This area was much later employed as the core of a great late Eighteenth/Nineteenth Dynasty necropolis, which destroyed any superstructures, but left elements of the substructures of the ancient tombs to be subsumed into those of the later sepulchers.[57]

However—perhaps because Saqqara only became an option relatively late in his reign—Khasekhemwy followed Peribsen in being buried at Umm el-Qaab, thus apparently abandoning—or repurposing—the enclosure at Hierakonpolis. His Abydene monuments are the largest of their respective types there. The actual tomb (V—figs. 32d, 46)[58] was, as usual, constructed in a pit and composed of mud brick, and in its initial form had much in common with the tomb of Peribsen. As such, it was entirely built of brick, in a pit in the desert gravel some five meters deep. However, the central room was then replaced by one of limestone, sunk two meters below the original floor level, the latter being the baseline for storerooms to the north (two) and south. The whole was approached by a ramp from the south.

FIGURE 46 The tomb of Khasekhemwy (V) at Umm el-Qaab with, inset, a fragment of one of the tomb's stelae.

A subsequent series of extensions then added further rooms on the north, a new group of ten on the south bringing the total number of rooms to fifty-eight. Finally, two pairs of rooms were added on each side of the access ramp at the southern end of the tomb. Two skeletons lay in a contracted pose to the east of the burial chamber, seemingly representing the last known manifestations of the custom of burying retainers with the kings that had peaked back in the time of Djer, and had steadily declined since. Although now sixty-eight meters long by twelve meters broad, the tomb even then occupied an area only 15 percent of that of the Saqqara tomb of Hetepsekhemwy.

Almost every chamber still contained material when excavated (see page 152), including jars of stone and pottery (predominantly in the northern half of the tomb), together with considerable numbers of vessels and other items in copper (fig. 47). Among the most impressive of these items was a gold and carnelian scepter, while some

FIGURE 47 Copper vessel and model tools from the tomb of Khasekhemwy (Liverpool 14.10.01.50a–j).

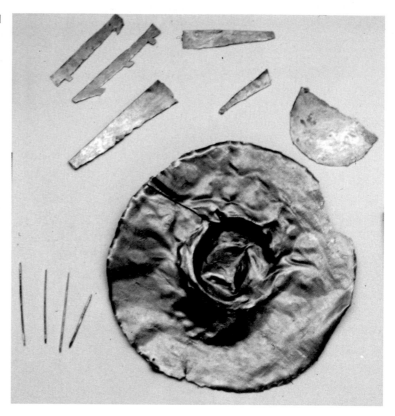

of the stone jars carried gold foil lids. The tomb would appear to have been marked by a rectangular tumulus, perhaps covering about half of the area of the substructure, which may have been clad in limestone. Of the stelae that delineated the tomb's offering place, some granite fragments from one were found to the south of the tomb itself, while the second (fig. 46, inset) was found, broken, in a secondary context some two kilometers to the east.[59]

Khasekhemwy's remote funerary enclosure, known today as the Shunet el-Zebib, is the only one of its genre at Abydos still standing (fig. 48),[60] with its paneled walls rising up to eleven meters above the desert surface. It was a much more massive structure than earlier examples, with a further outer wall enclosing the main paneled structure; compared with the Hierakonpolis enclosure, it covered more than two and a half times as much area. Its survival is presumably due to it being the last such enclosure built at Abydos, and thus not subject to dismantlement by a successor before building his own monument. As with previous enclosures, it seemingly housed no permanent structures other than a small brick building, but since much of the interior of the enclosure was reused as a cemetery for sacred ibises in Late and Ptolemaic times, it is possible that other elements may have been thus obliterated.[61]

FIGURE 48 The Shunet el-Zebib, Khasekhemwy's funerary enclosure at Abydos, showing the paneled inner walls.

3 THE THIRD DYNASTY

Although its products include one of the most significant of all ancient Egyptian monuments—the Step Pyramid at Saqqara—the Third Dynasty is in many ways as obscure as the Second, with the order and identification of its kings remaining distinctly problematic.[1] The state of the king lists for the period indicates the scope of the problem:

Abydos	Saqqara	Turin	Manetho
Nebka	—	Nebka; […] yrs	Necherôphês; 28 yrs
Djoser-sa[…]	Djoser	Djoser-itet; 19 yrs	Tosorthros; 29 yrs
—	—	—	Tyr(e)is; 7 yrs
—	—	—	Mesôkhris; 17 yrs
—	—	—	Sôÿphis; 16 yrs
Teti	Djoser-teti	Djoser-ty; 6 yrs	Tosertasis; 19 yrs
—	Nebkare	—	Akhês; 42 yrs
sds	—	[*ḥwḏf*]3; 6yrs	Sêphuris; 30 yrs
Neferkare	Huni	Hu[ni]; 24 yrs	Kerpherês; 26 yrs

In contrast to the earlier dynasties where, apart from the third quarter of the Second Dynasty, there is a broad agreement between these later sources, here there are few points of correlation, in names, numbers, or both.

The most straightforward equations are seen with the two Djoser kings. This is due to both their relative positions and their name forms, which are also found in other ancient contexts (see pages 126, 128, 131). As noted earlier concerning its occurrence in lists of the Second Dynasty (pages 47–48, above), "*ḥwḏf3*" seems to signify the existence of a gap in a source document, with "*sḏs*" likely to have a similar significance ("*sḏ sy*"— "damaged").[2] That the sources available to the compilers of the lists thus presented them with problems is further indicated by the lack of agreement over the position of "Nebka"/"Nebkare"/"Necherôphês"—three lists placing him at the beginning of the dynasty, the fourth near the end. However, the discovery of sealings bearing the Horus-name Netjerkhet—certainly to be identified with Djoser (see just below and pages 148–49)—in the tomb of Khasekhemwy at Abydos[3] makes it clear that Nebka cannot have reigned before Djoser and must indeed have ruled later in the dynasty.

Linking the list of Manetho with the pharaonic lists is replete with problems, both over the Greek source giving double the number of kings, and equating its names with those in the pharaonic lists. However, "Tosorthros" is fairly transparently "Djoser"/"Djoser-sa"/"Djoser-itet," and "Tosertasis" is the equivalent of "Teti"/"Djoser-teti"/"Djoser-ty." "Necherôphês," "Kerpherês," and "Sêphouris" are probably to be derived from "Nebka," "Neferkare," and "*sḏs*," respectively. "Akhês" may be a misplacement of the Turin list's Second Dynasty "Aaka," but the rest of the names on Manetho's list have no obvious equivalents. All this most likely reflects the corrupt state of available sources for the dynasty even in New Kingdom times, given the confusion over the placement of Nebka and the inclusion of "kings" who were actually notations of gaps in source documents.

Djoser

Although contemporary material only refers to him by his Horus-name, Netjerkhet, by the New Kingdom the first king of the new dynasty was being referred to as "Djoser," the name by which he is most commonly known today (see pages 122–23, below). As already noted, it now seems clear that he was the direct successor of Khasekhemwy. That the latter's wife, Nimaathap, was Djoser's mother seems fairly transparent on the basis that sealings of hers, which call her "King's Mother," were found with others naming Djoser in a huge mastaba at Beit Khallaf (K1), just north of Abydos (fig. 49).[4] Although there is no certainty about the tomb's ownership, since sealings of a range of individuals were found inside, the sepulcher's sheer size and elaborate internal arrangements (fig. 50) make it difficult to assess as other than a royal tomb.[5] If so, Nimaathap seems the most obvious candidate for its ownership.

That Djoser's reign was felt to be an important point in Egyptian history by New Kingdom scribes is indicated by the fact that his title is exceptionally inscribed in red ink in the Turin Canon (T4.5—fig. 107). He also seems to have stood at the beginning of a new column in one of the Canon's precursor documents.[6] The Canon gives a reign

FIGURE 49 Beit Khallaf tomb K1 with, inset, one of its seal impressions naming the King's Mother Nimaathap.

length of nineteen years, although his age at death is lost. The Third Dynasty is the last for which ages at death were included.

While the king is simply "Djoser" in the Saqqara king list, in the Canon it is expanded to "Djoser-i[te]t," while at Abydos the extant cartouche reads "Djoser-sa," but something has been erased above the two existing signs. One can only assume that this is the correction of some error—perhaps a sun disk inserted to give the name the New Kingdom–type format "X-Y-Re" that is most commonly found in the king lists (cf. page 181 n7, below).

Annals of the first five years of the reign are preserved on the Palermo fragment, beginning with the last nine months and twelve days of Khasekhemwy's last year, for which only the usual accession ceremonies are recorded. A royal Appearance and the king's "introduction into the *snwt(i)*-shrine" are recorded for the following year, with Djoser's first Following of Horus and the creation of a figure of Min marking the subsequent one. The remaining two years note the next Appearance and the foundation of a building, and the subsequent Following of Horus, before breaking off. Although the Turin Canon gives Djoser a nineteen-year reign, there seems to be no change-of-reign year division in the appropriate position on Annals CF1, the combination of the two sections suggesting that Turin's "19" years were an error for the *29 preserved in Manetho.

PLAN

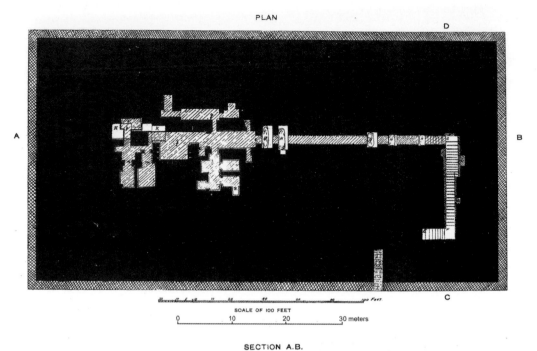

SECTION A.B.

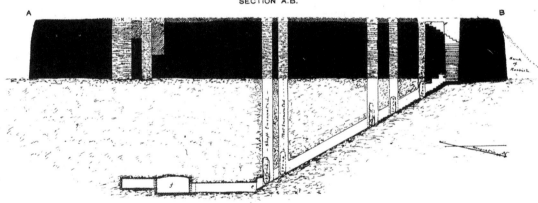

SECTION C.D.

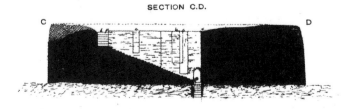

REFERENCES.

A B, C D SECTION LINES
E   TOP OF STAIRWAY, BROKEN AWAY
E F G DESCENDING STAIRWAY
G   STAIRWAY PASSES SOUTH UNDER ARCH
H···H SHAFTS FOR LOWERING PORTCULLIS STONES
K K WELLS FOR OFFERINGS
L   SLOPED WAY OF ACCESS
F G STAIRS FILLED WITH OFFERINGS
a b RECESSES FOR OFFERINGS
c   RECESS USED BY PLUNDERERS
d   GUIDE FOR PORTCULLIS STONE
G e PASSAGE DESCENDING UNDERGROUND
f   LARGE STONE-WALLED CHAMBER
g   GALLERY STORED WITH GRAIN IN SACKS
k   CHAMBERS FILLED WITH VESSELS OF OFFERINGS
m n p CHAMBERS FOR OFFERINGS
S   CHAMBER IN WHICH WAS SEALING OF PER-AB-SEN

FIGURE 50 Plan and section of Beit Khallaf K1.

Non-funerary material dating to Djoser's reign includes fragments of relief from a sanctuary at Heliopolis (figs. 51, 53) and a tableau at the Wadi Maghara in the Sinai (fig. 52a). This representation marks the earliest known royal expedition to this mining area, henceforth an important source of copper and turquoise. Apart from the king's mother, a wife, Hetephirnebty—probably a daughter of Khasekhemwy[7]—and a daughter, Intkaes, are known from a number of sources. These include a relief from the king's Heliopolis structure (fig. 53) and boundary stelae from the Step Pyramid complex.[8]

Southern officials of the reign are known from sealings in tombs K1 and K5 at Beit Khallaf, with the anonymous K3 and K4 also dated to Djoser's time. Meanwhile the First/Second Dynasty private necropolis at the northern end of Saqqara continued to grow westward under Djoser. Among the tombs dated by sealings to his reign is S2405, belonging to an official named Hesyre, and incorporating a number of innovative decorative elements, in particular some superb wooden reliefs (fig. 54) and the first known painted frieze of objects.[9] Dated by the same means are S2305 and S3518;[10] although neither preserved the name of their owner, a possibility for the latter tomb is considered below (pages 86–87, 161–62). Other tombs of similar design in the same area (see fig. 25) are also likely to date to the reign of Djoser.

However, in spite of the inherent interest of the aforementioned material, and the implications of Hesyre's reliefs for artistic progress in Egypt at this time, the key

FIGURE 51 Fragmentary relief from a structure of Djoser at Heliopolis (Turin S.2671).

FIGURE 52 Drawings of reliefs from the Wadi Maghara showing kings of the Third Dynasty: a. Djoser; b–c. Sanakhte; d. Sekhemkhet.

monument for the assessment of Djoser's reign is his tomb. As already noted, until the end of the Second Dynasty, the Egyptian royal tomb had comprised two distinct and separate elements—the burial place itself and a ceremonial enclosure. While both of these elements were retained by Djoser, they were now combined into a single monument. Not only this, but the combined monument was built entirely from limestone—albeit using blocks whose size approximated conventional mud bricks; furthermore, the superstructure over the burial place would go through an evolution that ultimately created the first ever pyramid (figs. 55a, 56).

FIGURE 53 Fragment of relief from a structure of Djoser at Heliopolis, showing the lower part of a seated figure of the king and representations of his wife Hetephirnebty and his daughter Intkaes (Turin S.2671).

The enclosure wall followed the basic model seen at the Shunet el-Zebib, with a paneled exterior and a principal entrance at the southern end of the east wall (fig. 57). This led, via an elaborate colonnade (fig. 58), to an open courtyard (figs. 59, 60) containing elements associated with the ritual run that formed part of the royal jubilee ceremonies. A complex of shrines in the adjacent "Heb-sed Court" was also associated with these

FIGURE 54 Detail of the paneled façade of the tomb of Hesyre (S2405) at Saqqara, and two of the wooden panels (Cairo CG1426–27) that adorned it.

activities (fig. 61), while many of the other structures within the pyramid enclosure also seem to belong to jubilee or coronation rituals. Most of these buildings were solid dummies, imitating constructions from organic materials. This suggests that their prototypes may have been the temporary structures that may have been erected within the Early Dynastic enclosures of Abydos and Saqqara.

Taking these elements together with the presence in the subterranean portions of Djoser's complex of reliefs of the king taking part in jubilee-related ceremonies (fig. 69), it seems possible that these ceremonies may, at this point in Egyptian history, have formed a basis for the conception of the dead king's revivification. Given the clear affinities between the Step Pyramid complex and the enclosures associated with earlier royal tombs, it may be that these were also intended as the venues for a posthumous jubilee, perhaps carried out as part of the funerary rituals. Unfortunately, the lack of any textual material relating to the king's posthumous destiny prior to the appearance of the Pyramid Texts at the end of the Fifth Dynasty makes any assessment of the beliefs potentially underlying the earliest royal funerary monuments highly problematic.

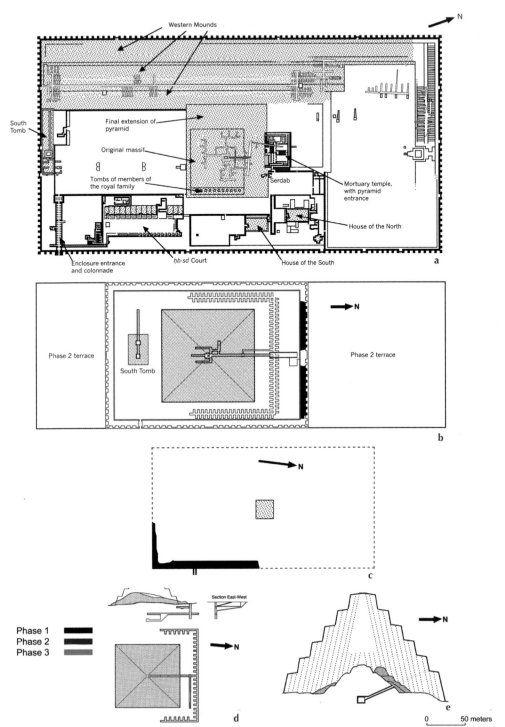

FIGURE 55 The royal tombs of the Third Dynasty: a. the Step Pyramid (Djoser); b. the pyramid of Sekhemkhet; c. El-Deir (Sanakhte?); d. the Layer Pyramid (Khaba?); e. the Brick Pyramid (Huni?).

FIGURE 56 Model of Djoser's Step Pyramid complex at Saqqara (Brussels).

FIGURE 57 Entrance to the Step Pyramid complex and its southern wall.

FIGURE 58 Entrance colonnade to the Step Pyramid complex.

It has been suggested that the Step Pyramid enclosure was originally laid out to a somewhat smaller and simpler plan, and was only later extended to the north and west to achieve its final form.[11] However, closer analysis of the data would seem to make this unlikely, although it seems clear that numerous detail changes were made throughout the construction process.[12]

The area occupied by the enclosure was separated from the surrounding plateau by cuttings on all four sides (see fig. 25), the southwestern section apparently being taken over from works accompanying the building of the Second Dynasty royal funerary monuments

FIGURE 59 The southern face of the Step Pyramid from the southern court, with the outline of the original low superstructure clearly visible.

in that area (see pages 41–44, 46–47, above).[13] This part of the "dry moat" is split on the south side, suggesting that the ancient approach to the entrance to the complex was past the Second Dynasty enclosures, then along the northern fronts of the Second Dynasty royal tombs themselves, and finally on to the wide terrace on the east front of the Step Pyramid enclosure, as defined by the eastern arm of the "dry moat."

The Step Pyramid itself, eventually sixty meters high, on a base of 121 by 109 meters, was constructed in the center of the enclosure. It was begun as a low square structure, which was then enlarged laterally, subsequently being transformed into a four-stepped pyramid, and then into the final six-stepped rectangular structure (figs. 62 top, 65). While the original monument was constructed from horizontal layers of masonry, the additional

FIGURE 60 Southern court of the Step Pyramid complex, with the entrance to the Heb-sed Court in the center, and the entrance colonnade and South Tomb (embedded in the enclosure wall) on the right.

FIGURE 61 Dummy shrines on the west side of the Heb-sed Court.

FIGURE 62 Top: detail of the southeast corner of the Step Pyramid, showing the original square monument (built using horizontal rows of blocks) and the two initial eastward extensions, using masonry sloped inward perpendicular to the external slope of the monument. The same was true of the accretion layers of the pyramid phase, shown (bottom) on the north side.

stonework was laid in inward-sloping layers (fig. 62 bottom), a technique previously seen at the Gisr el-Mudir, and which would be used in all subsequent pyramids down to the Bent Pyramid of Seneferu at the beginning of the Fourth Dynasty. Although the core of Djoser's monument was built from limestone quarried nearby, this was faced with much finer stone from the Tura quarries on the opposite side of the Nile. This pattern of material usage continued in all subsequent stone-built pyramids.

A temple built against the north face of the pyramid, but entered from the east (fig. 63 top), followed a plan reminiscent of one first found in the tomb of Merka, back in the reign of Qaa (page 39, above). Just outside its entrance was placed a statue of the

FIGURE 63 The Step Pyramid from the northwest, showing the remains of the mortuary temple. The *serdab* (location marked with an arrow) is shown at the bottom, with a view through one of the "eyeholes" to the modern cast of the statue within.

king, enclosed in a windowless room known as a *serdab* (figs. 63 bottom, 64), presumably to allow offerings to be placed without actually entering the temple. This image of the king is near-life size and the earliest such statue known. It was originally painted and equipped with inlaid eyes.

The substructure of the pyramid centered on a burial chamber constructed at the bottom of a vertical shaft, which would be filled in once the chamber had been built. Access was via a sloping passage from the north (figs. 65e–f, 66 left, 67), which terminated in a now-destroyed room built of limestone, under whose floor was a cist constructed of granite blocks, accessed via a "stopper" in its roof (fig. 66 right).[14] When the first stage of the monument was laid out, this sloping passage led directly north to an entrance, but when the superstructure was extended in this direction, the approach was shifted to the western end of a new transverse room (fig. 65 no. 4), giving access to the definitive entrance in the western court of the mortuary temple (fig. 65a).

Human remains, including a foot, were found in the cist, with molded wrappings of a type often found during the Old Kingdom.[15] However, there are questions about whether all belonged to the same individual, while radiocarbon determinations make them some two thousand years or more too recent for any to actually represent the remains of Djoser. Nevertheless, their archaeological context in the difficult-to-access cist and embalming technique is problematic if they indeed come from Late/Greco-Roman intrusive burials elsewhere in the pyramid.[16]

The burial cist was surrounded, at a slightly lower level, by a complex of galleries. Most were fairly rough, but two sets were lined with fine limestone, their doorways adorned with the name and titles of the king, and their walls inlaid with countless faience tiles, to imitate matting (figs. 68, 69). The outermost group, not fully complete when work was abandoned (fig. 65m–n), also incorporated a series of stelae, showing the king in ritual poses related to the jubilee (fig. 69).[17]

Originally outside the eastern boundary of the first massif over the royal tomb, but then covered by its extension and transformation into a pyramid, were nine shaft tombs (fig. 65 nos. I–IX), with corridors penetrating westward below the level of the main substructure.[18] That they were originally intended for the burial of members of the royal family is indicated by the presence of alabaster sarcophagi, or fragments thereof, in tombs I, II, IV, and V. The two unbroken examples are in tomb V, whose walls had originally been lined with wood paneling. The sarcophagus at the far end of the tomb was found to contain a gilded plywood inner coffin and the skeleton of a child, probably male and around nine years of age; it lay on its left-hand side.[19] Two sarcophagi of identical design (fig. 103) were found reused in the Twelfth Dynasty pyramid complex of Senwosret III, and are likely to have been extracted from these galleries (pages 120–22, below).

FIGURE 64 The statue of Djoser from the *serdab* of the Step Pyramid (Cairo JE49158).

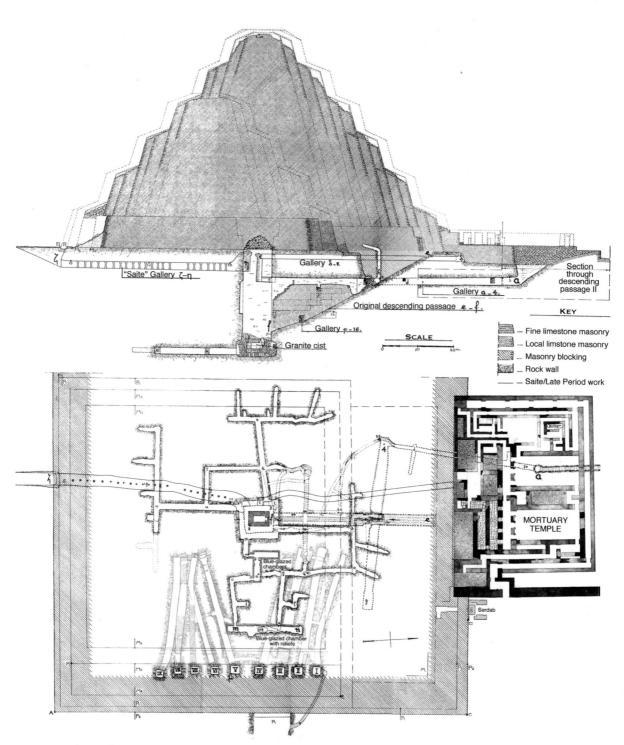

FIGURE 65 Plan and section of the Step Pyramid.

FIGURE 66 Views down the last section of the entrance passage of the Step Pyramid and down onto the burial cist; inset: blocks from the ceiling of the destroyed chamber above the cist.

However, in addition to their roles as the burial places of the royal family, the galleries, in particular VI and VII, were used as repositories for huge quantities of broken stone vessels, dating from the beginning of the First Dynasty down to the end of the Second Dynasty. The meaning of these deposits has been much debated, one suggestion being that some derive from the clearance of tombs plundered during the civil wars of the Second Dynasty. Further deposits of stone vessel fragments were made in the long galleries under the western side of the enclosure.

Yet more subterranean galleries lie under the northeast and northern parts of the enclosure.[20] The former (listed as Saqqara tomb 86/A4) were found to contain embalming material dating from the New Kingdom, but clearly formed part of the original Third Dynasty pyramid complex, and may originally have been intended as further royal family tombs. This is also likely to be the case with the second set of galleries, which contained sealings of Djoser and Khasekhemwy. This same location was chosen some eight centuries

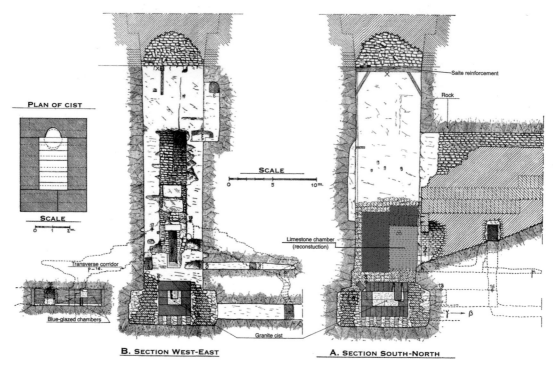

PLAN OF CIST

SCALE
0   1   2ᵐ.

Transverse corridor
P - 16.

Blue-glazed chambers

B. Section West-East

SCALE
0   5   10ᵐ.

Saïte reinforcement

Rock

Limestone chamber
(reconstuction)

Granite cist

A. Section South-North

FIGURE 67 Sections of the central part of the substructure of the Step Pyramid.

later for the burial places of members of the family of Senwosret III, the basic layout of whose funerary complex was derived from that of Djoser (see pages 120–22).

A further set of galleries was situated below a mastaba built into the south wall of the enclosure (figs. 69, 70). This so-called "South Tomb" duplicated the key elements of the substructure of the Step Pyramid itself on a reduced scale, including the "stoppered" burial cist and the faience-paneled rooms, with reliefs of the king (fig. 71). With no trace of a burial—and a granite cist too small in any case to hold a body—the South Tomb's purpose has been much debated, one popular idea being that it may have housed Djoser's embalmed viscera. However, one thing that seems clear is that the South Tomb was the prototype for the "subsidiary pyramids" that would be built to the south of almost all pyramids from the beginning of the Fourth Dynasty to the middle of the Twelfth. None of these were demonstrably used for viscera—and, indeed, from the middle of the Fourth Dynasty onward it is certain that viscera were interred in the main pyramid's burial chamber. It must thus be admitted that the purpose of both the later subsidiary pyramids and Djoser's South Tomb remains obscure (see page 94, below, for the anomalous situation at the complex of Sekhemkhet).

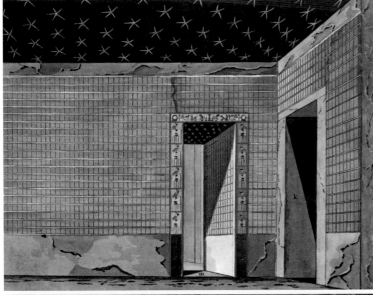

FIGURE 68 The western inner blue-glazed chamber of the Step Pyramid in 1821, and the eastern chamber, looking into the western, in 2020. This shows the removal of the inscribed doorway between them in 1843, and the loss of almost all faience tiles, many examples of which are in museums around the world.

Imhotep

Later tradition associated Djoser with one Imhotep (pages 131–34, below), who by the Late Period was regarded as a great sage and had been deified as a patron of physicians and scribes.[21] Contemporary confirmation of Imhotep's existence and exceptional standing comes from a statue base of Djoser found in the entrance colonnade of the complex, which names not only the king himself, but also the "Chancellor, First after the King, Administrator of the Great Palace, Nobleman, High Priest at Heliopolis, Chief Sculptor and Vase-maker," Imhotep (fig. 72). This kind of citation of a commoner on a royal statue

FIGURE 69 The northern part of the eastern blue-glazed chamber of the Step Pyramid, as reconstructed in the Imhotep Museum, Saqqara, and, bottom left, the southern (left-hand) niche, still in situ under the pyramid. The latter and the central stelae had grids drawn over them in ink in much later times (see page 129).

is quite exceptional, and clearly indicates that tradition was right in its characterization of Imhotep's importance.

The earliest evidence for Imhotep's posthumous regard dates to the New Kingdom,[22] being later linked with a later sage, Amenhotep-son-of-Hapu, a high official of the reign of Amenhotep III.[23] In the work of Manetho, the extant entry for Djoser attributes to

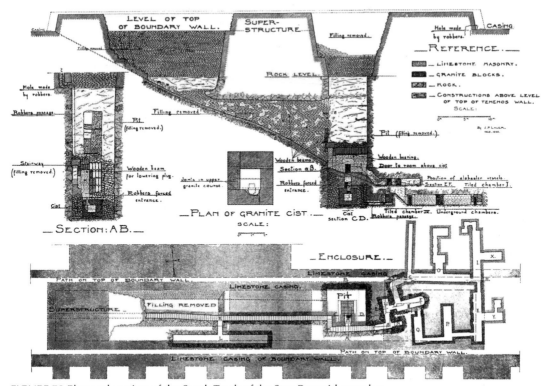

FIGURE 70 Plan and section of the South Tomb of the Step Pyramid complex.

the king the statement that "because of his medical skill has the reputation of Asclepios among the Egyptians and who was the inventor of the art of building with hewn stone. He also devoted attention to writing." As these attributes closely align with those of Imhotep from the Late Period onward, it has generally been assumed that Imhotep's name dropped out of the entry during the transmission of the Manethonic text (page 133). On this basis, tradition will also have had Imhotep as the originator of stone architecture, with the implication that he was responsible for the construction of the Step Pyramid complex.[24] Interestingly, no formal title associating him with royal works is given on the aforementioned statue base, but this may simply be a reflection of a status that made him an ultimate de facto authority for a wide range of activities, regardless of his specific titles, which may actually reflect ones gained incrementally during his career.[25]

FIGURE 71 Northern stela niche from tiled room II under the South Tomb.

FIGURE 72 Base of statue of Djoser, found in the entrance colonnade of the Step Pyramid complex, including the name and titles of Imhotep (Imhotep Museum, Saqqara, ex-Cairo JE60487).

No tomb preserves Imhotep's name, but it would seem most likely that he would have been buried in the northern Saqqara cemetery (fig. 25) that, as we have already seen, had progressively spread westward from the original row of First Dynasty noble tombs at the eastern edge of the escarpment. Intriguingly, two of the largest examples attributable to the Third Dynasty, S3518 (figs. 73, 130) and S3050, have an orientation significantly different from the vast majority of tombs in the area. While most tombs essentially follow the nearly north–south alignment of the original First Dynasty tombs, these two are oriented significantly east of north—just like the Step Pyramid complex (probably owing to the need to align it with the Second Dynasty rock-cutting defining the "royal precinct" directly to the south). Might one of them have been the tomb of Imhotep?

A further suggestive feature is that S3518 stands directly above the later temple complex of the Sacred Animal Necropolis that grew up in the area during the Late Period. The main gallery for the burial of the sacred baboons of Thoth directly intersects one of the two burial shafts of the ancient tomb, and two of the galleries' branches run under or just west of S3518's façade. Through his position as a patron of learning, Imhotep was linked to Thoth (cf. page 135, below), and images of Imhotep (fig. 116 left) were among the kinds of votive offerings deposited in the temple complex.[26] There is accordingly a strong likelihood that the temple complex lay close to Imhotep's tomb—

FIGURE 73 Saqqara tomb S3518—a candidate for the tomb of Imhotep—on the western edge of the Third Dynasty necropolis at Saqqara, and overlooking what would later be the Sacred Animal Necropolis (fig. 130), whose baboon galleries intersect S3518's southern burial shaft. In the distance are the Fifth Dynasty pyramids of Abusir, and in the middle ground the grove of palm trees marks the beginning of the wadi that comprised the principal approach to the Saqqara necropolis for much of its history.

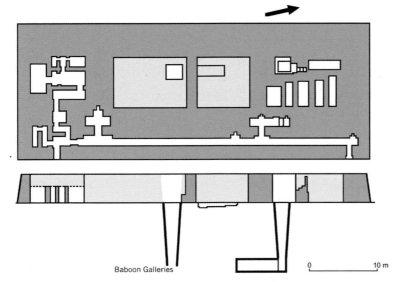

Baboon Galleries

0   10 m

and S3518 stands directly above the temple, as well as being directly connected to its baboon catacomb. Taken with its orientation and date, a strong case can therefore be made for S3518 being the tomb of Imhotep, although, in the absence of any surviving relevant texts, this is not susceptible to absolute proof.

Sekhemkhet

It seems fairly clear that the next place in the royal succession should be taken by Sekhemkhet, the owner of an unfinished step pyramid complex at Saqqara (fig. 74), whose architecture and position clearly indicate a chronological position soon after the

FIGURE 74 View from the north end of the pyramid complex of Sekhemkhet at Saqqara, showing the original northern enclosure wall, the pyramid entrance, and the remains of the unfinished structure itself. In the distance are (from the left) the monuments of Isesi; Senwosret III; Nemtyemsaf I; Shepseskaf; Pepy II; and the two of Seneferu at Dahshur.

FIGURE 75 Graffito of Imhotep on the enclosure wall of Sekhemkhet.

monument of Djoser. Furthermore, an inscription found in the pyramid would appear to read "may the Nebty Djoser-ti live!" (fig. 80 top), a name that must be the prototype of the "Djoser-ty" of the Turin Canon (T4.6), with the variants "Djoser-teti" and "Teti" of the Saqqara and Abydos lists (S14, A16). He would thus also be the "Teti" included on a later writing board that lists a number of the predecessors of the Fifth Dynasty King Neferirkare (fig. 97).

While these names directly follow that of Djoser in the pharaonic king lists, Manetho interposes a Tyr(e)is, Mesôkhris, and Sôÿphis between Tosorthros (Djoser) and Tosertasis (Djoser-ty/teti), for whom there are no obvious candidates. This would seem to be simply evidence of the disordered state of the transmission of the history of the Third Dynasty, rather than concealing real kings.[27]

Additional support for placing Sekhemkhet directly after Djoser may come from a construction graffito on the enclosure wall of the monument, which mentions an Imhotep (fig. 75), who seems most likely to be the great figure of Djoser's reign,

FIGURE 76 The two Wadi Maghara reliefs of Sekhemkhet; the king's *serekh*s in the upper image have been cut out in recent times (cf. early twentieth-century drawing, fig. 52d).

overseeing work on the complex of a close successor. Apart from the pyramid, the king's known monuments are restricted to two reliefs in the Wadi Maghara (figs. 52d, 76).[28]

The pyramid complex of Sekhemkhet was constructed just southwest of the Step Pyramid, and west of the Second Dynasty royal tombs; interestingly, the complex conforms to the orientation of the Gisr el-Mudir. It comprised a rectangular enclosure, with what was planned to have been a seven-stepped pyramid in the center, and a "south tomb" between the pyramid and the southern enclosure wall (fig. 55b). While superficially similar to the Step Pyramid complex, it marked a significant development from it, a key aspect being a square, rather than rectangular, pyramid. Rather larger blocks than the

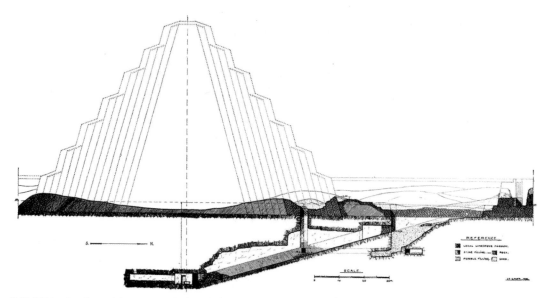

FIGURE 77 Section of the pyramid of Sekhemkhet.

mud-brick simulacra that formed the basis for the construction of Djoser's monument were employed, while wholly tunneled, much more regularly formed substructures were cut under the pyramid and south tomb (fig. 77).

The complex was, however, abandoned at a fairly early stage of the project, consistent with the six-year reign assigned to "Djoser-ty" by the Turin Canon. Only the lowest part of the pyramid core had been constructed by then, but the complex's design had been changed at least once, probably not long before the king's death. The original enclosure, measuring 229 by 165 meters, had been laid out much closer to the perimeter of the pyramid itself than had been the case at the Step Pyramid. A few parts of its paneled wall had been cased (fig. 78 top), but most of them had progressed no further than the rough core (fig. 78 bottom) when it was buried in an extended terrace that added 165 meters to the north end and 83 meters to the south end of the monument. This gave overall dimensions of 475 by 165 meters. Presumably the intention was that this would be given a paneled exterior wall, but this was never begun.

The substructure was approached via a slope in front of the center of the pyramid's north face, perhaps intended to be within the precincts of a mortuary temple, as had been the case at the Step Pyramid. Interestingly, two attempts had been made to cut the subterranean corridors. The first had been abandoned after reaching a depth of ten meters; the floor of the ramp was then raised and a new cutting begun. This tunnel (most of the ceiling of which subsequently collapsed) then descended to a burial chamber

FIGURE 78 Two sections of the enclosure wall of Sekhemkhet, the upper essentially complete, but the lower with only the core masonry in place.

under the center of the pyramid, with a number of passages surrounding it. Around a third of the way down the corridor it was intercepted by a vertical shaft, perhaps planned to accommodate a vertical portcullis, lowered through the superstructure, of a kind found in a number of Second and Third Dynasty tombs (e.g., at Beit Khallaf K1). At the same point, a doorway in the west wall gave access to a passage leading back northward to give access to a U-shaped set of galleries. These run across the front of the north face under the entrance slope, and then parallel to the northern halves of the east and west faces of the pyramid. These were lined with 132 small storage chambers (fig. 79 left), holding many stone vessels, among which were sealings of the pyramid's owner. Just beyond the shaft was found a deposit of stone vases and another of precious material, including bangles (fig. 80 bottom), a shell-shaped container, a wand, and a bead bracelet, all in gold.

FIGURE 79 Left: storerooms in Sekhemkhet's pyramid; right: the burial chamber and calcite sarcophagus.

FIGURE 80 Major finds from the substructure of Sekhemkhet's pyramid: ivory label with the Nebty-name Djoser-ti, and three of the gold bracelets (Cairo JE92679, JE92655-53, -56, -70).

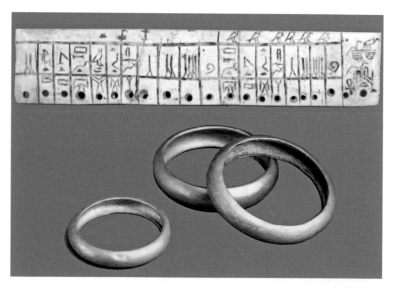

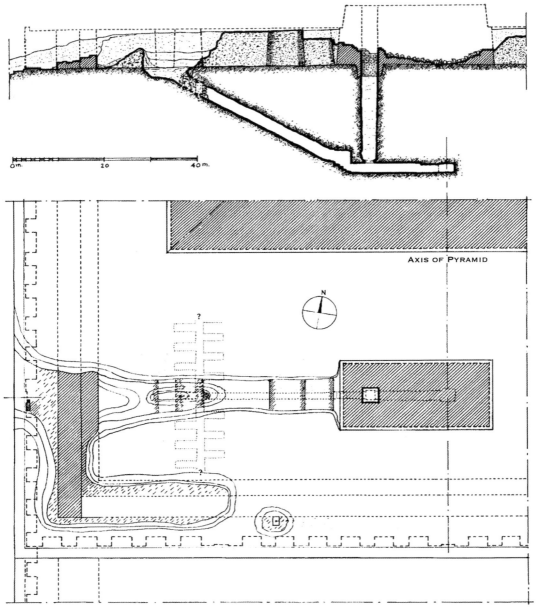

FIGURE 81 Section and plan of South Tomb of Sekhemkhet.

Much further down the sloping passage, which was blocked with rubble, lay an unfinished trident-shaped complex of rooms under the center of the pyramid. Accessed via a stone-blocked doorway, this included the burial chamber, which held an alabaster sarcophagus of unique form. This had a sliding panel at one end sealed with plaster, with the remains of what has been interpreted as a funerary wreath on top (fig. 79 right).[29] This was the first free-standing stone sarcophagus to be used in a king's burial—and apparently the last until the reign of Khufu. Unfortunately, the sarcophagus proved to be empty, with no trace of a body anywhere in the pyramid, in spite of the considerable amount of funerary equipment found, and the fact that the descending passage had been blocked in antiquity. The explanation of this mystery remains wholly obscure.

The south tomb of the complex differed from that of Djoser in being built halfway between the pyramid and the (original) south wall of the enclosure, rather than against the latter. Like Djoser's example, the substructure of the south tomb of Sekhemkhet was a reduced version of that under the king's pyramid (fig. 81), with a vertical shaft descending to the main gallery, and apparently the same kind of U-shaped gallery of storerooms, although excavations terminated before this was verified. The question of the purpose of such "south tombs" is further complicated by the presence in Sekhemkhet's of a contemporary coffin and skeleton of a child aged eighteen to twenty-four months in the substructure.[30] The child is certainly too young to be the "missing" king from the pyramid's sarcophagus: perhaps it was a child of the king, buried here for want of any completed royal-family tomb provision within the rest of the enclosure.

Sanakhte

Following "Teti/Djoser-teti/Djoser-ty," the pharaonic lists diverge. Those of Turin and Abydos continue with "names" that, as noted earlier, were actually notations of defects in their source documents. However, the Saqqara list continues with the name "Nebkare," which is clearly a "correction" (cf. page 65, above) of the "Nebka" that the other lists place—wrongly, given the aforementioned evidence of Djoser's sealings in the tomb of Khasekhemwy—at the beginning of the dynasty. It may also be noted that "Nebka" is mentioned after Djoser in the story cycle of Papyrus Westcar (page 122, below), which appears to place its protagonists in chronological order.

What appears to be this name is also the earliest royal name to be found written within a cartouche in a contemporary context: a broken seal impression in tomb K2 at Beit Khallaf (fig. 82). At the top left of the piece is the lower part of the cartouche, with what can only be the remains of a terminal *k3*-sign, and thus wholly consistent with the name being restored as "Nebka." The sealing also includes the Horus-name Sanakhte, who is also known from two representations at the Wadi Maghara (figs. 52b–c, 83). That Sanakhte dates soon after Djoser is indicated by the presence of seal impressions including his name in the mortuary temple of the Step Pyramid.[31] Another indication is the fact that the Beit Khallaf cemetery seems to have been in use for a very restricted period of time, with four (K1, K3, K4, and K5) of the five tombs there datable by sealings

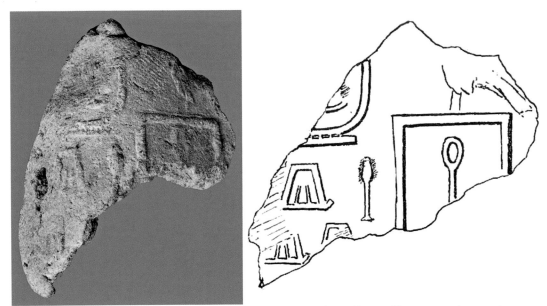

FIGURE 82 Sealing fragment from Beit Khallaf K2, with *serekh* of Sanakhte and lower part of cartouche (Garstang E.5251).

FIGURE 83 Reliefs from Wadi Maghara showing Sanakhte (left: Cairo JE38565=CG57101; right: BM EA691); see also fig. 52b, c.

to the reign of Djoser.[32] All this makes Sanakhte's placement as Sekhemkhet's successor highly probable.

Although the king is named in sealings in K2, this was clearly a private tomb,[33] with two sets of substructure—one for the husband, one for the wife. This plan is very similar to many other private tombs of the Third Dynasty, including S3518, the putative sepulcher

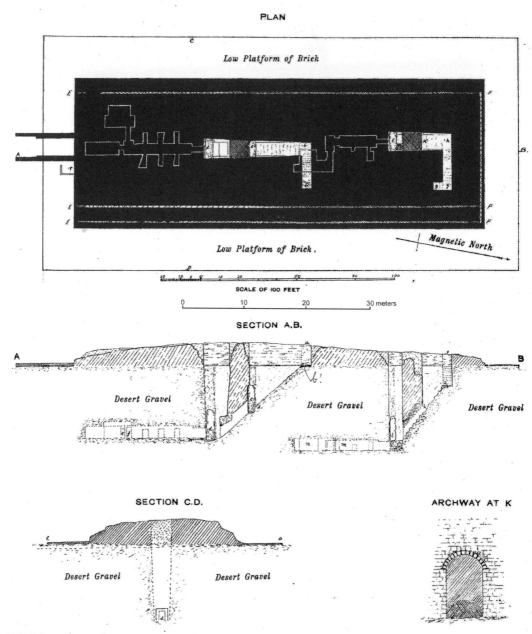

PLAN

Low Platform of Brick

Low Platform of Brick.

Magnetic North

SCALE OF 100 FEET

0   10   20   30 meters

SECTION A.B.

A   B

Desert Gravel   *Desert Gravel*   *Desert Gravel*

SECTION C.D.   ARCHWAY AT K

Desert Gravel   *Desert Gravel*

FIGURE 84 Plan and sections of Beit Khallaf K2.

of Imhotep, albeit 25 percent larger than the latter (fig. 84). The main burial chamber contained the skeleton of a man of exceptionally large stature for ancient times—1.86 meters tall.[34] No indication of his identity was found either in the substructure or in the remains of the superstructure.

As regards the actual funerary monument of Sanakhte, a strong candidate is a brick structure, known today as El-Deir, 2.5 kilometers northwest of the mid-First Dynasty Cemetery M at Abu Rowash (fig. 85).[35] It comprises a brick enclosure 330 by 170 meters, with a 20-meter-square central massif of the same material, built upon a knoll of rock, and still standing 4.15 meters high in 1902 (fig. 55c).[36] While other structures were built

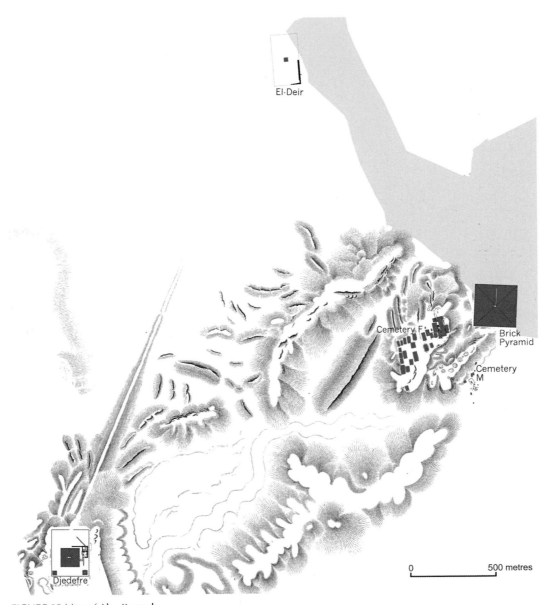

FIGURE 85 Map of Abu Rowash.

FIGURE 86 Satellite photograph of El-Deir at Abu Rowash (2009), with Macramallah's plan superimposed; inset: view of remains of central massif from northwest (2021).

over the site down to Coptic times, early Old Kingdom pottery has nevertheless been found there. In addition, the scale and form of the original monument—particularly its combination of a central structure with a large rectangular enclosure—strongly suggest that it was a royal tomb of the period directly following Djoser.

The reversion to brick may not be a significant issue in relative dating, as a brick pyramid would be built at the end of the dynasty, not far from El-Deir. This choice of material may have been related to the location of both monuments on the very edge of the desert, with easy access to the raw materials of mud brick. Unfortunately, El-Deir has apparently not been examined archaeologically since 1931, and has been badly damaged by irrigation schemes in the area. However, some brickwork still survives, and the southern part of the site is presently clear of major modern encroachment (fig. 86). The continuing existence of a funerary domain of Nebka is attested by the Saqqara tomb of its priest Akhetaa (datable on style to the late Third or very early Fourth Dynasty),[37] and a mention in the mortuary temple of the Fifth Dynasty king Niuserre.[38]

Khaba

Given the paucity of material relating to the majority of the Third Dynasty, the typology of the royal tombs plays an important role in determining their historical sequence. The great rectangular enclosure of El-Deir fits in well with the Step Pyramid and pyramid of Sekhemkhet, but by the beginning of the Fourth Dynasty such enclosures were long gone and replaced by the "classic" arrangement of a mortuary temple against the eastern side of the pyramid, joined to a valley building at the edge of the cultivation by a causeway, with the enclosure wall closely hugging the base of the pyramid itself.

The earliest monument that may have had this layout is the Layer Pyramid at Zawiyet el-Aryan (figs. 55d, 87).[39] There is no sign of a rectangular enclosure around the pyramid and, indeed, it lies on the edge of a steep incline from the desert down to the edge of the fields, a rather different site from those of earlier monuments and wholly unsuitable for the kind of enclosure found around the aforementioned royal tombs of the first half of the Third Dynasty. Four mud-brick walls perpendicular to the east face may represent traces of an eastern mortuary temple, while some blocks that might have formed part of a valley building were formerly visible near the edge of the desert.[40]

Looking at the substructure, its features suggest construction not long after the pyramid of Sekhemkhet, sharing the latter's U-shaped storage galleries, something that is not found in any other known pyramids. The pyramid is, however, much smaller than Sekhemkhet's (84 meters versus 120 meters square), and has a unique layout for the rest of its substructure. Thus, the entrance lies toward the eastern end of the north face, leading westward to a shaft, from which the main axis runs southward. As at Sekhemkhet's monument, it

FIGURE 87 The Layer Pyramid at Zawiyet el-Aryan, from the northeast.

appears that plans were changed as to the depth at which the substructure should be cut. However, at Zawiyet el-Aryan the decision was to go deeper, rather than less so, as had been the case at Saqqara. Accordingly, the original entrance slope directly abutted the shaft, with the axial passage driven south just below the level at which the slope ended. This corridor was cut horizontally, but was abandoned before it had penetrated significantly under the superstructure. There may have been concerns that the corridor was too close to the surface for safety, in particular with the supercumbent weight of the masonry above it.

Thus, the shaft was deepened and a new entrance to the pyramid cut further east, with a tunnel that intercepted the shaft much lower down than the original. Just below this point, a new main corridor was cut southward, with another running north to give access to the U-shaped storage gallery, differing from that of Sekhemkhet in having chambers opening only from the inner faces of the gallery. The southern corridor was continued to a point under the center of the pyramid, where it was seemingly abandoned. A stairway was then cut in the floor halfway along (fig. 88), descending to a deeper level at which the definitive corridor to a burial chamber below the center of the pyramid was cut. No trace of any interment was found within the pyramid.

Although atypical in many details, the substructure of the Layer Pyramid may be seen as representing a development of that of the pyramid of Sekhemkhet. In particular, the unusual arrangement of the entrance passage should probably be regarded as a solution to the awkward access to the U-shaped store galleries in Sekhemkhet's sepulcher. Accordingly, placing the Layer Pyramid not long after the latter, and directly after the apparently last known rectangular enclosure at El-Deir, seems a reasonable assessment on the basis of current knowledge.

No indication of the name of the owner of the Layer Pyramid has come from the structure itself. However, numerous stone vessels inscribed with the *serekh* of a King Khaba were found in the large mastaba Z500, which lay just under a quarter of a kilometer to the north of the pyramid. On this basis, the latter is usually attributed to Khaba, although it is by no means certain that the mastaba and pyramid are absolutely contemporary. Khaba's name is also found on a vessel fragment from Abusir, another possibly from Dahshur, and one of unknown provenance.[41] Seal impressions with his name have been found in the town area at Hierakonpolis, as well as in a domestic context at Elephantine, and in a mastaba at Quesna in the southern Delta.

Whether or not Khaba was indeed the builder of the Layer Pyramid, the monument's position seems archaeologically secure, and thus its owner must have fallen within the "*ḥwḏf3/sḏs* Periods" of the Turin and Abydos lists. It is of course unclear how many names might have been lost and, combined with the confusion between the lists on the position of Nebka(re), all this suggests that surviving records were so problematic by the New Kingdom that little can be achieved by further discussion at this remove.

FIGURE 88 View of the interior of the Layer Pyramid, from the bottom of the entrance passage, looking along the middle horizontal passage, with the stairway and the beginning of the lower horizontal passage, to the burial chamber, at the bottom.

Huni

A number of later sources place a King "Huni" at the end of the Third Dynasty. This is found most explicitly in the Middle Kingdom Papyrus Prisse, which includes the didactic Instructions of Kagemni, in which we read: "Then the person of the Dual King Huni died and the person of the Dual King Seneferu arose as king."[42] The succession Huni→Seneferu is also to be found in the Turin and Saqqara lists, but Abydos names Seneferu's predecessor as a "Neferkare" (which passed into Manetho as "Kerpherês"). This is difficult to explain, unless it is some kind of confusion with the "Nebkare" found in the Saqqara list, exacerbated by the problems with the source document attested by the "sḏs" notation immediately before.

The Turin entry for Huni is unusual in that his name and length of reign (24 years) are followed by a broken notation reading "the one who has built sšm [...]." It has been suggested that a problematic fragment of the papyrus, which has been alleged to include part of a mention of Imhotep, might be part of this line, and make it a record of that worthy's death.[43] However, this reconstruction has now been shown to be impossible, as the text on the other side of the fragment in question would be wholly out of place in the tax list upon the back of which the Turin Canon was copied.[44] For another possibility, see page 106, below.

Contemporary and near-contemporary material naming Seneferu's predecessor is rare, but that which survives shows that during his lifetime and immediately afterward that predecessor's name was written in the somewhat problematic form (⊕). There has been considerable debate as to how this should be transliterated.[45] The first group of signs is identical to the writing of nswt, the generic term for "king" during the New Kingdom, and as a result it has been proposed that the cartouche should be read simply as "King H" (nswt ḥ), with the final character an abbreviated writing of ḥwi/ḥïi, "smite/strike."[46] While a rather different proposal would read "Ny-śwtḥ" ("The one belonging to the One [who causes] to seize"),[47] this has met with little support.[48]

However it should be transliterated and interpreted, the royal name has hitherto been found in four places, all in either contemporary or Old Kingdom contexts. The first is on a curious conical piece of granite, found on the island of Elephantine (fig. 89), with the name in a cartouche, linked with what seems to be the name of a palace or fortress.[49] Second, the burial chamber of tomb AS54 at Abusir South contained a fragment of a stone vessel with the name, but with no cartouche (fig. 90).[50] Both of these attestations seem to be contemporary with the king's reign, but the other two are both retrospective, and refer to estates in the king's name. The earlier is in the early Fourth Dynasty tomb chapel of Metjen (fig. 96),[51] the later is in one of the entries in the Annals for the Fifth Dynasty king Neferirkare.[52]

The discovery at Abusir proves crucial in understanding the true makeup of the royal name. The form "Huni" found in Middle Kingdom and later sources seems to have been based on an assumption that the "*nswt*" element was a case of including a kingly title within the cartouche, and thus capable of being ignored,[53] the residual "H" being expanded into "Huni" ("The Smiter"). However, the Abusir inscription (fig. 90, bottom) cites the king as "*nswt-bîty nswt-ḥ*"—"the Dual King *nswt-ḥ*"—showing that the "*nswt*" was indeed an integral part of his actual name, *not* an abbreviation of his royal title. Accordingly, one might best translate the name as "The Royal Smiter."[54] As for other parts of Huni's titulary, it is likely that his Horus-name was Qahedjet, which appears on a relief in the Louvre Museum whose style seems to be appropriate for the late Third Dynasty (fig. 91).

FIGURE 89 Inscription naming Huni from the base of the granite "cone" from Elephantine (Cairo JE41556).

The aforementioned "cone" has often been associated with a small step pyramid on Elephantine (fig. 92), although there is no record of how close to it the piece was actually found.[55] If the pyramid indeed dates the latter to Huni's reign, it may point to a similar dating for some other similar small step pyramids. These line the Nile from there down to the mouth of the Fayyum, at Edfu South, El-Kula (fig. 93a), Naqada (fig. 93b), Abydos South (Sinki, fig. 93c), Zawiyet el-Maytin/Sultan (fig. 93d), and Seila.[56] The latter is firmly attributed by inscribed material to the reign of Huni's successor, Seneferu.[57] Therefore it may be that the series—whose meaning remains very much a moot point,[58] since they show no indication of having been intended for burials—was the product of the two reigns.

As regards the actual tomb of Huni, for many years he was frequently associated with the inner step pyramid(s) of the pyramid at Meidum,[59] in spite of all the material from the site dating explicitly to the time of Seneferu. Apart from nagging doubts that Seneferu could have built *three* large pyramids (the one at Meidum, plus the Bent and Red Pyramids at Dahshur), plus one small one (Seila), totaling over 3.5 million cubic meters of stone, the attribution was based on the apparent

FIGURE 90 Abusir South tomb AS54, dated to the reign of Huni by the inscribed vessel shown at the bottom.

lack of an alternative candidate for the funerary monument of a king who, according to the Turin Canon, lasted some two and a half decades.

This latter issue was resolved in 1986/7 when the long-lost Brick Pyramid at Abu Rowash was reidentified (page 144, below).[60] Lying something over a kilometer south of El-Deir (fig. 85), all that remains today is a rock knoll (fig. 94a), into which a sloping corridor runs from the north to a wholly rock-cut burial chamber. However, in the early nineteenth century masses of mud brick still adhered to the knoll (fig. 94b), keyed in by trenches cut in its surface. Extrapolating from the latter, the monument can be reconstructed as having been planned as a brick step pyramid of great size (fig. 55e).[61]

FIGURE 91 Relief panel showing Qahedjet, perhaps the Horus-name of Huni (Louvre E.25982).

The forms of both the pyramid—step pyramids are unknown after the early part of Seneferu's reign—and the wholly rock-cut substructure (a type unknown after Khufu)[62] make it impossible to place the Brick Pyramid at any point other than in the later part of the Third Dynasty. Huni is, of course, the obvious candidate for its owner.

This dating is further supported by the placement of the entrance to the pyramid. This will originally have lain some twenty-five meters above the ground, at the juncture between the first and second steps of what was probably a six-stepped monument. This

FIGURE 92 The small step pyramid at Elephantine.

contrasts with the ground-level entrances of all earlier royal tombs, but is a feature of early Fourth Dynasty pyramids, although not later ones. The plan is extremely simple, with a single chamber under the center of the pyramid itself. The base dimensions of the latter can be reconstructed as some 215 meters square, making it by far the biggest pyramid attempted up to that time, and the fourth largest pyramid of all time. The surprising thing, of course, is the use of brick—not again used for pyramid construction until the Middle Kingdom. However, it has been argued above that Sanakhte had reverted to this medium for the building of El-Deir, and that proximity to the cultivation would have made mud brick attractive in both its case and the nearby Brick Pyramid.

The approach of building the pyramid around an existing rock knoll (also seen at El-Deir) may also have favored the use of the well-tried medium of mud brick for the rest of its core, although the outer casing will doubtless have been of fine quality Tura limestone from the opposite bank of the river.[63] The pyramid seems, however, never to have been finished, as by the end of the Old Kingdom enough of the rock core was exposed to allow the cutting of small tombs into it.[64] Yet the distant memory of a giant brick pyramid of the Old Kingdom may lie behind the Greek historian Herodotus' story of Asychis, "the successor of Mykerinos (Menkaure), who . . . , wishing to go one better than his predecessors, built a pyramid of brick to commemorate his reign, and on it cut an inscription in stone to the following effect: 'Do not compare me to my disadvantage with the stone pyramids. I surpass them as far as does Zeus the other gods. They pushed a pole to the bottom of a lake, and the mud that stuck on it they collected and made into bricks. That is how they built me.'" Indeed, it has been suggested the extraordinary Brick Pyramid was the "*sšm* [...]" mentioned in the Turin Canon's obscure comment regarding Huni.[65]

FIGURE 93 The small step pyramids at: a. El-Kula; b. Naqada/Nubt; c. Abydos South/Sinki; d. Zawiyet el-Maytin/Sultan

FIGURE 94 The Brick Pyramid at Abu Rowash, from the southwest in 1985 (top) and in the 1840s (middle), and from the northwest at the same time (bottom).

Given the obscurity of its kings, it is not surprising that only a handful of officials can be assigned with confidence to the latter part of the Third Dynasty. Various private tombs have been dated to the period, but most have been so devastated by plunderers that their owners are rarely identifiable, the exceptions being Saqqara tombs S3036X and S3037/38X, of Irisetjet and Khuire,[66] and S3073 of Khabausokar, which can be placed stylistically around the end of the dynasty.[67]

In contrast to the obscurities of the Third Dynasty, the inception of the Fourth Dynasty brings forth a sudden blaze of light: with certain minor exceptions, the royal succession is essentially clear, dynastic relationships can be reconstructed, and the great officials of state are known by name. The great pyramids of Dahshur and Giza are a concrete memorial to long reigns and mastery of the techniques of stone building, but they rest entirely upon the foundations laid by the preceding Third Dynasty. In view of this debt owed by Egyptian monumental architecture to Imhotep, it is not surprising that he was remembered down to the Ptolemaic Period, when he became a god, the very son of Ptah, the creator craftsman-god who presided over the city of Memphis.

4 LIMBO

There can be no question that the accession of Seneferu—and thus the death of Huni—marks a whole new era of Egyptian history. In place of the paucity of monuments of the latter part of the Third Dynasty, we find large high-status cemeteries appearing alongside the no fewer than three major pyramids built by the new king, beginning a sequence that continues until the end of the Old Kingdom. These contribute to a comprehensive prosopography of the Egyptian governmental classes being available for much of the remainder of the period.[1] Documentation also becomes sufficiently plentiful that the royal succession over the next few centuries is largely secure, with only a few relatively minor issues.

Concepts of kingship also seem to have been consolidated under Seneferu, to be seen in the standardization of the royal titulary in fourfold form, with the most commonly used version of the king's name now consistently enclosed in a cartouche and preceded by the title *nswt-bity*. The only substantive later change to the royal titulary would be the addition of a further cartouche name during the Fifth Dynasty, which became permanent (save among the local Theban kings of the Eleventh Dynasty) during the Sixth. This fivefold titulary would endure down into Roman times.

This sudden ubiquity of the cartouche name, and its synonymity with Egyptian kingship, probably resulted fairly rapidly in a retrospective attribution of cartouches to previous kings who had not actually possessed them (or at least no evidence survives of them having done so). The earliest known examples would seem to be those assigned to Sened and Peribsen in the tomb of Shery, which in Peribsen's case simply involved the enclosure of his *serekh* name in a cartouche (figs. 36, 95). The situation regarding Sened is less clear, owing to the paucity of contemporary material relating to that king. Perhaps related to Shery's cult of Peribsen is a cylinder seal bearing the king's name in a cartouche.[2] Other cults and funerary estates that survived down to the Fourth Dynasty

FIGURE 95 Central panel of the false door of Shery (see fig. 36), acquired by Oxford's Ashmolean Museum in 1683 from the Rev. Robert Huntington (1637–1701), who had visited Egypt in 1678/79 and 1681. The cartouche of Sened is visible at the top (AN1683.479).

included that of Huni. This is mentioned in the tomb of Metjen, whose responsibilities also included the cult of Queen Nimaathap. An estate of Huni was still extant under the Fifth Dynasty king Neferirkare (see page 102).

The attribution of cartouche names to early kings is next attested by a writing board found in the Fifth Dynasty tomb G1011 at Giza (fig. 97).[3] This includes four identical columns, each containing the same six cartouches. From the top, these are of the Fifth Dynasty kings Neferirkare and Sahure, the Fourth Dynasty kings Khaefre and Djedefre, and of "Teti" and "Budjau." Since the upper four names are arranged in descending chronological order, it follows that the bottom pair must denote pre-Djedefre monarchs, and thus that "Teti" is not the Sixth Dynasty founder of that name. In the Abydos list, the name "Teti" was the name assigned, as noted above (page 88), to Sekhemkhet, the name being probably derived from his Nebty-name, Djoser-ti. "Budjau" appears in the Abydos list as the first king of the Second Dynasty, and thus would be Hetepsekhemwy. However, unlike in the case of Sekhemkhet, no contemporary designation of Hetepsekhemwy in any way resembles "Budjau" (apart from his Horus-name, we only have the simple Nebty-name, "Hetep"). That it may have been an ad hoc designation by an Old Kingdom scribe is perhaps suggested by the fact that the Saqqara and Turin lists give Hetepsekhemwy the wholly different name "Netjerbau."

Around the same time as the writing board was being produced, it is likely that the compilation of the Annals Stone(s) (fig. 98) was underway. It seems probable that at least the principal stone was erected at Memphis, whence the only provenanced fragment

FIGURE 96 The chapel from the tomb of Metjen (LS6) at Saqqara LS6 (Berlin ÄM1105).

comes (see page 159, below). Given that the final king covered by the latter appears to have been Neferirkare,[4] the last king included on the writing board, the Annals clearly enshrine what was known—or was believed to be known—about the history of Egypt down to the mid-Fifth Dynasty.

The number of copies of the Annals that may have once existed has been the subject of much debate. The surviving fragments show variations in thickness and workmanship, and some may be incompatible with others as regards the overall layout of the original

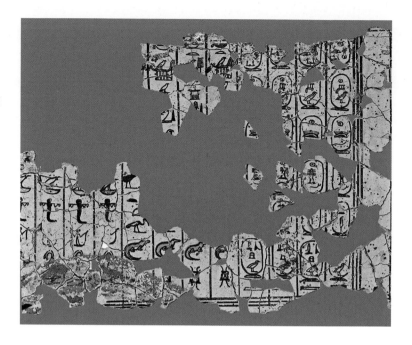

FIGURE 97 Detail of writing board from Giza tomb G1011, including the columns containing the repeated cartouches of, from the top, Neferirkare, Sahure, Khaefre, Djedefre, "Teti," and "Bedjau" (Cairo JE37734).

monument. Additionally, some pieces are alleged to have been found in Middle and Upper Egypt—and the one with a secure (Memphite) provenance seems incompatible with all the others. A suggestion has been that at least some of the fragments might come from a Twenty-fifth Dynasty copy. Accordingly, what we may have is an Old Kingdom original, set up at Memphis, and at least one copy—either broadly contemporary or much later—set up in the south.[5]

Questions as to the reliability of the Annals have already been noted, ultimately grounded on our ignorance of what kinds of documents were available to the compilers. In favor of significant reliability is the inclusion of inundation data throughout the dynastic part of the Annals, suggesting that a full year-by-year register of this important metric survived in the archives, although the other annual information may have been compiled from more diverse sources.

On the other hand, there remains throughout the possibility of some conscious "editing" of history. This would be the case in the early Nineteenth Dynasty, when the late Eighteenth Dynasty "Amarna" kings were excluded from the monumental king lists, making Horemheb the direct successor of Amenhotep III. But even then, numbers of years were maintained by the early Rameside kings retrospectively allocating the regnal years of the excluded monarchs to Horemheb.[6] This suggests that even if "bad" kings were taken out of such lists, care was taken to avoid upsetting the cumulative number of years in any

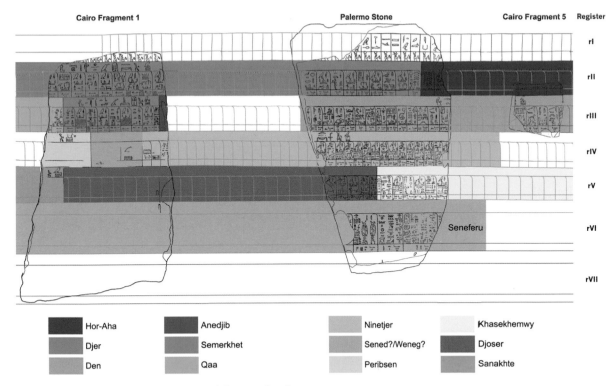

FIGURE 98 Reconstruction of the recto of the Annals, after Barta.

formal chronicle. This may be the origin of the "King *ḥwḏf3*"—"King Gap"—of the Second and Third Dynasties and "King *sḏs*"—"King Damaged"—of the latter dynasty.

In compiling the Annals, cartouches were again provided retrospectively, although only two, those attributed to Djer and Semerkhet, remain on the surviving fragments. These correspond to those employed for those kings in the Abydos and Saqqara lists, respectively, supporting the hint from the Giza writing board that the cartouche names employed in the Rameside lists do indeed go back to the Old Kingdom, rather than being later confections.[7]

The Tomb of Osiris

Following the production of the Annals during the later Old Kingdom, little is known about Egyptian engagement with the legacy of their earliest monarchs until the late Middle Kingdom, although a remembrance of Djoser is demonstrated by a statue being dedicated to him by Senwosret II.[8] Then, however, a wholly new strand emerges, focusing on the equation of one of the tombs of the earliest kings with that of Osiris, god of the dead.

By then, the royal cemetery of Umm el-Qaab had long since been plundered. This probably occurred more than once, perhaps most recently when the necropoleis of Abydos were ransacked by the Herakleopolitan forces of the Tenth Dynasty king, Akhtoy V, during the civil war with the kings of Thebes that ended the Second Intermediate Period.[9] But during the Middle Kingdom there was an upsurge in devotion to Osiris, manifested in the construction of large numbers of tombs and cenotaphs, particularly on the "Staircase/Terrace of the Great God." This lay southwest of the Osiris temple complex at Kom el-Sultan, along the southern edge of the Northern Cemetery, close to the Early Dynastic funerary enclosures, and overlooking the beginning of the wadi that led west through the desert toward Umm el-Qaab.[10] This wadi had by this time become the venue for an annual "passion play" based around aspects of the Osiris myth.[11]

Details of this are provided by the Abydene stela of one Ikherneferet (fig. 99 left), sent by Senwosret III to undertake renovations in the temple of Osiris and take part in the festival. This included "clear(ing) the ways of the god to his tomb before Peqer," the contemporary

FIGURE 99 Left: stela of Ikherneferet (Berlin ÄM1204); right: stela of Wegaf and Neferhotep I (Cairo JE35256); from Abydos.

name for Umm el-Qaab. There, at some point prior to Senwosret III's reign, one of the ancient royal tombs had been identified as that of the god. The earliest Middle Kingdom remains in the area comprise an offering table dedicated by Senwosret I to Montjuhotep III of the Eleventh Dynasty, followed by a stela fragment of the time of Amenemhat II. Whether those responsible believed the tomb chosen—that of Djer—to have been the god's *actual* tomb is unclear. Indeed, it may be that it was chosen for its convenient location and accessibility to the notables and pilgrims who took part in the festival. To allow them to descend into the burial chamber, a stairway was added on its western side (fig. 20c).

By the early Thirteenth Dynasty there were concerns that the sacred way toward Umm el-Qaab was being impinged upon by the tombs and cenotaphs of those who wished to be buried close to the "Terrace of the Great God." Accordingly, under King Wegaf,[12] steps were taken to protect it, a set of four stelae being erected that delineated *t3 ḏsr*—the sacred part of the wadi leading toward "[the god's] tomb before Peqer." The one surviving example (fig. 99 right) prescribes the penalty of burning for any trespass within the prohibited area—probably referring to any attempt to have any structure built there. On the other hand, the stela confirms the legitimacy of the rest of the area as a place for one's tomb or cenotaph: it was only the sacred wadi area that is the subject of concern.

Royal interest in Osiris's tomb and cult deepened under Wegaf's successor, Khendjer.[13] First, he commissioned one Amenysonbe to "cleanse" and restore the god's temple.[14] Second, he added to the former tomb of Djer a recumbent figure of the god, presumably to provide a focus for the climax of the festival and for pilgrims (fig. 100).[15] This depicted Osiris lying on a bier, the two sides of which are formed of the bodies of

FIGURE 100 The Osiris bed from the tomb of Djer at Umm el-Qaab (Cairo JE32090).

FIGURE 101 The Abydos
stela of Neferhotep I
(Cairo JE6307).

lions, of a type familiar in Egyptian funerary usage. Raptors, probably representing Sokar, guard each corner, and another, representing Isis, straddles the god's loins, impregnating herself in order to bear Horus. The "Osiris bed" presumably lay within a stone shrine built in the center of the chamber, only a few fragments of which have been identified.

Khendjer's fourth successor, Neferhotep I, also concerned himself with Osiris's affairs—and may actually have been buried at Abydos.[16] A sandstone stela, found near the entrance to the Osiris temple, records how the king undertook research into the archives of the temple of Re-Atum at Heliopolis to check on the correct forms due to Osiris. Having done so, the king proceeded to Abydos to take part in the annual festival. This having taken place, he began the renovations that his archival investigations deemed necessary, and exhorted the priesthood to maintain them (fig. 101). It was doubtless as part of this work that the stelae of Wegaf were appropriated in Neferhotep's name. Perhaps also due to Neferhotep is the erasure of Khendjer's inscriptions on the Umm el-Qaab Osiris bed, although this could equally have been due to Khendjer's immediate successor, Imyromesha, who seems to have denied Khendjer burial in his Saqqara pyramid.[17]

The importance of the Umm el-Qaab cemetery as a pilgrimage center continued through to at least the Third Intermediate Period times. Two priests dedicated a hawk to the god's "tomb" during the reign of Amenhotep II;[18] one of them, Iuiu, also dedicated a shabti, a trend that was followed by many others in following years. Votive pottery was deposited above Djer's former sepulcher, inscribed vessels multiplying in number during the later New Kingdom and Third Intermediate Period.[19] Of particular interest are a group of ostraca from the latter period, naming kings such as Pasebakhanut II, Shoshenq I, Osorkon I, and Osorkon II.

The pull of the ancient necropolis and pilgrimage spot was doubtless one of the reasons why even high-status Thebans sought burial at Abydos during the Third Intermediate Period. Perhaps most surprisingly, these included the High Priests of Amun Menkheperre[20] and Iuput,[21] whom one would have expected to have been interred at Western Thebes, opposite their temples at Karnak. Pontifical families followed suit, including Menkheperre's son, Pasebakhanut A.[22]

High-status popularity of the area around the wadi leading to Umm el-Qaab continued into the Twenty-fifth Dynasty, with a number of ladies of the Nubian royal family finding rest in the same area as Pasebakhanut.[23]

During the Twenty-sixth Dynasty, a shrine was erected up at Umm el-Qaab by King Wahibre (Apries), part of the stela from this being found in the tomb of Queen Merneith.[24] Other fragments indicate work by one Pefdjauneith under Ahmose II. Interest in Umm el-Qaab continued into Ptolemaic times, with references surviving to an oracle of Osiris there.[25] Use of the wadi seems to have receded by Roman times,[26] when a new access route direct from the Sethy I temple supersedes it, probably connected with the contemporary shift of focus of the main Osiris cult from the temple at Kom el-Sultan to the Sethy I temple.

The worship of Osiris continued until the end of paganism, when his role as savior was taken over by Christ. Iconoclasts of the new religion came to further ransack the remains of the old god's "tomb" at Umm el-Qaab, which would then slumber until the last years of the nineteenth century AD.

The Past as Validation for the Present

The involvement of Senwosret III in the regulation of the Osiris festival was not the king's only engagement with the monuments of the monarchs of the remote past. Most strikingly, the design of his pyramid complex at Dahshur (fig. 102)[27] reversed centuries of development of such structures by adopting, in its final form, the kind of great rectangular enclosure last seen in the middle of the Third Dynasty. While many of the details, such as the employment of a causeway and the placement of a mortuary temple on the east side, followed more recent traditions, the overall form mirrored early Third Dynasty practice. Specific borrowing from Djoser's complex is almost certainly to be seen in, for example, the presence of royal family tombs in a highly unusual catacomb

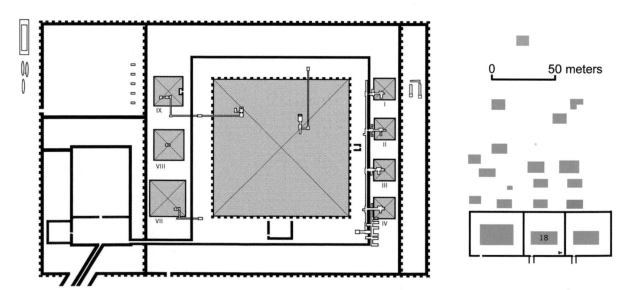

FIGURE 102 Plan of the pyramid complex of Senwosret III at Dahshur. The two shafts with Third Dynasty calcite sarcophagi, between the two northern enclosure walls, are marked in red, and the Fourth Dynasty tomb shaft containing the Djoser boundary stela, within the enclosure of tomb 18, is marked in blue.

under the east end of the enclosure. In addition, Senwosret III's sarcophagus, and others of the period, adopted a paneled frieze around the lower part of the coffer that, by the inclusion of the indication of a doorway in one of the bastions on the front left of the sarcophagus, confirms this to be an imitation of the Step Pyramid enclosure wall.

But not only did Senwosret III's complex recall the Step Pyramid architecturally and artistically, it also seems to have incorporated actual material from that ancient monument.[28] At the north end of the complex, between an inner and outer enclosure wall, were two shaft tombs (marked in red on fig. 102). Each contained a calcite sarcophagus (fig. 103) identical to the examples that had been found—both whole and in fragments—in royal-family tombs I, II, IV, and V below the Step Pyramid (page 79, above). Apart from four calcite jars buried with one of them, neither tomb showed any signs of having been used for a burial, while no evidence for a wider Third Dynasty cemetery has ever been found in the area.[29]

Accordingly, it seems likely that the two sarcophagi had been moved from elsewhere with some kind of talismanic function. Given both their similarity to those found under the Step Pyramid and the architectural links between Senwosret III's pyramid complex and the Step Pyramid, it seems difficult to doubt that one or more of the royal family shafts under the Step Pyramid had been entered under Senwosret III and two of their sarcophagi extracted and transported to the site of the new royal tomb. Not only this, but a boundary stela of Djoser, of the same type as found at the Step Pyramid enclosure (page 67), was also found north of the Senwosret III enclosure,[30] and may have been moved at the same time, the ensemble perhaps intended to form a physical link between the Twelfth Dynasty ruler's funerary monument and the ancient building which had

FIGURE 103 Third Dynasty calcite sarcophagus from northern section of the complex of Senwosret III at Dahshur (Cairo CG28102).

served as its inspiration.[31] Ironically, Senwosret III seems not to have been buried in his Dahshur pyramid; rather, his burial place appears to have been a tomb of innovative design at Abydos[32]—presumably to aid his posthumous participation in the festival on which he had lavished attention in life.

A further appeal to the remote past seems to have arisen during the late Second Intermediate Period during the codification of a number of texts of both sacred and secular natures. The reign of Den—in the guise of "Khasty"—is given as the point of origin not only for a remedy in the Ebers[33] and Berlin Medical Papyri[34] but also for Chapters 54, 64, and 130 of the Book of the Dead, suggesting some especial renown for Den's era.

The late Middle Kingdom/Second Intermediate Period also sees early kings appear in the literary setting of the story cycle of magical exploits preserved in Papyrus Westcar.[35] The first two stories are set in the reigns of Djoser and Nebka and, as previously noted, their placement in this order, in a document in which the stories are set progressively closer to the present day, supports reversing the order of the two kings in the later king lists.

New Kingdom Times

An odd remembrance of an Early Dynastic king seems to be present on an item datable to the interface between the Second Intermediate Period and the New Kingdom. The vaulted lid of a rectangular coffin of an unknown woman, found on the Dra Abu'l-Naga hill at Western Thebes during 1862/3, but now lost,[36] was decorated by eight cartouches. These were arranged in pairs, the first containing the name of Sened. The cartouche paired with it was unreadable, but the other pairs contained royal names ranging from the Middle Kingdom to the period of the coffin's manufacture. Their interpretation is problematic but, in any case, Sened's inclusion sheds interesting light on the remembrance and reception of this obscure king over a millennium after his death.

A rather different interaction with a period that now lay a millennium in the past is to be seen in the graffiti applied by New Kingdom visitors to ancient monuments. A considerable number are known from the Step Pyramid enclosure, in particular the so-called Houses of the North and the South, opposite the southeast corner of the pyramid itself (fig. 104).[37] These texts date from the reign of the early Eighteenth Dynasty king Amenhotep I down to the Twenty-sixth Dynasty, with the majority written during the New Kingdom (e.g., fig. 105). Clearly, such structures were now tourist attractions, the visitors being well aware that the Step Pyramid complex was the work of a King "Djoser."[38]

Broader and deeper knowledge of the earliest kings of Egypt by the New Kingdom is indicated by the so-called king lists that survive in copies dating to the early Nineteenth Dynasty (fig. 106). These represent the most comprehensive enumerations of former kings of Egypt to survive from pharaonic times. In their edited monumental forms in

FIGURE 104 The Houses of the South and North in the Step Pyramid complex.

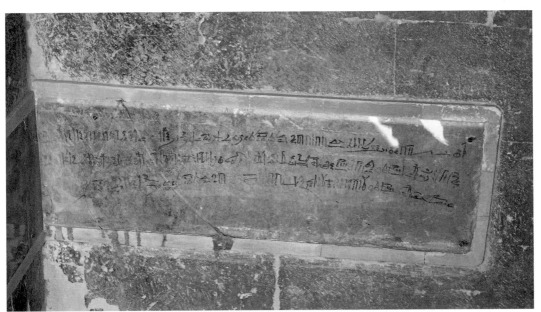

FIGURE 105 Graffito from the House of the North in the Step Pyramid enclosure, dating to the reign of Rameses II: "Year 47, II month of *prt*, day 5. The Scribe of the Treasury, Hadnakhte, son of Suner, his mother being Tawosret, came to make an excursion and amuse himself on the West of Memphis, together with his brother, the Scribe of the Vizier, Paanakhti: 'O all Gods of the West of Memphis, and the Gods presiding over the Sacred Land, Osiris, Isis, and the great Spirits of the West of Ankhtawi, give a good lifetime serving your *ka*s, and may I receive a good burial after a good old age, in sight of the West of Memphis, like a great honored one, and like yourself!' By the scribe of the Treasury of the Lord of the Two Lands, Hadnakhte, true of voice, and the scribe of the Vizier, Paanakhti."

royal temples (see below), they may have been intended to explicitly link the kings of the new dynasty, who seem to have lacked any royal blood,[39] to the kings of the past. A desire to reach back into the distant past may also be seen in the kings chosen to be represented in the procession of statues of former pharaohs in the Min-festival reliefs of Rameses II in his memorial temple, the Ramesseum. There, the "legitimate" kings of the New Kingdom, from Ahmose I to Rameses II himself,[40] are followed by Montjuhotep II (second unifier of Egypt, at the beginning of the Middle Kingdom) and finally "Meni" (fig. 117). Interestingly, the later surviving version of the festival tableaux in the memorial temple of Rameses III at Medinet Habu begins the sequence of statues with Amenhotep III. It is unclear whether this indicates a difference of emphasis regarding legitimacy or, more prosaically, simply a question of available space. More comprehensive than the monumental lists, and clearly preserving a version of the full king-list tradition that lay behind the monumental lists, is the Turin Canon (fig. 120). This comprised a chronicle from the mythical reigns of the gods down to, presumably, the early Nineteenth Dynasty, although the last surviving names come from the late Second Intermediate Period.[41] The extant document is by no means a formal archival item, having been written on the back of an existing accounts papyrus of the time of Rameses II, presumably as a working reference document of some kind. Each individual ruler was given a cartouche name, with a record of reign length[42] and, down to Djoser, a record of their age at death. However, only a handful of entries now preserve anything approaching a complete entry, the vast majority being represented by nothing more than fragments.

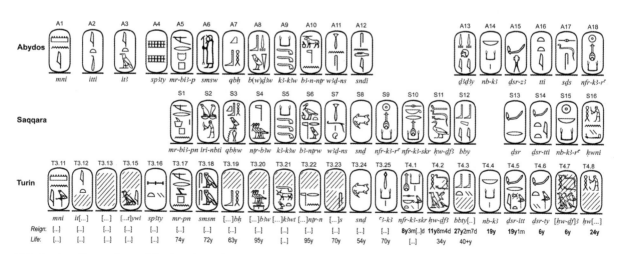

FIGURE 106 Comparison of the first three dynasties as presented in the three Rameside king lists.

Although the exactitude with which many reign lengths are given implies a high degree of reliability, there are a number of cases where the lengths of reign appear to be contrary to data contemporary with the reign in question. This underlines the fact that we know nothing about the source material of the compiler of the Canon, although elaborate proposals have been made for its editorial history. The latter is underpinned by the inconsistency in the ways that reign lengths are recorded, implying different source documents, as well as entries that will have marked the beginning of a column in some source document. Likewise unclear, as already noted (pages 111–12), not only for the Turin Canon, but also the monumental king lists, are the origins of the cartouche names used prior to the Fourth Dynasty; some certainly go back to the Old Kingdom, or can be derived from contemporary names, but most have no obvious prototypes.

The first three dynasties cover the lower part of what is now known as Column 3 of the papyrus, and the upper part of Column 4 (fig. 107).[43] A total of twenty-two entries cover monarchs between Meni and Huni, of which all but one have at least some signs—or enough traces to restore some signs—surviving.

The monumental king lists are essentially enumerations of deceased rulers in receipt of an offering, conveniently placed in chronological order. The most extensive pair, covering back to the unification, were placed in the temples of Sethy I and Rameses II at Abydos, although nothing of the latter prior to the middle of the First Intermediate Period now survives (see fig. 119). However, that of Sethy I is undamaged (fig. 123), and gives eighteen names from Meni to the predecessor of Seneferu (fig. 108).

The Abydos list is largely consistent with that given in the Turin Canon, the names corresponding to the First Dynasty being essentially identical, except for omitting the "extra" king close to the beginning of the Turin list (page 14, above). The same is true of the Second Dynasty section, except that the Abydos list omits the three kings that follow Sened in the Canon. The two lists have the same number of kings for the Third Dynasty, but with significant variations in the names quoted.

The final monumental list comes from a private tomb at Saqqara, belonging to the Overseer of Works Tjenry, who served under Rameses II (fig. 122).[44] The most striking thing about this list is that the earliest king mentioned is "Merbiapen" (Anedjib); after him come fifteen names down to Huni (fig. 109). The omission of the earlier kings has been suggested as relating to traditions of royal legitimacy in the north, as opposed to the Abydos region—but it seems more likely this was simply a matter of space available on the wall. This was certainly what lay behind the failure of this list to include the First and Second Intermediate Periods.[45] The Saqqara list has, in any case, other oddities, such as placing the Eleventh and Twelfth Dynasties in reverse order. Accordingly, it seems unlikely that anything should be read into the omission of the early First Dynasty kings.

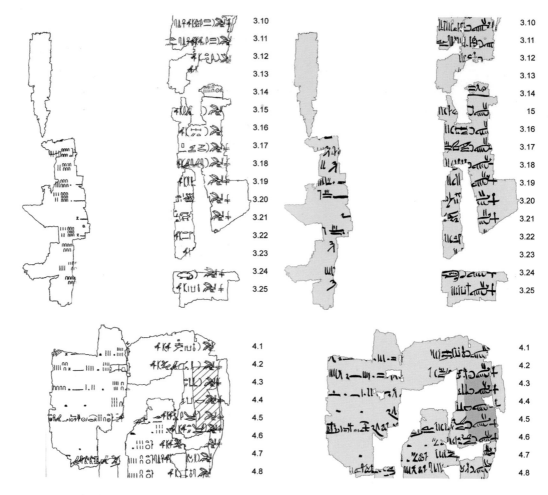

FIGURE 107 The first three dynasties as presented in the Turin Canon.

Of the names actually included, the Saqqara list agrees with the Turin Canon down to the end of the Second Dynasty in all essentials, but its Third Dynasty has one less name than either the Turin or Abydos lists, and shifts a version of the latter two sources' first king of the dynasty to the penultimate position (pages 64, 94, 101, above).

Interest in ancient kings in early Rameside private contexts is further indicated by a block from the tomb of the Custodian of the Treasury, Mahu, which depicts "Djoser-nub," "Teti" (probably Sekhemkhet), the Fifth Dynasty Userkaf, and a king whose name and figure are lost (fig. 110). The pairing of Djoser and Sekhemkhet would endure until at least Twenty-sixth Dynasty times (page 131, below).

The variations among the Turin, Saqqara, and Abydos lists, all carved or written at around the same time, are curious, and suggest that a number of listings of the early kings

First Dynasty

Second Dynasty

FIGURE 108 The first three
dynasties as presented in the
Abydos king list of Sethy I.

Third Dynasty

FIGURE 109 The first three dynasties as presented in the Saqqara king list.

FIGURE 110 Block from the Rameside tomb of Mahu in the Teti cemetery at Saqqara, showing Kings Djoser-nub, Teti, and Userkaf (Cairo JE33258).

of Egypt were by then in circulation. The significant differences lie in the latter parts of the Second and Third Dynasties, and the problems with the source documents indicated by, as already discussed (pages 47–48, 64, 101, 116), the inclusion of the "names" "*ḥwdf3*" and "*sḏs*" in the listings. However, the editors of the monumental lists were clearly less diligent than those of the Turin list, those of the Abydos list simply omitting the "problematic" part of the Second Dynasty altogether—jumping straight from Sened to Djadjy (Khasekhemwy).

To the End of Antiquity

Unfortunately, nothing akin to these early Rameside king lists has survived from the remaining years of Egypt's independence. On the other hand, continuing interest in aspects of the earliest times is evidenced by an elaborate scheme to explore the substructure of the Step Pyramid. Thus, a whole new passage (figs. 65ζ–η, 111) was driven under the south face of the monument, equipped with pillars made of reused material going back to the New Kingdom. It reached the center of the structure and seems to have been used to empty the central constructional pit of its rubble filling, to gain access to the galleries at the lowest levels of the pyramid. A further, less spacious, passage was driven from the north (fig. 65δ–ε), presumably as part of the same project.

Its objectives seem to have included the copying of at least some of the carved tableaux below the pyramid, two of which preserve copy grids. These may give a hint at the date of the "excavation." This is because, while a generalized Old Kingdom–based "archaism" is to be found in Egyptian art (and literature) from the eighth century onward,[46] datable explicit copying of the Third Dynasty style is only to be found in a series of reliefs of King Osorkon IV (c. 736–after 716 BC), found at Tanis (fig. 112 left),[47] and a pair of votive or "trial" plaques (fig. 112 right)[48] that are so similar in execution that they can only have been made at the same time.[49] It is unclear whether they were directly copied from the Step Pyramid reliefs, or whether the latter merely provided models,[50] but the stylistic fidelity is such that the material was confidently originally dated to the Third Dynasty, before doubts set in. That they were actually reproductions of the ancient style was finally confirmed by the discovery of the Tanis blocks.[51]

FIGURE 111 The "Saite" southern gallery under the Step Pyramid at Saqqara, probably actually cut during the late eighth century BC.

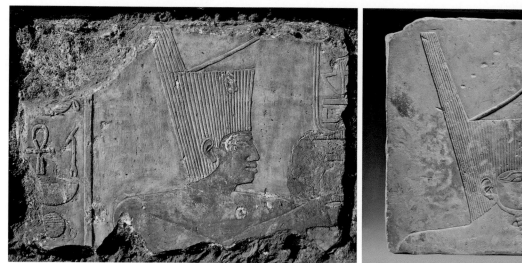

FIGURE 112 Left: Block of Osorkon IV at Tanis, carved in Third Dynasty style; right: contemporary trial piece in the same style (MMA 11.150.30).

This direct copying from the remote past was within the context of a movement that begins during the middle years of the eighth century BC. This featured the adoption of simplified royal names on the model of Old/Middle Kingdom schemes, replacing the elaborate, multi-epitheted forms that had been standard since Rameside times.[52] The phenomenon may be seen as part of an attempt to "reset" the Egyptian monarchy after the crises and civil conflict of the late ninth/early eighth centuries.[53] These new name styles are first found under Takelot III in the south, and Shoshenq V in the north, and although not the same kind of "carbon copies" seen under Osorkon IV, we find reliefs produced under the latter that have a strong Third Dynasty "feel" under the fifth Shoshenq.[54] It is accordingly to the reign of Shoshenq V that we might attribute the penetration of the Step Pyramid substructure and the copying of its decoration,[55] with the artists of the following reign inspired to produce true facsimiles.

A further product of this early example of archaeological investigation is to be seen by a mention of Djoser—as the "Dual King, Nebty Netjerkhet-nub"[56]—on a stela dedicated by a certain Padubast during the later eighth century. This was found at the Serapeum, the catacomb of the sacred Apis bulls,[57] this citation of the king being a direct quote from the lintel inscriptions of the reliefs below the Step Pyramid.[58] This suggests that the results of the investigations below that monument were in wide circulation during the late eighth century, not just for use in royal representations.

The southern gallery[59] was later used for the burial of some thirty uncoffined mummies, probably of Ptolemaic or Roman date,[60] with other burials of this date also made elsewhere in the pyramid substructure. Another ancient monument that was reused as a burial catacomb in Twenty-sixth Dynasty times was the tomb of Ninetjer,[61] where some chambers near the entrance were enlarged into two mass burial vaults. More coffins were deposited in the main corridor, while shaft tombs were sunk in various other rooms; such reuse of older monuments was common at Saqqara from the Twenty-sixth Dynasty onward. Indeed, the tomb of Ninetjer had already received intrusive burials as early as the later Eighteenth Dynasty, when shafts belonging to the extensive late Eighteenth/early Nineteenth Dynasty cemetery to the south also penetrated some of the Second Dynasty private tombs in that area (see page 58). Such large-scale reuses of earlier monuments for communal burials have been found across the Saqqara plateau.

Continuing interest in Djoser during the Twenty-sixth Dynasty is underlined by the existence of priests of his cult, a certain Ahmose being "Prophet of the Dual King Netjerkhet-Djoser and Libation-priest of Djoser-Teti" (fig. 113), again cultically linking these two kings (cf. page 126).[62] A further pairing of cults of ancient kings is found in the case of one Senebef, who was a "Prophet of the Dual King Djoser" and "the Dual King Meni."[63] A cult of the latter was in any case still current in early Ptolemaic times, when the priest Nesynuwer was Prophet not only of the founder of the Egyptian monarchy, but also of the "Dual King Titet"—presumably the "Iteti" whom the Abydos list makes the successor of Meni.[64] In addition, a probably Twenty-sixth Dynasty bronze survives representing Sened,[65] and the Twenty-seventh Dynasty genealogy of the architect Khnumibre not only includes Imhotep as an ancestor, but includes alongside him a cartouche of Djoser (fig. 114).

The Greek Writers

Roughly contemporary with Khnumibre's genealogy is the work of the fifth-century BC Greek traveler and historian Herodotus. In his writings, he notes that he was told that "the first human king of Egypt . . . was Min, in whose time all of

FIGURE 113 The statue of Ahmose, a Twenty-sixth Dynasty priest of the cults of Djoser and Sekhemkhet (Berlin ÄM14765).

FIGURE 114 The Wadi Hammamat, and its graffito 92, giving the alleged descent of the Twenty-seventh Dynasty architect Khnumibre from Imhotep, who appears on the right, along with a cartouche of Djoser.

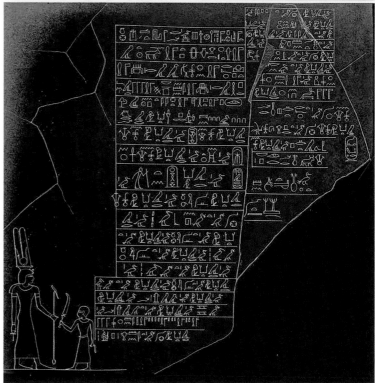

Egypt save the Thebaid was a marsh," and that he reclaimed the site of Memphis by erecting earthworks to the south of the city, and founding the temple of Hephaestus (Ptah) there. Two centuries later, Diodorus Siculus (first century BC) adds that he "taught the people to worship the gods and offer them sacrifices"—and also introduced them to the luxuries of tables and couches.

It is in the wake of Egypt's takeover by the Macedonian Ptolemaic Dynasty in the fourth century BC that we find the next documented attempt to produce a comprehensive chronicle of the Egyptian monarchy—although Herodotus states that his guides possessed a scroll from which they were able to recite the names of the 350 kings who followed "Min." This was the *Aegyptiaka* of Manetho, apparently put together in the third century BC.[66] It comprised a narrative history of the country from the times of the gods, in doing so formally introducing numbered dynasties to distinguish the various ruling houses. Unfortunately, no copy of the original work, or even a fragment thereof, has yet come to light, but it was used as a source by a number of later writers, preserving elements of it. Some only gave short extracts, but the Jewish historian Josephus (AD 37–c. 100) included, allegedly verbatim, full quotations relating to the end of the Second Intermediate Period and parts of the New Kingdom.

On the other hand, the Christian chronographers Sextus Julius Africanus (c. AD 160–c. 240) and Eusebius of Caesarea (AD 260/65–339/40) quoted comprehensively an "epitome" of the original *Aegyptiaka*, which gave just a list of kings, with their reign lengths and in some cases short notes on the reign in question. Of the two, Africanus's version is generally regarded as the more accurate; that of Eusebius further summarized some parts, and made amendments to others.

No copies of the original works of either Africanus or Eusebius survive, but a direct fifth-century AD Armenian translation of Eusebius is known, while the extant work of the Byzantine chronicler George Syncellus (eighth century AD) quotes both their versions of Manetho. Since what we refer to as "Manetho" has come down to us via multiple redactions and editorial lenses, the omission of important words, inconsistencies between these various versions, the pharaonic king lists, and the original monuments, should not come as a surprise. Despite their problems, these extracts from Manetho would form the bedrock of knowledge regarding the ancient history of Egypt down to the nineteenth century AD, and continue to be an important topic of scholarly discourse down to the present day. The full Manethonian successions according to Africanus and Eusebius for the first three dynasties are given in appendix 4.

Manufacturing History

In the Manethonic list, Djoser appears as "Tosorthros"/"Sorthros." He continued to be an important figure from the past during the Ptolemaic Period, and is strikingly coupled with Imhotep in the so-called Famine Stela on Sehel Island, just upstream of Aswan (fig. 115).[67] Ostensibly dated to Djoser's Year 18, the text begins with the king's concern at the lack of an inundation for seven years, the resulting famine, and consequent breakdown in law and order. Imhotep, in the role of a lector-priest, is tasked with commissioning

FIGURE 115 The Famine Stela on the island of Sehel, just south of Aswan.

priestly research into the birthplace of Hapi, the personification of the inundation, and to discover which god presides over it. The answer is that it is under the authority of Khnum, and Imhotep travels to his sanctuary at Elephantine, where he dreams of the god, who promises to reinstate the Nile flood. On being informed of this, Djoser decrees the restoration of the temple of Khnum and the institution of appropriate offerings, endowing its priesthood with all the revenues of the northern half of Lower Nubia, plus a share of those from the broader region. The stela is very clearly of Ptolemaic date (perhaps the reign of Ptolemy V, 205–180 BC), and was doubtless prepared by the contemporary priests of Khnum to support a claim to the revenues of what was by then known as the Dodekaschoinos—yet another case of using the remote past as a validation of the present.

The employment of Imhotep—by now a fully fledged divine being (fig. 116)[68]—in the narrative fits in well with his status in Late and Greco-Roman times. A number of other narratives survive from this time, perhaps most notably a purported "Life" written in the second century AD.[69] This presents a series of fantastic episodes, including a magical duel with an Assyrian sorceress, which took place while he was in her country on a quest to retrieve fragments of the body of Osiris.

FIGURE 116 Left: Late Period bronze figure of Imhotep (MMA 26.7.852); right: Imhotep as represented in the temple of Deir el-Medina (temp. Ptolemy VI); the corresponding pillar on the other side of the temple shows Imhotep's New Kingdom equivalent, Amenhotep-son-of-Hapu.

Beyond this, Imhotep (Imuthes in Greek), in his guise as the Greek god of medicine, Asklepios, is widely described as the son of Hephaistos (i.e., Ptah), and also linked in one horoscope with Hermes, the Greek equivalent of the Egyptian god Thoth. This latter association is also found in the demotic Book of Thoth, the Imhotep/Thoth link fitting well with the close association of the Late Period catacomb of the sacred baboons of Thoth at Saqqara with the putative tomb of Imhotep (page 86, above). Although the cult of Imhotep died out with the rest of Egyptian paganism during the fourth century AD, aspects of his fictionalized life became merged into tales of the Judaic/Christian/Islamic figure of Joseph, in particular his role in seven years of famine, and also as an interpreter of dreams.

Also from the second century AD come mentions of the mysterious Second Dynasty king "Neferkasokar" in material deriving from the so-called Book of the Temple—a

Demotic treatise dealing with the planning and building of such structures. This work seems to have originally been written somewhat earlier in Middle Egyptian and then later translated into Demotic.[70] This includes a "historical" introduction that tells how, as a result of a seven-year famine, Neferkasoker undertook a program of temple restoration throughout the country, the resulting decree being found by Prince Hordjedef—a son of Khufu and remembered as a great sage. This ancient decree is nominally the basis of the treatise.

The motif of seven-year famine is, of course, highly reminiscent of that in the Famine Stela, with it being used here in exactly the same way as a frame and justification for the royal act that is then described. Clearly, by Greco-Roman times the legend of a major famine during the earliest times had become a trope that could be applied to a number of kings attributed to this era, with once again the intention of giving authority to the accompanying text by its attribution to a distinguished personality of the remote past. Thus, even as the curtain began to descend on ancient Egypt, a few echoes of historical figures of the earliest dynasties remained, albeit as near-spectral guarantors of the antiquity of texts, rather than as genuine historical figures.

5 RESURRECTION

The memory of Djoser and Imhotep survived to the very end of the ancient Egyptian culture. Those of Den and Neferkasokar also endured well into Greco-Roman times as alleged fonts of medical and religious spells, and issues of temple planning. However, any true understanding of the earliest centuries of pharaonic civilization had long since been lost, even before the triumph of Christianity at the end of the fourth century had severed all remaining explicit links with the past. In contrast with later periods, where large numbers of standing monuments reminded people of the existence of their now-forgotten builders, almost all monuments of the first pharaohs had utterly vanished and would not reappear until the end of the nineteenth century AD.

The Dawn of Archaeology

The first phase of the decipherment of hieroglyphs in the 1820s led to fairly rapid steps in reconstructing significant parts of the sequence of kings. It was also possible to assign monuments to many of them, as far back as what would prove to be the beginning of the second millennium BC. However, this was by no means true for earlier periods, especially in the case of the earliest dynasties, where Manetho remained the only source. The one exception was that his "Menes" and Herodotus' "Min" were immediately recognized as identical with the "Meniy" shown in the Min-festival reliefs at the Ramesseum (fig. 117; see page 124, above).[1]

On the other hand, the pioneering 1820s saw the first modern entry into the Step Pyramid. This took place in 1821 when twenty-five local laborers, under the direction of Youssef Masarra (c. 1785–after 1842)*, were able, after some three weeks' labor, to facilitate access by the Prussian Johann Freiherr von Minutoli (1772–1846)*, together with his assistant, Girolamo Segato (1792–1836)*. The latter produced a fairly accurate set of plans of the parts of the monument they penetrated (fig. 118, top), together with drawings of the outer set of "blue chambers" and the texts on their door lintel (figs. 68,

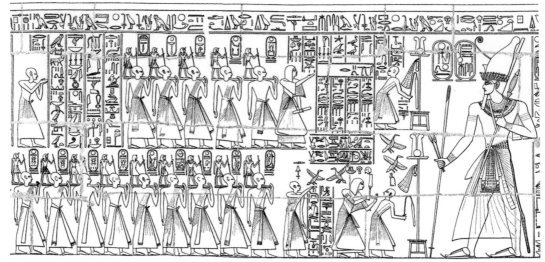

FIGURE 117 Section of the Min-festival reliefs on the inner face of the Second Pylon of the the memorial temple of Rameses II (the Ramesseum), showing the procession of statues of ancestral kings. From the top left: "Meni" (highlighted); Montjuhotep II; Ahmose I; Amenhotep I; Thutmose I, II and III; Amenhotep II; Thutmose IV; Amenhotep III; Horemheb; Sethy I; Rameses II.

118 bottom). James Burton (1788–1862)* soon followed Minutoli into the labyrinth and also copied the texts on the doorway of the "blue chambers," which he published soon afterward.[2] These rooms were judged by Gardner Wilkinson (1797–1875)*, writing a few years later, to be later additions to the pyramid substructure,[3] an erroneous idea that would be repeated by later scholars into the twentieth century.

During 1837–39, Richard Howard Vyse (1784–1853)* and his associate John Perring (1813–69)* undertook extensive excavations at Giza, and also made a comprehensive survey of the pyramids of the Memphite region.[4] In doing so, they made the first record of the Brick Pyramid at Abu Rowash, which at that time still retained significant amounts of brickwork.[5] They were also the first to note the existence of the nearby El-Deir, calling it "traces of an ancient square building."[6]

Perring was also responsible, in the summer of 1839, for undertaking clearances below the Step Pyramid, penetrating most of those parts of the interior of the monument missed by Minutoli and Segato, and producing more accurate and detailed plans, which would remain standard for a century.[7] He also opened the eighth-century gallery under the southern part of the pyramid, in which he found thirty uncoffined mummies. Perring's publication included comments on the doorway texts by Samuel Birch (1813–85)*, who noted that they had been "much defaced" in the decade since being first copied, and that they contained the "titles and standard [i.e., *serekh*] of a monarch, which may

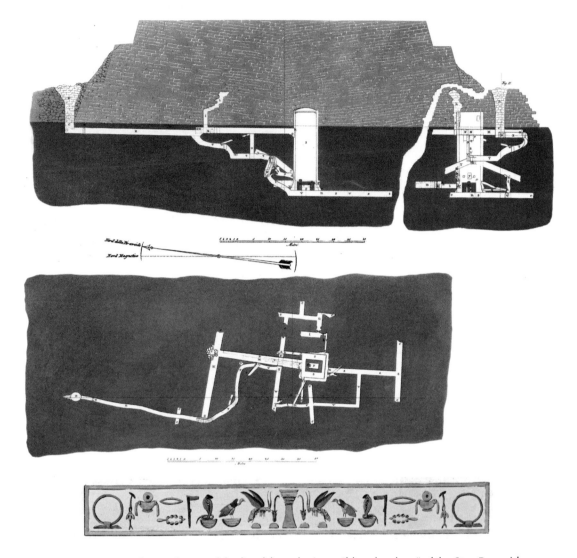

FIGURE 118 Section, plan, and copy of the lintel from the inner "blue chambers" of the Step Pyramid at Saqqara, as made during Minutoli's exploration of 1821. It is interesting to compare the galleries and chambers entered at this time with the full extent of the pyramid's substructure (fig. 65).

belong to the founder of the pyramid." However, in the absence of any other known example of the royal name within the *serekh* (Netjerkhet), Birch could only conclude that "the date of the monarch . . . has not yet been determined by any inscription, nor has it been ascertained whether he preceded, or was posterior to Cheops [Khufu]."[8] This uncertainty about the date of the pyramid would endure for some time. Nevertheless, Birch was able to recognize the secondary nature of the southern gallery on the basis of texts found on blocks reused in making its supporting pillars.

The Abydos and Turin Lists

As regards sources of royal names, Manetho had by now been supplemented by two of the early Rameside lists. Unfortunately, the monumental example, from the temple of Rameses II at Abydos, found in 1819 by William John Bankes (1786–1855)*, was only preserved (and then only partially) as far back as the First Intermediate Period (fig. 119).⁹ The Turin Canon had been acquired by Bernardino Drovetti (1776–1852)* around 1818, allegedly in good condition,¹⁰ but by the time it had reached Turin in 1824 it had been reduced to fragments—including the section that included the earliest dynasties.

That October, Jean-François Champollion (1790–1832)*, who had published the first substantive attempt to sketch a method of hieroglyphic decipherment two years previously, began to sort through the masses of fragmentary papyri held by the Turin museum,¹¹ eventually finding and extracting forty-eight fragments of the Canon. However, while Champollion copied the fragments and noted their content, no attempt was yet made at a formal reconstruction.

FIGURE 119 The Abydos king list of Rameses II (BM EA117) restored to its original location, from which it was removed in 1837.

The first steps toward this were taken by the German Gustav Seyffarth (1796–1885)*, a scholar who had developed his own method of decipherment,[12] and who would soon become Champollion's bitter enemy. However, following Seyffarth's first visit to Turin in May 1826, there was a degree of collaboration, as the German began a minute examination of the fragments, arranging them with reference to their fibers and color as well as the hieratic signs on them, and finding additional pieces among those set aside (or not seen) by Champollion. As a result, Seyffarth was able to make the first mounting of the fragments. In doing so, he was able to put together a considerable number of groups of fragments, with many joins that have stood the test of time. However, when it came to placing groups relative to one another where no direct links could be perceived, errors arose, in particular with those relating to the earlier part of the Canon where no cross-checking was possible, owing to the loss of the first part of the Abydos list (fig. 121). Accordingly, the first attempt at reconstructing the Canon provided little useful basis for the resurrection of the first three dynasties. On the other hand, while Seyffarth made errors in arranging the columns covering later dynasties as well, his layout was broadly correct from the later Old Kingdom onward.

Unfortunately, the feud between Champollion and Seyffarth had by now exploded, with the former unwilling to accept the fundamental correctness of the latter's work, although this had been done on purely scientific principles, without any influence from Seyffarth's system of decipherment. On the other hand, Seyffarth's assessment of the actual names was of course impacted by his views on transliteration.[13] For example, the cartouche at T3.16, which is now known to read "Spaty" (Den), was interpreted as "Pi" and equated with Manetho's "Phios"—that is, Pepy I of the Sixth Dynasty. Seyffarth's credibility was also undermined by his coming to believe that the Canon was not merely a version of Manetho's work in Egyptian, but an original autograph manuscript by Manetho himself.

The Canon was thus effectively left in limbo until November 1841, when Samuel Birch read a paper on it to the Royal Society of Literature in London.[14] In this, he notes the presence of "Menes," and equates the following king, "Itet," with the "Athoth" (Athôthis) of Manetho (a link already made by Champollion). However, Birch then moved on to names much later in the papyrus, and makes no further comment on what it revealed regarding the earliest kings.

The same year, Richard Lepsius (1810–84)* had made his second visit to Turin (following one in 1835), in particular to make a facsimile of the Canon, as restored by Seyffarth. This was published in 1842, in a volume also including a copy of the Abydos list.[15] No commentary was included, but this at last made the papyrus available to the wider world of Egyptology, and through Lepsius's imprimatur removed something of

FIGURE 120 The current reconstruction of the fragments of the Turin Canon (Turin C.1874), with the segments containing the first three dynasties highlighted.

the stigma that the papyrus had acquired through Seyffarth's role in its reconstruction. On this basis, the next significant discussion of the contents of the Canon came in two papers read by Edward Hincks (1792–1866)* in 1846.[16] These focused, however, on identifying the Sixth and Twelfth Dynasty portions, but also noted that the arrangement of fragments as published by Lepsius contained clear errors (see further below).

Fieldwork Renewed

Soon after he had made his facsimile of the Turin Canon, Lepsius had proceeded to Egypt at the head of the great Prussian archaeological expedition, which lasted from 1842 to 1845. During this, Lepsius would find the tomb of Metjen at Saqqara, with its mentions of the funerary estates of Huni and Queen Nimaathap, and become the next major explorer of the galleries below the Step Pyramid, in February 1843. This included the removal of the inscribed doorway of the "blue chambers," which was subsequently installed in the Ägyptisches Museum in Berlin.[17] The expedition also surveyed the whole structure.[18]

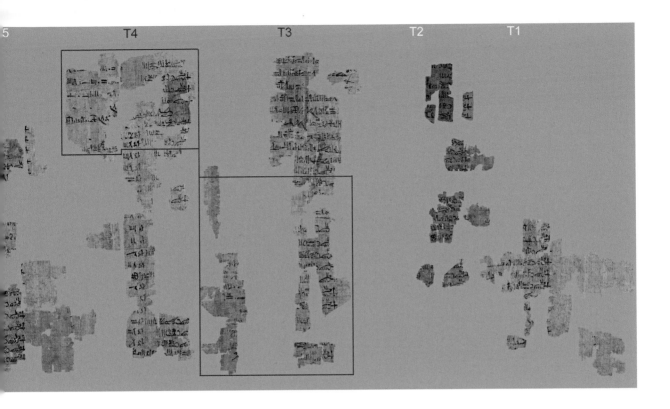

A contemporary opinion regarding the date of the Step Pyramid was that it was one of the pyramids stated by Manetho to have been erected at "Kôkômè" by the First Dynasty "Ouenephês" (i.e., Djer). This place name was by some interpreted as being derived from the Egyptian *k3-km*, "black bull," and an attempt was also made to link the royal titles on the "blue chambers" doorway to epithets of the Apis bull. These had been revealed by the excavation of the New-Kingdom-to-Ptolemaic catacomb of the Apis, the Serapeum, during the early 1850s. In addition, these excavations also brought to light the stela of Padubast, with its "quotation" from the texts of Djoser below the Step Pyramid (see page 130, above).[19] On this basis, Heinrich Brugsch (1827–94)*, writing in 1876, speculated that the Step Pyramid's "hollow body concealed the bleached bones of bulls and inscriptions chiselled in the stone relating to the royal name of Apis, was a common grave of the holy bulls which in days gone by King Uenephes consecrated in pious faith of these animals."[20] While these conclusions were wide of the mark, by thus placing the pyramid back in the First Dynasty, Brugsch nevertheless recognized the likelihood that it was the oldest then-known monument in Egypt.

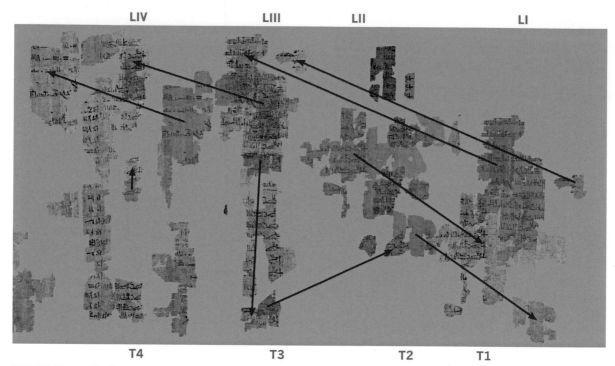

FIGURE 121 Seyffarth's original reconstruction of the first columns of the Turin Canon (in blue) compared to the current one. Lepsius column numbers are given at the top, current ones at the bottom.

Lepsius had also examined the Brick Pyramid at Abu Rowash, publishing the only two images of it to show brickwork still in situ (our fig. 94, bottom).[21] This had all been quarried away, as either building material or fertilizer, by the beginning of the twentieth century, and the pyramid's very existence was sometimes doubted until Nabil Swelim (1935–2015)* reidentified it in 1985, and published it soon afterward.[22]

Papyrus Progress

An additional fragment of data regarding the earliest dynasties became available with the publication of Papyrus Prisse in 1847,[23] with its passing mention of the Huni–Seneferu succession, while a new facsimile of the Turin Canon was made by Gardner Wilkinson in 1849, which he published in 1851.[24] This did not differ significantly from that of Lepsius, although Wilkinson spotted the misplacement of T3.11–13, and suggested that T4.1–4 might "contain the last kings of the Third Dynasty" (rather than, as actually the case, the last kings of the Second), with ḥwḏf3 identified as perhaps the Sephuris of Manetho. The latter was a remarkably prescient observation, given that "Sephuris" seems indeed to correspond with the "name" ḥwḏf3—but actually the one at T4.7, rather than the one at T4.2. Having made these observations, Wilkinson was unfortunately forced to make T4.5 and T4.6 the first kings of the Fourth Dynasty, thus linking Djoser-it with Manetho's "Sôris" (Seneferu), and making Djoser-ty an otherwise unattested "Sôris II." Wilkinson realized that this created problems, admitting that, after all, "it is not certain that these are the third and fourth dynasties."

Moving on to T3.24–25, which were misplaced as the next lines in the Seyffarth reconstruction, Wilkinson recognized the name of Sened as one "found at tombs near the pyramids": one of these will clearly have been Shery, fragments of whose tomb had long been in Oxford and Florence,[25] but no other tombs including Sened's name are known today. Wilkinson's analysis was, however, hampered by his opinion that the Second and Third Dynasties were contemporaneous, and thus that the Second Dynasty was not present in the Canon. This was based on Manetho's characterization of the kings of the two dynasties as respectively "of Thinis" and "of Memphis." Wilkinson also labored under the related misapprehension that the Fifth Dynasty (characterized by Manetho as "of Elephantine") was also absent from the Canon, having run in parallel with the Fourth Dynasty ("of Memphis").

Wilkinson's publication also included a section by Hincks, in which he noted the confused state of the initial columns as then arranged, in particular the need to move most of LII in front of LI, to make Meni and his immediate successors the precursors of the human kings of LIII. Hincks also inserted a new column (in which he placed a fragment containing what later transpired to be the reign lengths from Merpen to Aaka) between this and LIV. However, he maintained Wilkinson's misidentification of T4.1–4 as the end of the Third Dynasty, continuing to view the two Djoser-kings as the first rulers of the Fourth Dynasty.

New Lists

Further progress with the Canon in general,[26] and questions surrounding the earliest dynasties in particular, required some means of verifying the ordering of the fragments, as well as a source of undamaged versions of the cartouches attributed to the earliest kings. These desiderata were provided a decade later by two discoveries of Auguste Mariette (1821–81)*, appointed in 1858 director of Egypt's Antiquities Service and the new museum in the Cairo suburb of Bulaq. First, during the winter of 1859–60, he uncovered at Saqqara the tomb of Tjenry, datable to the reign of Rameses II, one of whose walls was adorned with a king list (fig. 122).[27] This was damaged, and missing the latter parts of the Fourth and Eighteenth Dynasties, but the beginning was intact. Mariette was able to collate this with the Turin Canon and Manetho to demonstrate that the Saqqara list began halfway through the First Dynasty and that, while there were variations among the three sources, they were essentially consistent with one another.

FIGURE 122 The Saqqara king list (Cairo JE11335 = CG34516).

He was able to continue this work of correlation soon afterward, when the clearance of the temple of Sethy I at Abydos revealed not only a king list, but one that went all the way back to "Meni." Its initial publication in 1866 thus provided a complete list of cartouche names for the earliest kings of Egypt (fig. 123). This permitted Emmanuel de Rougé (1811–72)* to produce the first major study of the first six dynasties,[28] which included probably the first mention in print of the Palermo fragment of the Fifth Dynasty Annals (fig. 124). This had been in the eponymous city since around 1859—although it would not be donated to its museum until 1877—and a lithographic copy had been made in 1865.[29] However, de Rougé's reference was only regarding one part of the Fifth Dynasty section, which seems to have been the only part that attracted any attention until some decades later (page 157, below).

Although an apparently continuous run of cartouches was now available back to "Meni," there was little that de Rougé could do with those prior to Seneferu in historical terms. All he could do was discuss the differences among the various source documents. For example, there was the inclusion of the name of Huni in the Saqqara and Turin lists,

FIGURE 123 The Gallery of Lists in the temple of Sethy I at Abydos, with the king list on the left-hand wall, and Mariette's original drawing of it.

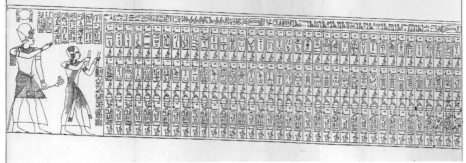

but its omission from the Sethy I list, and Huni's mention as Seneferu's predecessor in Papyrus Prisse.[30] De Rougé's problem derived from the fact that none of the royal names in question occurred on any known monuments contemporary with the period during which the kings had allegedly lived. Indeed, their very reality was a matter for debate for some considerable time: as Flinders Petrie (1853–1942)* put it in 1894: "The first three dynasties are a blank, so far as monuments are concerned; they are as purely on a literary basis as the kings of Rome or the primeval kings of Ireland." Commenting on the king lists, he opined that "a people who could put into regular chronologic order, as rulers of the land, the lists of their gods, were quite capable of arranging human names as freely and as neatly."[31]

FIGURE 124 Recto of Palermo Stone (Palermo, Museo Archeologico Regionale Antonino Salinas 1028).

The Fog Begins to Lift

However, in February 1889, Charles Wilbour (1833–96)* had rediscovered[32] the boulder atop the granite island of Sehel, just south of Aswan, on which the Famine Stela (pages 133–34, above) had been inscribed (fig. 126).[33] He was perplexed by the juxtaposition of what was clearly a Greco-Roman relief with a name he read initially as "Kharser," being joined in his confusion by Archibald Sayce (1845–1933)*, who accompanied Wilbour when he revisited the site a year later.

Abydos		Saqqara		Turin		Manetho		
							Africanus	Eusebius
A1	Meni			T3.11	Meni	I.1	Mênês	Mênês
A2	Itti			T3.12	It[...]	I.2	Athôthis	Athôthis
				T3.14	[...]	I.3	Kenkenês	Kenkenês
A3	Ita			T3.15	[...t]iywi	I.4	Ouenephês	Ouenephês
A4	Spaty			T3.16	Spaty	I.5	Ousaphaidos	Ousaphaïs
A5	Merbiap	S1	Merbiapen	T3.17	Merpen	I.6	Miebidos	Niebaïs
A6	Semsu	S2	Irinebti	T3.18	Semsem	I.7	Semempsês	Semempsês
A7	Qebeh	S3	Qebhu	T3.19	[...]bh	I.8	Biênekhês	Oubienthês
A8	Budjau	S4	Netjerbau	T3.20	[...]baw	II.1	Boêthos	Bôkhos
A9	Kakau	S5	Kakau	T3.21	[...]kawt	II.2	Kaiekhôs	Khôös
A10	Baennetjer	S6	Banetjeru	T3.22	[...]netjer	II.3	Binôthris	Biophis
A11	Wadjnes	S7	Wadjnes	T3.23	[...]s	II.4	Tlas	-
A12	Sendi	S8	Senedj	T3.24	Senedj	II.5	Sethenês	-
				T3.25	Aka	II.6	Khairês	-
		S9	Neferkare			II.7	Nepherkherês	-
		S10	Neferkasokar	T4.1	Neferkasokar	II.8	Sesôkhris	Sesôkhris
				T4.2	Hudjefa			
A13	Djadjay	S11	Beby	T4.3	Bebty[...]	II.9	Khenerês	-
A14	Nebka			T4.4	Nebka	III.1	Nekherôphês	Nekherôkhis
A15	Djoser-sa	S12	Djoser	T4.5	Djoser-itet	III.2	Tosorthros	Sesorthos
						III.3	Tyreis	-
						III.4	Mesôkhris	-
						III.5	Sôÿphis	-
A16	Teti	S13	Djoser-teti	T4.6	Djoser-ty	III.6	Tosertasis	-
						III.7	Akhês	-
A17	Sedjes	S14	Nebkare	T4.7	[Hudjef]a	III.8	Sêphouris	-
A18	Neferkare	S15	Huni	T4.8	Hu[...]	III.9	Kerpherês	-

FIGURE 125 Comparison of the pharaonic and Manethonic king lists.

Heinrich Brugsch at first read the cartouche as "Ahaser,"[34] but as this name was otherwise unknown, it added little to the debate. However, Georg Steindorff (1861–1951)* quickly spotted that the cartouche in fact read "Djoser," and was accompanied by a *serekh* which contained the long-mysterious name from under the Step Pyramid: Netjerkhet. Thus the date of the Step Pyramid could finally be verified.[35] The Menethonic note linking "Tosorthros" (Djoser) and the invention of stone architecture also now took on a much greater significance, since he was now identified as the owner of the monument that had long been seen as the most ancient standing structure in Egypt.

FIGURE 126 The location of the Famine Stela, with a detail of the figure of Djoser.

In 1894, the existence of the Wadi Maghara relief of Djoser (fig. 52a) was noted for the first time in print by Georges Bénédite (1857–1926)*. He based his communication on casts taken by Pierre-Victorien Lottin de Laval (1810–1903)* in 1850.[36] The reliefs in this area had been noted by earlier travelers, including Alessandro Ricci (1792/5–1834) and Lepsius, but Lottin's records were the first extensive ones to be made, and his work was followed by a major survey sponsored by the Palestine Exploration Fund (PEF) during 1868–69.[37] This was by no means an epigraphic mission, and while some reliefs were copied, many were not, and the copies actually made were often poor. On the other hand, the PEF work recorded both of the Sekhemkhet tableaux (fig. 76). The second of these was not noted again until 1973,[38] having been missed by the Egypt Exploration Fund team that undertook extensive copying work under the direction of Flinders Petrie during 1904–1905.[39] Indeed, Raymond Weill, in pioneering studies of the Sinai texts, denied the very existence of this tableau.[40]

The journey back beyond Djoser, into the earliest years of Egyptian history and its prehistory, was also just beginning. During his 1893/94 season at Koptos (Qift), Petrie found, under the Ptolemaic pavement, three colossal statues of the god Min (fig. 5) that he had little hesitation in ascribing to prehistoric times.[41] On the other hand, Petrie had much more difficulty in so dating other material found at Koptos, and also at the settlement and burial sites he dug on the opposite bank of the Nile at Naqada and nearby Ballas during the spring of 1895, assisted by James Quibell (1867–1935)*. Thus he attributed these crouched burials and the objects found in them to an invading "New Race" of the early First Intermediate Period.[42]

By contrast, the following year Jacques de Morgan (1857–1924)* had no doubts that material he found at El-Amrah, near Abydos, and closely resembling the "New Race" artifacts, belonged to prehistoric times.[43] In March 1897, at Naqada itself, he excavated the so-called Royal Tomb (page 21, above),[44] revealing material that could be related to some of his "prehistoric" assemblage—as well as that now being found at Abydos by Émile Amélineau (see just below)—and yielding the serekhs of Aha and Narmer, together with the "Menes tablet" (pages 14–15, above). Gustave Jéquier appended to de Morgan's publication of the tomb an extensive overview of current research into the earliest years of Egyptian history. This included advance copies of some of the illustrations for the first volume of Amélineau's report on his work at Abydos, and some comments on the similarities between the paneled architecture seen at Naqada and in Mesopotamia.[45] The Naqada tomb was later replanned (in one day!) and studied architecturally by Ludwig Borchardt (1863–1938)* in 1897,[46] and re-excavated by John Garstang (1876–1956)* in 1904.[47]

Nevertheless, it was not until the end of Petrie's 1897/98 work in the early First Intermediate Period cemeteries—which showed no trace of any "New Race" material—that the British archaeologist would grudgingly accept that de Morgan had been right.[48] To his credit, once convinced, Petrie embarked on a statistical analysis of the material from the prehistoric graves using the technique of seriation. This allowed them to be placed in a broad chronological order down to the beginning of history,[49] producing the first meaningful scheme for ordering Egypt's Predynastic cultures.

The Early Dynastic Kings Revealed

Meanwhile, in November 1895, Émile Amélineau (1850–1915)* had moved on from a previous season's clearance work in the temple of Sethy I at Abydos to excavating in the nearby necropoleis. His early discoveries included the tomb of the Twenty-second Dynasty high priest of Amun, Iuput A (cf. page 119, above).[50] In the new year, he moved two kilometers out into the desert to Umm el-Qaab, long known to the local inhabitants as a source of antiquities, and where there was evidently a local custom to go there on Good Friday to obtain playthings for the children.

Between 9 February and 18 March 1896, Amélineau discovered, in the south central part of the site, four large tombs and many subsidiary graves. The first of the big tombs proved to be that of Den, its ownership clear from a carved stone fragment found there (fig. 23d). Its interior showed signs of a massive fire—as did other monuments found. Part of the tomb of Qaa, and the sepulchers of Semerkhet and Djet, were then uncovered, yielding stela bearing the kings' names, most notably the fine example of Djet (fig. 23b), along with seal impressions and vessels in stone and pottery. Other fragments included the *serekh*s of additional kings, including Anedjib (in the tomb of Qaa), and another that Kurt Sethe (1869–1934)* and Gaston Maspero (1846–1916)* saw as the origin of the cartouche name Merpaben/Merbiap/Merpen of the king lists,[51] thus providing a direct link between them and the new discoveries.

The next season, beginning in November 1896, Amélineau investigated a depression to the south of where he had worked earlier in the year.[52] There he revealed the huge tomb of Khasekhemwy (fig. 46). This was correctly recognized as having been built in at least two phases, but the excavator's conclusions on its ownership were received poorly by the scholarly community. Based on the unique Horus-and-Seth-topped *serekh* of the tomb's owner, as revealed by seal impressions, Amélineau concluded that the two parts of the tomb were the actual sepulchers of Horus and Seth, who he argued had been real people, albeit later deified.

By contrast, Maspero immediately recognized that a king of the first three dynasties was involved. He also equated the Queen Nimaathap mentioned on sealings from the tomb with a lady of that name whose funerary cult had long been known from the early Fourth Dynasty tomb of Metjen (page 112, above). However, the current scholarly view, given the date of Metjen's sepulcher, was that Nimaathap's royal son had been Seneferu. Accordingly, Maspero assigned the Umm el-Qaab tomb and Khasekhemwy to the late Third Dynasty. This conclusion was rejected by Amélineau, who continued to hold on to his theory that it was indeed the sepulcher of the two gods, even arguing that the remains of the two skeletons found in the tomb were theirs.

Petrie would later point out that as there were plenty of examples of funerary cults flourishing long after their subjects had died, there was no underlying problem in allowing Nimaathap—and with her Khasekhemwy—to take her more archaeologically likely place at the end of the Second Dynasty.[53] This placement of the queen and the king was confirmed soon afterward by the discovery of Nimaathap's name alongside that of Djoser in Beit Khallaf tomb K1 (page 63).

Amélineau's belief that at least some of the tombs he was finding belonged to individuals who subsequently became gods was continued when, on 30 December 1897, he found a new tomb.[54] He was now working at the highest point of Umm el-Qaab, which was also the center of the vast scatter of potsherds that gave the site its name. A statuette of Osiris was the first find, and then the outline of the mud-brick chambers of

FIGURE 127 The "Osiris bed" as found by Amélineau in the tomb of Djer. The stairway installed for the convenience of pilgrims is clearly visible in the upper image.

a tomb. This proved to be similar in design to that of Djet, and like other tombs at the site (and elsewhere) had been burned in remote antiquity (page 40, above).

Having previously uncovered various material in the sepulcher's storerooms, on 2 January 1898, in the southwest corner of the tomb, Amélineau's workmen uncovered a black basalt sculpture, lying on its left side—the so-called Osiris bed (figs. 100, 127). Full-scale clearance of the tomb occupied 5 to 12 January, during which a skull was found in a chamber on the east side of the tomb. Amélineau promptly proclaimed the tomb (and the skull) to have belonged to Osiris himself. He based this on the votive ostraca naming Osiris found above the tomb, the "bed"—which he insisted on calling a "sarcophagus"—and a belief that the entrance stairway to the sepulcher (marked in red on fig. 20c and visible in fig. 127 upper) was the "Staircase of the Great God," mentioned in many texts referring to the Osiris cult (cf. page 116, above). He thus believed that he had found not only the tombs of Osiris, Horus, and Seth, but their mortal remains as well.[55] Needless to say, Maspero was not supportive of the idea, pointing out that the "sarcophagus" was no such thing, and in any case of a much later date than the tomb (he estimated no earlier than the Eighteenth Dynasty—but see page 117, above).

Amélineau continued to clear the subsidiary graves around the "Tomb of Osiris," and then to uncover that of Peribsen, to the northwest of the preceding monument, starting on 19 January 1898. However, this would be his last substantive work at the site, as after his departure from Abydos in March 1899, permission to excavate would be granted—apparently without any notice being given to Amélineau—to Flinders Petrie by the newly (re)appointed Director of Antiquities: Amélineau's constant critic, Gaston Maspero.

Petrie had long coveted Abydos, but had been frustrated by Amélineau's possession of a five-year permit. The then–director of antiquities, Victor Loret (1859–1946)*, had been unwilling to overturn this in favor of an application made by the Egypt Exploration Fund (EEF) on Petrie's behalf. Now, Maspero, who was incidentally also a vice president of the EEF, happily gave a permit to the Briton:[56] Amélineau would later state that he only found this out in March 1900 when he made inquiries about resuming his work after events had detained him for twelve months in France.[57]

Beginning at the end of November 1899, the 1899/1900 and 1900/01 seasons were occupied with the complete re-excavation of the tombs cleared by Amélineau (including sifting his spoil heaps), together with the clearance of the tomb of Merneith, which had been entirely missed by the Frenchman, along with smaller sepulchers.[58] Significant amounts of new material were recovered, including both funerary stelae of Peribsen (fig. 37),[59] while proper survey indicated that many of Amélineau's plans were inaccurate at best.[60] The two volumes that published Petrie's results came out within weeks of the ends of each of his excavation seasons:[61] in contrast, the last installment of Amélineau's reports did not come out until 1905. Petrie's archaeological and historical conclusions would form the basis for all future understanding of the Early Dynastic Period.

An example of how incompletely Amélineau had cleared the tombs was one of Petrie's most spectacular finds, in the tomb of Djer:

> While my workmen were clearing the tomb, they noticed amongst the rubbish which they were moving a piece of the arm of a mummy in its wrappings. It lay in a broken hole in the north wall of the tomb [in chamber I]. The party of four who found it looked in to the end of the wrappings and saw a large gold bead . . . .

They did not yield to the natural wish to further search or remove it; but laid the arm down where they found it until Mr. Mace[62] should come and verify it. Nothing but obtaining the complete confidence of the workmen, and paying them for all they find could ever make them deal with valuables in this careful manner. On seeing it Mr. Mace told them to bring it to our huts intact, and I received it quite undisturbed. In the evening the most intelligent of the party was summoned up as a witness of the opening of the bandages, so that there should be no suspicion that I had not dealt fairly with the men. I then cut open the linen bandages, and found, to our great surprise . . . four bracelets of gold and jewellery . . . . When recorded, the gold was put in the scales and weighed against [gold] sovereigns before the workman, who saw everything. Rather more than the value of gold was given to the men, and thus we ensured their goodwill and honesty for the future.[63]

The arm (fig. 128) was sent to the Egyptian Museum in Cairo, where the bracelets were quickly put on display, but the bones were discarded on arrival by the curator, Emile Brugsch (1842–1930: as Petrie wryly remarked, "a museum is a dangerous place").[64] The arm has usually been called that of a woman, in which case it might belong to the same individual as Amélineau's so-called "head of Osiris." On the other hand, there is nothing definite against it having been the last remains of Djer himself.

While work had been going on at Umm el-Qaab, another ground-breaking excavation had been underway at Hierakonpolis, hitherto all but ignored, apart from a visit by Gardner Wilkinson during the earlier part of the nineteenth century and a brief note by Urbain Bouriant (1849–1903)* in 1885.[65] Alerted by the appearance of material apparently from there on the Luxor antiquities market, in 1897 James Quibell and Frederick Green (1869–1949)* began work under the auspices of the Egyptian Research Account. First, they examined the so-called Fort (i.e., Khasekhemwy's enclosure: fig. 43) and a few Predynastic graves near the edge of the desert, before moving to the Kom el-Ahmar (Red Mound) in the cultivation. This was the site of the former temple, the last standing trace of which (a Ptolemaic gate) had been demolished for its stone some three decades earlier.

However, concealed under the foundations were found first an Old Kingdom golden-headed cult image of the local form of Horus, and then a pit holding a copper-covered statue of the Sixth Dynasty king Pepy I, a pottery lion—and the schist statuette of Khasekhem, by far the oldest royal image yet found (figs. 41 left, 129). To the east a further group of objects was discovered—the so-called Main Deposit (see fig. 2, inset)—comprising a huge number of other pieces of discarded temple equipment, some of them stretching back to before the dawn of Egyptian history, and including the Narmer Palette, the "Scorpion" macehead, and the limestone statuette of Khasekhem (figs. 13, 11, 41 right).

FIGURE 128 The mummified arm from the tomb of Djer, and its gold and turquoise bracelets (Cairo CG52008-11).

The following season, Green, now working at Hierakonpolis on his own (Quibell having now joined the Egyptian government's Antiquities Service), found a deeply buried revetment that had defined the raised platform upon which the first temple at the site had been built, elements of which had included blocks from the reign of Khasekhemwy (page 56, above). This was clearly where the material found the previous year had originally been dedicated, becoming buried when later generations of temple

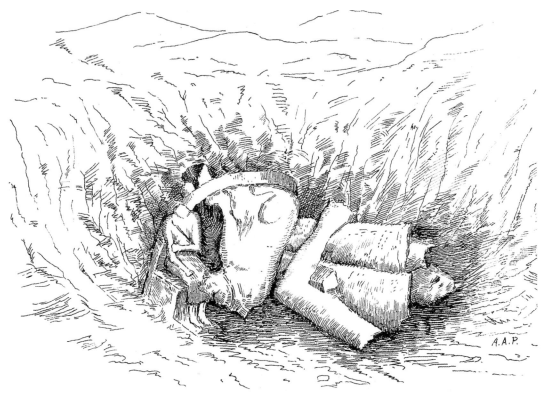

FIGURE 129 The schist statue of Khasekhem (fig. 41 [right]) as found at Hierakonpolis in 1898. The other items visible in the deposit are parts of a copper statue of the Sixth Dynasty king Pepy I.

builders had set to work (fig. 44). Furthermore, just over a kilometer south of the temple site, he also found the decorated Predynastic tomb 100 (fig. 4).[66]

It was also in 1899 that the first substantive Egyptological discussion of the Palermo Stone appeared from the pen of Édouard Naville (1844–1926),[67] although a preliminary publication had been made in a local archaeological journal in Sicily in 1895.[68] This was followed by a full publication (by Heinrich Schäfer) and commentary (by Naville) during 1902/03.[69] Additional fragments of the Annals would come to light over the coming decades (see page 159).

A further important piece of fieldwork, carried out during the 1900/01 season, was the investigation of the tombs at Beit Khallaf by John Garstang, also working for the Egyptian Research Account. Tomb K1 had been noticed in the past, but not examined, so was now opened for the first time in modern times. The discovery of sealings with the name of Djoser resulted in the sepulcher being proclaimed his and, in view of the presence of a skeleton in it, the Step Pyramid demoted to a mere cenotaph of the king.[70] The much more denuded tomb K2 was also investigated, and attributed to Sanakhte—who was regarded as a "new" king: his presence at Wadi Maghara had yet to be published. On the other hand, the likelihood that the broken cartouche found in the tomb was that of the "Nebka" who appeared in the Abydos and Turin king lists was recognized.

The Field Widens

Knowledge of two important monuments of the early dynasties came about through the work of Alexandre Barsanti (1858–1917)* early in the new century. First, in March 1900, he was tasked by Maspero to open the Layer Pyramid at Zawiyet el-Aryan.[71] This had resisted Maspero's own efforts in the 1880s, and although de Morgan had located the entrance stairway in 1896, he had gone no farther.

Then, in December 1901, the presence of a pre-Djoser royal tomb in the north of Egypt was revealed when Barsanti, while working in the pyramid complex of Unas at Saqqara, uncovered a series of underground galleries containing sealings of Hetepsekhemwy and Reneb.[72] These were analyzed by Maspero,[73] who placed them stylistically after the First Dynasty, but was unable to say whether they might be late Second or early Third Dynasty in date. However, the two names were recognized as being found alongside that of Ninetjer on the shoulder of a statue found at Memphis in 1888, belonging to a certain Hetepdief (fig. 34). Since Ninetjer had by now found a secure place as third king of the Second Dynasty, the allocation of the sealings and the tomb at the start of the dynasty was clear.

The beginning of the following year saw the first excavation of the area of El-Deir at Abu Rowash, which was threatened by the construction of military barracks nearby, although the work concentrated on the Coptic remains at the site.[74] Two years later, in 1904, Edward Ayrton (1882–1914)* and Charles Currelly (1876–1957)* found the first of the pre–Shunet el-Zebib royal funerary enclosures (that of Peribsen—the so-called Middle Fort).[75] Nearly two decades later, those of Djer, Djet, and Merneith, plus the anonymous "Western Mastaba," would be found by Petrie during the winter of 1921/22:[76] one row of graves had previously been uncovered by Eric Peet (1882–1934)* in 1911, but their context had not been recognized.

The progress made in the study of earliest dynasties over the little more than a decade since Petrie's pessimistic pronouncement of 1894 is illustrated by the fact that in 1908 Raymond Weill (1874–1950)* was able to complete a 515-page doctoral thesis on the monuments and history of the Second and Third Dynasties—the first book-length study of the topic.[77] In addition, the previous year Henri Gauthier (1877–1950)* had produced the first volume of his monumental *Livre des rois d'Égypte*, listing all the attestations of the pharaohs of the first dozen dynasties, and with some sixty pages dedicated to the kings of the first three dynasties. There nevertheless remained issues, Gauthier (for example) placing Narmer at the head of the Second Dynasty. The interest in the period was further underlined when Naville undertook new excavations at Umm el-Qaab during 1908/10. He investigated some apparently virgin areas, recleared the tomb of Peribsen, albeit with few new results, and confirmed that no undiscovered tomb remained in the main part of the site.[78] Most of Cemetery U to the east would remain hidden until the 1980s.

In 1909, Joseph Gautier (1861–1924)* found, on the island of Elephantine at Aswan, the curious "cone" of Huni, which was mentioned in print the same year by Borchardt, although no photograph would be published of it for nearly half a century.[79] In 1910, the Egyptian Museum in Cairo acquired, on the antiquities market, three new fragments of the Annals,[80] allegedly found near Minya in Middle Egypt. Soon afterward, a further piece was purchased, having been discovered at Memphis during the harvesting of ancient mud brick for use as fertilizer.[81] Yet another fragment was purchased by Petrie around the same time, supposedly found somewhere in Upper Egypt.[82] The most recent acquisition of an Annals fragment came in 1963.[83]

In 1914 and 1915 Henri Gauthier published studies on the Annals fragments that incorporated the new Cairo pieces, including the first attempt to tie together the largest of these with the one in Palermo.[84] The following year, three further studies of the Annals were published, by Georges Daressy (1864–1938),* Frederick Read (b. 1863), and Flinders Petrie; two more came in 1917, by Ludwig Borchardt and Seymour de Ricci (1881–1942)*. All subsequent work on the Annals has been based in some way on these pioneering studies, the reconstruction in our figure 98 being largely based on one produced by Winfried Barta (1928–92)* in 1981.[85]

The years directly prior to the outbreak of the First World War had seen the first systematic investigations of the early tombs at Saqqara. While a few had been seen during Mariette's work at the beginning of the 1860s, James Quibell, now working for the Egyptian Antiquities Service, began excavations at the northeastern extremity of the necropolis, where a series of Second and Third Dynasty tombs came to light— including that of Hesyre (page 70, above), originally found by Mariette, but long since lost. Suspended following Quibell's posting to the Egyptian Museum at the beginning of 1914, excavations in the area were not resumed until 1930. Cecil Firth (1878–1931)* then undertook a season before his premature death.

Firth had been engaged on the excavation of the Step Pyramid complex since 1924, with the assistance of the architect Jean-Philippe Lauer (1902–2001)* from 1926 onward. On Firth's death, he was succeeded by Quibell, who had acted as his assistant after his retirement from the Antiquities Service in 1925, and who completed the publication of the work[86] before his own death in 1935. Among the myriad discoveries was the statue base of Djoser also naming Imhotep (pages 85–86, above), and potential fragments of the king's mummy—first in 1926 by Battiscombe Gunn (1883–1950)* and then by Lauer in 1934. Lauer continued with the restoration of the structures in the complex and completed further volumes of its publication over the subsequent decades, being still involved as an advisor until his death.

The excavations in northeastern Saqqara were taken up again by the Antiquities Service in 1935 under the direction of Bryan Emery (1903–71)*, beginning a systematic scheme of work that revealed the large First Dynasty tombs along the eastern edge of the escarpment. Interrupted by the Second World War, Emery was finally able to resume activities in 1952, now under the auspices of the Egypt Exploration Society, only to have to stop again in 1956 on account of the Suez Crisis, when Anglo-French forces attempted to seize the Suez Canal.

The uncovering of the First Dynasty cemetery greatly enhanced the material available from the period,[87] but also led to some long-term confusion, since the size of many of the tombs found was significantly greater than those of the kings at Umm el-Qaab. The idea thus arose that the Saqqara sepulchers might be the actual burial places of the earliest kings, the Abydene structures being no more than cenotaphs.

A solution to the conundrum of size was put forward in 1966 by Barry Kemp,[88] who pointed out that while the actual burial monuments at Abydos were smaller, if one added the area covered by the associated monumental enclosures, the aggregate size of a given king's installation far overshadowed that of any of the candidate tombs at Saqqara. There was also a problem in that in some cases a number of tombs datable to the reign of a single king existed there, with none sufficiently larger than the rest to obviously belong to the king himself. It therefore seems clear that, while the Saqqara tombs were of high-status individuals, they were not those of kings.[89]

Elsewhere at Saqqara, in 1936, Neguib Macramallah (1903–49)* found a group of graves datable to the reign of Den, west of the Step Pyramid (see page 36). Then, in 1938, Selim Hassan (1886–1961)*, working on the Fifth Dynasty causeway of Unas, found the tomb of Ninetjer, containing large numbers of Late Period coffins and mummies;[90] his investigation was, however, rather summary. The tomb was rediscovered, and a proper examination begun, by a joint Berlin–Hanover expedition led by Peter Munro (1930–2009)* in the spring of 1980, the concession later passing to the German Archaeological Institute in Cairo, culminating in the final publication of the tomb in 2014. A private cemetery of the same date to the south of the royal necropolis was revealed quite by accident early in the twenty-first century, when Dutch-led excavations in the Eighteenth/Nineteenth Dynasty necropolis in that area found parts of Second Dynasty tombs incorporated into the substructures of the much later sepulchers.

Away from Saqqara, Macramallah had carried out work out at Abu Rowash's El-Deir in 1931, again as a result of threats to the site, this time the installation of a drainage pipe. He identified the central brick massif, and the southeastern quadrant of the enclosure wall, although his provisional identification was as a fort of the Middle Kingdom. This was the last time that the monument seems to have been examined, and it has subsequently suffered further damage from drainage work[91] and the encroachment of modern housing.

Between 1942 and 1954, the extensive Early Dynastic cemeteries at Helwan, directly across the river from Memphis, were investigated by Zaki Saad (1901–82)*, funded directly by Egypt's King Faruq.[92] New work, by the Australian Centre for Egyptology from Macquarie University, began in 1997 under the direction of Christiana Köhler.[93]

One of the most spectacular discoveries of a monument of the earliest dynasties came in September 1951, when Zakaria Goneim (1911–59)* began the excavation of what proved to be the unfinished pyramid of Sekhemkhet.[94] While much important material and data was gathered, there was the disappointment of finding the seemingly intact sarcophagus empty when opened on 26 June 1954.

The discovery of the pyramid had wider implications, since it led to the recognition that a name on the Sinai tableau previously assigned to Semerkhet of the First Dynasty was actually that of *Sekhem*khet.[95] This discovery brought forward attested Egyptian activity in this part of the Sinai by two centuries,[96] although earlier names have been found elsewhere on the peninsula.

Emery's Egypt Exploration Society work at Saqqara resumed in 1964, to the west of the First Dynasty cemetery, at the point where the escarpment descended into the great "access wadi" that culminated in the Gisr el-Mudir. Here, in 1956, Emery had made some initial investigations of an area covered with fragments of jars that had formerly held Late/Greco-Roman Period mummified ibises, and the remains of a tomb datable to the Third Dynasty. The renewed work revealed not only further tombs of the latter date, but also a temple complex and an associated vast necropolis for the burial of sacred and votive animals. There were separate catacombs for ibis, baboon, falcon, and cow mummies, the latter the mothers of the Apis bull (fig. 130).

Given the presence of Third Dynasty tombs, and Imhotep's association with some of the cults in evidence at what was dubbed the "Sacred Animal Necropolis," Emery was confident that Imhotep's tomb could be found in the area. However, by the time of his death in 1971 he had been unable to identify the sepulcher—although tomb S3518, found during the winter of 1968/69 directly above the entrance to the Baboon galleries, and with part of its substructure penetrating them, has (as discussed above, pages 86–87) a range of features that make it a strong candidate for Imhotep's long-lost burial place.

FIGURE 130 The Sacred Animal Necropolis at Saqqara. Tomb S3518 lies on the ridge in the middle of the photograph.

Various other excavations during more recent decades have revealed more data about the earliest pharaohs and those they ruled, as well as about the period that preceded the unification. Key for our understanding of the mortuary history of the First and Second Dynasty kings have been the re-excavation of areas of the royal funerary enclosures at Abydos by American teams, and the re-excavation of the tombs at Umm el-Qaab by the German Archaeological Institute in Cairo. The application of modern methods has allowed not only amplification and revision of the results obtained by Amélineau and Petrie, but also the uncovering of hitherto unsuspected monuments. Another significant discovery has been the discovery by the Czech team at Abusir of the first tomb unequivocally dated to the reign of Huni (pages 102–104, above).

Thus, the resurrection of the founders of Egypt's greatness is an ongoing process. While a surprising amount is known about this remote period, there remain various obscurities and "spare" royal names. In particular, the "dark age" of the Second Dynasty and the time immediately before Huni in the Third remain all but impenetrable in the current state of knowledge, and one can only hope that excavations will reveal more data that will allow us to tell more of the story of the first pharaohs.

APPENDIX 1:

CHRONOLOGY

All dates prior to 690 BC are approximate to a greater or lesser degree.
Only kings mentioned in the text are listed.
LE = Lower Egypt only
UE = Upper Egypt only

PALEOLITHIC		300,000–8000 BP
EPIPALEOLITHIC		8000–6000
PREDYNASTIC PERIOD		
Upper Egypt	*Lower Egypt*	
	Omari/Merimde/Fayyum A	c. 6000–4100
Badarian/Naqada I–IIB	Maadi-Buto I–IIa	c. 4400–3600
Naqada IIC–IID2	Maadi-Buto IIb–IIIa	c. 3600–3350 BC
PROTODYNASTIC PERIOD		
Naqada IIIA–B	Maadi-Buto IIIb–IV	c. 3350–3150
EARLY DYNASTIC PERIOD		
Dynasty 1		3150–2810

    Narmer
    Hor-Aha
    Djer
    Djet
    Den
    Anedjib
    Semerkhet
    Qaa

Dynasty 2   2810–2675
    Hetepsekhemwy
    Reneb
    Ninetjer
    ?
    Sened   } NB: between Ninetjer and
    Weneg   Khasekhem(wy) the number
    Peribsen   and order of succession of
    Sekhemib   kings is uncertain
    ?
    Khasekhem(wy)

OLD KINGDOM

Dynasty 3   2675–2600
    Djoser
    Sekhemkhet
    Sanakhte
    Khaba
    Huni
Dynasty 4   2600–2470
    Seneferu
    Khufu
    Djedefre
    Khaefre
    Menkaure
Dynasty 5   2475–2360
    Sahure   2469–2457
    Neferirkare   2457–2447
    Niuserre   2437–2426
    Isesi   2418–2390
    Unas   2390–2360
Dynasty 6   2360–2195
    Teti   2360–2348
    Pepy I   2346–2300
    Nemtyemsaf I   2300–2293
    Pepy II   2293–2200

FIRST INTERMEDIATE PERIOD

Dynasties 7/8		2200–2100
Neferirkare II		
Dynasties 9/10 (LE)		2100–2000
Akhtoy V	c. 2100	
Merykare		
Dynasty 11a (UE)		2080–2014

MIDDLE KINGDOM

Dynasty 11b		2014–1943
Montjuhotep II	2010–1962	
Montjuhotep III	1962–1950	
Dynasty 12		1943–1780
Senwosret I	1923–1878	
Amenemhat II	1881–1845	
Senwosret II	1848–1838	
Senwosret III	1838–1797	
Dynasty 13		1780–1650
Wegaf		
Khendjer		
Imyromesha		
Neferhotep I		

SECOND INTERMEDIATE PERIOD

Dynasty 14 (LE)		1700–1650
Dynasty 15 (LE)		1650–1535
Dynasty 16 (UE)		1650–1590
Dynasty 17 (UE)		1585–1540

NEW KINGDOM

Dynasty 18		1540–1278
Ahmose I	1540–1516	
Amenhotep I	1516–1496	
Amenhotep II	1415–1386	
Amenhotep III	1377–1337	
Akhenaten	1337–1321	
Horemheb	1308–1278	

Dynasty 19		1278–1176
Sethy I	1276–1265	
Rameses II	1265–1200	
Dynasty 20		1176–1078
Rameses III	1173–1142	

THIRD INTERMEDIATE PERIOD

Dynasty 21		1078–941
Pasebakhanut II	967–941	
Dynasty 22		943–736
Shoshenq I	943–922	
Osorkon I	922–888	
Osorkon II	872–831	
Shoshenq V	773–736	
Dynasty 23		736–666
Osorkon IV	736–710	
Dynasty 24		734–721
Dynasty 25		754–656

SAITE PERIOD

Dynasty 26		664–525
Wahibre	589–570	
Ahmose II	570–526	

LATE PERIOD

Dynasty 27		525–404
Dynasty 28		404–399
Dynasty 29		399–380
Dynasty 30		380–342
Dynasty 31		342–332

HELLENISTIC PERIOD

Dynasty of Macedonia		332–310
Dynasty of Ptolemy		310–30
Ptolemy V Epiphanes	210–180	
Ptolemy VI Philometor	180–145	

ROMAN PERIOD

	30 BC–AD 395

APPENDIX 2:

ROYAL NAMES

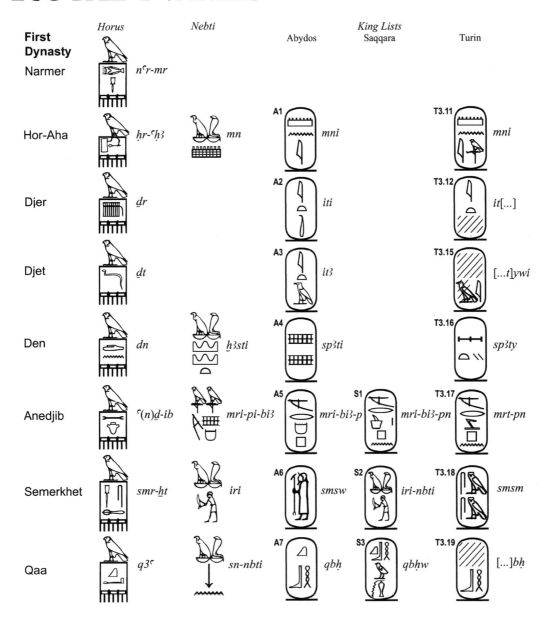

First Dynasty	Horus		Nebti		Abydos		King Lists Saqqara		Turin	
Narmer		n⁽r-mr								
Hor-Aha		ḥr-⁽ḥ3		mn	**A1**	mni			**T3.11**	mni
Djer		ḏr			**A2**	iti			**T3.12**	it[...]
Djet		ḏt			**A3**	it3			**T3.15**	[...t]ywi
Den		dn		ḫ3sti	**A4**	sp3ti			**T3.16**	sp3ty
Anedjib		⁽(n)ḏ-ib		mri-pi-bi3	**A5**	mri-bi3-p	**S1**	mri-bi3-pn	**T3.17**	mrt-pn
Semerkhet		smr-ḫt		iri	**A6**	smsw	**S2**	iri-nbti	**T3.18**	smsm
Qaa		q3⁽		sn-nbti	**A7**	qbḥ	**S3**	qbḥw	**T3.19**	[...]bḥ

167

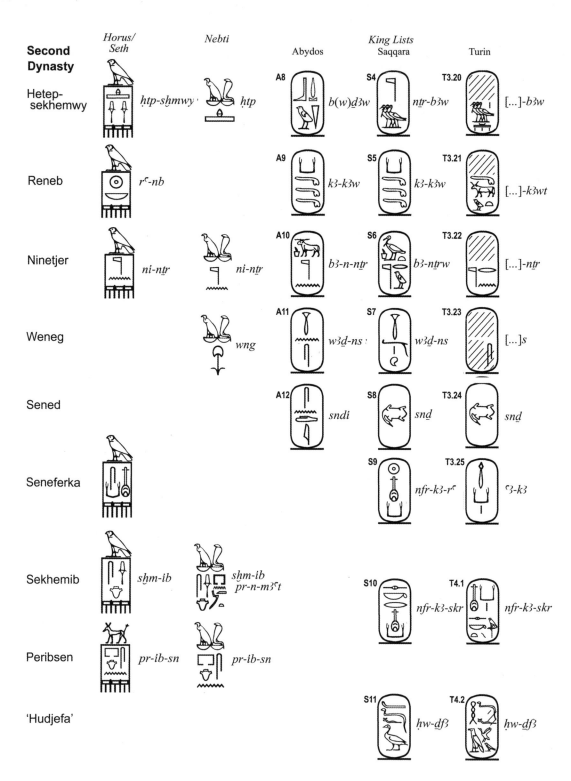

Second Dynasty	Horus/Seth		Nebti		Abydos		King Lists Saqqara		Turin	
Hetep-sekhemwy		ḥtp-sḥmwy		ḥtp	A8	b(w)ḏ3w	S4	nṯr-b3w	T3.20	[...]-b3w
Reneb		rˁ-nb			A9	k3-k3w	S5	k3-k3w	T3.21	[...]-k3wt
Ninetjer		ni-nṯr		ni-nṯr	A10	b3-n-nṯr	S6	b3-nṯrw	T3.22	[...]-nṯr
Weneg				wng	A11	w3ḏ-ns	S7	w3ḏ-ns	T3.23	[...]s
Sened					A12	sndi	S8	snḏ	T3.24	snḏ
Seneferka							S9	nfr-k3-rˁ	T3.25	ˁ3-k3
Sekhemib		sḥm-ib		sḥm-ib pr-n-m3ˁt			S10	nfr-k3-skr	T4.1	nfr-k3-skr
Peribsen		pr-ib-sn		pr-ib-sn						
'Hudjefa'							S11	ḥw-ḏf3	T4.2	ḥw-ḏf3

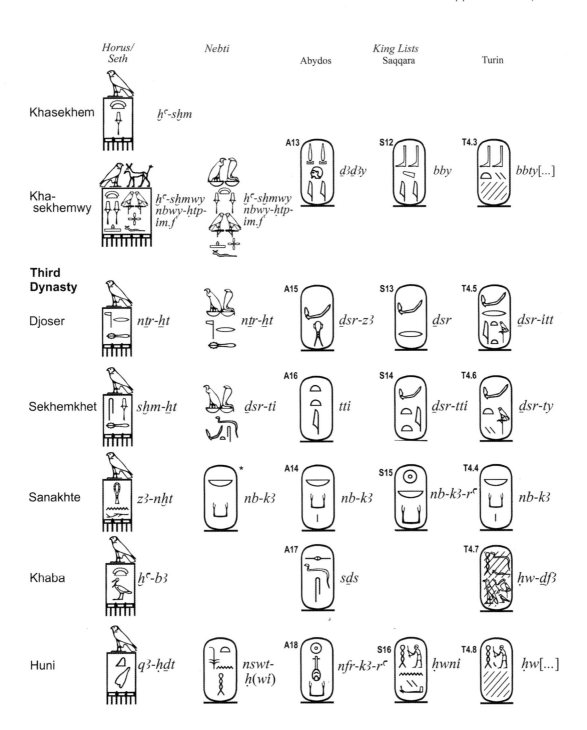

	Horus/ Seth	Nebti	Abydos	King Lists Saqqara	Turin
Khasekhem	ẖꜥ-šḥm				
Kha-sekhemwy	ẖꜥ-šḥmwy nbwy-ḥtp-im.f	ẖꜥ-šḥmwy nbwy-ḥtp-im.f	A13 ḏꜣḏꜣy	S12 bby	T4.3 bbty[...]
Third Dynasty					
Djoser	nṯr-ḫt	nṯr-ḫt	A15 ḏsr-zꜣ	S13 ḏsr	T4.5 ḏsr-itt
Sekhemkhet	šḥm-ḫt	ḏsr-ti	A16 tti	S14 ḏsr-tti	T4.6 ḏsr-ty
Sanakhte	zꜣ-nḫt	* nb-kꜣ	A14 nb-kꜣ	S15 nb-kꜣ-rꜥ	T4.4 nb-kꜣ
Khaba	ẖꜥ-bꜣ		A17 sḏs		T4.7 ḥw-ḏfꜣ
Huni	qꜣ-ḥḏt	nswt-ḥ(wi)	A18 nfr-kꜣ-rꜥ	S16 ḥwni	T4.8 ḥw[...]

Dimensions of Royal Tombs

King	Location	Superstructure base dimensions (meters)	Enclosure dimensions (meters)
Narmer	Umm el-Qaab B17/18	10* x 3*	?
Hor-Aha	Umm el-Qaab B10/15/19	12* x 9.5*	I: 33 x 22 II: 17.3 x 12.0 } (1080m²) III. 13.4 x10.5
Djer	Umm el-Qaab O	13.2* x 12*	~110 x ~65 (5265m²)
Djet	Umm el-Qaab Z	12* x 9.4*	~100 x ~60
Merneith	Umm el-Qaab Y	9* x 6.4*	~65 x 30+
Den	Umm el-Qaab T	15.2* x 8.9*	
Anedjib	Umm el-Qaab X	15.1* x 7.2*	
Semerkhet	Umm el-Qaab U	16.7* x 7.4*	
Qaa	Umm el-Qaab Q	24* x 12*	
	Abydos Donkey Enclosure		67 x 37.5 (2500m²)
	Abydos Western Mastaba		68 x 28
Hetepsekhemwy	Saqqara L-shaped	104 x 52?	200+ x 400?
Ninetjer	Saqqara Gisr el-Mudir	77* x 50*	~680 x 400
Peribsen	Umm el-Qaab P	18* x 15*	110 x 50
Khasekhemwy	Umm el-Qaab V	88* x 20*	137 x 77
Djoser	Saqqara	121 x 109	536 x 272
Sanakhte?	Abu Rowash	20 x 20	330 x 170
Sekhemkhet	Saqqara	120 x 120	536 x 194
Khaba (?)	Zawiyet el-Aryan	80 x 80	?
Huni(?)	Abu Rowash	~215 x ~215	?

* Dimensions of substructure, so minimum likely size.

APPENDIX 4:

THE FIRST THREE DYNASTIES ACCORDING TO THE SURVIVING EXTRACTS FROM MANETHO

Africanus

I.1	Μηνης	Mênês	62/60 yr
I.2	Αθωθις	Athôthis	57 yr
I.3	Κενκενης	Kenkenês	31 yr
I.4	Ουενεφης	Ouenephês	23 yr
I.5	Ουσαφαιδος	Ousaphaidos	20 yr
I.6	Μιεβιδος	Miebidos	26 yr
I.7	Σεμεμψης	Semempsês	18 yr
I.8	Βιηνεχης	Biênekhês	26 yr
			253 yr

II.1	Βοηθος	Boêthos	38 yr
II.2	Καιεχως	Kaiekhôs	39 yr
II.3	Βίνωθρις	Binôthris	47 yr
II.4	Τλας	Tlas	17 yr
II.5	Σεθενης	Sethenês	41 yr
II.6	Χαιρης	Khairês	17 yr
II.7	Νεφερχερης	Nepherkherês	26 yr
II.8	Σεσωχρις	Sesôkhris	48 yr
II.9	Χενερης	Khenerês	30 yr
			302 yr

Eusebius

I.1	Μηνης	Mênês	30 yr
I.2	Αθωθις	Athôthis	27 yr
I.3	Κενκενης	Kenkenês	39 yr
I.4	Ουενεφης	Ouenephês	42 yr
I.5	Ουσαφανς	Ousaphaïs	20 yr
I.6	Νιεβανς	Niebaïs	26 yr
I.7	Σεμεμψης	Semempsês	18 yr
I.8	Ουβιενθης	Oubienthês	26 yr
			252 yr

II.1	Βωχος	Bôkhos	—
II.2	Χωος	Khôos	—
II.3	Βίοφις	Biophis	—
II.4	-		—
II.5	-		—
II.6	-		—
II.7	-		—
II.8	Σεσωχρις	Sesôkhris	48 yr
II.9	-	-	—
			297 yr

III.1	Νεχεροφης	Nekherôphês	28 yr		III.1	Νεχερωχις	Nekherôkhis	—
III.2	Τοσορθρος	Tosorthros	29 yr		III.2	Σεσορθος	Sesorthos	—
III.3	Τυρεις	Tyreis	7 yr		III.3	—		—
III.4	Μεσωχρις	Mesôkhris	17 yr		III.4	—		—
III.5	Σωυφις	Sôÿphis	16 yr		III.5	—		—
III.6	Τοσερτασις	Tosertasis	19 yr		III.6	—		—
III.7	Αχης	Akhês	42 yr		III.7	—		—
III.8	Σηφονρις	Sêphouris	30 yr		III.8	—		—
III.9	Κερφερης	Kerpherês	26 yr		III.9	—		—
			214 yr					**198 yr**

NOTES

Note to Preface

1   See Maragioglio and Rinaldi 1967: 22–25; Edwards 1994; however, some scholars (e.g., the present writer [1981] and Swelim [1983; 2014–15]) continued to favor a Third Dynasty date for considerably longer.

Notes to Introduction

1   For overviews of Egyptian prehistory, see Midant-Reynes 2000 and Tassie 2014.

2   Vermeersch et al 1998.

3   On the question of climate change, see Kuper and Kröpelin 2006; see also Leplongeon 2017.

4   Wendorf and Schild 2001: 463–521.

5   Barich et al. 2014.

6   See previous note.

7   The modern designation of the earlier part of what was originally called the Amratian; the mode of transition between the Badarian and Naqada I remains a matter for debate.

8   On the various issues surrounding the chronology of the Predynastic, see F.A. Hassan 1988 and Hendrickx 2006; on subsistence issues of the transition, see Phillipps, Holdaway, Wendrich, and Cappers 2012.

9   Naqada IIA–B corresponds to the Late Amratian culture, while Naqada IIC–D corresponds to the Gerzean.

10   Formerly the Semainean culture; Naqada IIIA–B covers the period directly before the beginning of the First Dynasty, Naqada IIIC1 that from Narmer to Djer, Naqada IIIC2 from Djer to Anedjib, and Naqada IIID from the last part of the First Dynasty into the Second.

11   An overview of the history of the site is given by Adams 1995: 21–80; a full bibliography and up-to-date information on the ongoing work at the site is at www.hierakonpolis-online.org.

12   Kemp 1973: 38–43.

13   For this and Predynastic Abydos in general, see Hartung 2018.

14   A wide range of models have been put forward for the way in which the southern polity came into existence. Examples include those set out in Kaiser 1990; T.A.H. Wilkinson 2000b; Köhler 2014; 2014–15.

15   Cf. papers cited in previous note.

16   For the latter site, see the overviews in Ciałowicz 2011; Chłodnicki 2014.

17   Kołodziejczyk 2005; for an overview of the Predynastic in the Delta, see Tristant and Midant-Reynes 2011.

18   The Palermo fragment and other Annals Stones are fully published in T.A.H. Wilkinson 2000a.

19   Cf. Leprohon 2013: 17.

Notes to Chapter 1

1   Dreyer 1998a; 2011.

2   See Dreyer 1991; however, such gravel tumuli have been found above First Dynasty tombs at Kafr Hassan Dowud (Hassan et al. 2003: 42).

3   Nakano 1998; on the ware in general, see Hartung et al. 2015.

4   Davis 1992.

5   For a preference of this term over the more loaded "trade," see discussion in Hendrickx and van den Brink 2002; on interactions with Syria-Palestine, see Braun 2011.

6   https://www.uni-bonn.de/news/297-2020. It should be noted, however, that Castillos (2002: 74–75) and Lankester (2011) question the identification of the "scorpion" sign with the name of a king, the latter regarding him as actually Narmer.

7   The equation of the macehead owner with the tomb owner has been questioned in Dreyer 1998a: 17–18, in part on the basis of radiocarbon dates from U-j. However, while determination would push the tomb back into the thirty-fourth century, the other's range is compatible with a date in the thirty-first century, that is, not long before the most likely date of the Unification (see just below). There is in any case a wider issue of radiocarbon dates from the Old Kingdom and earlier appearing to be uniformly higher than seems historically credible (cf. page 16).

8   Porter and Moss 1937: 87; Kaiser and Dreyer 1982: 221–25.

9   B. Adams 1995: 49.

10   Taillet and Laisney 2012: 385–87.

11   Cf. Heagy 2014.

12   Garstang 1905b.

13   As first proposed by Borchardt (1898).

14   As first pointed out by Wiedemann (1898: 113).

15   Dreyer et al. 1996: 72.

16   Entry numbering in this book is that put forward in Ryholt 2004, correcting and superseding earlier reconstructions.

17   Dreyer 1987; Kaiser 1987.

18   Placing his Year 7 in 1831/30 BC: see Krauss 2006: 448–50; this is the earliest generally agreed absolute date in Egyptian chronology.

19   Spence 2000; 2001; Rawlins and Pickering 2001.

20   See Manning 2006: 338–50; Rowland 2013; cf. n7, above.

21   Cf. n7, above.

22   Other, rather different, interpretations of the palette have also been put forward, for example, O'Connor 2011.

23   Dreyer 2000.

24   Dreyer 1987; Kaiser 1987.

25   Dreyer et. al. 1996: fig. 26, pl. 14 b, c.

26   Williams 1988.

27   Taillet and Laisney 2012: 387.

28   Berlin ÄM22607 (Malek 1999: 1114–15).

29   Porter and Moss 1937: 88; Kaiser and Grossmann 1979: 157–58; Kaiser and Dreyer 1982: 220–21; Dreyer et al. 2003: 85–86.

30   Bestock 2012: 39–44.

31   Kaiser 1969; O'Connor 1989; Bestock 2009: 57–61; 2012: 38–45; see also page 70.

32   Dreyer et. al. 1996: fig. 26, pl. 14 b, c.

33   Porter and Moss 1937: 118–19; van Wetering 2012.

34   Porter and Moss 1974–81: 443–44.

35   Jeffreys and Tavares 1994.

36   Although other interpretations have been proposed (e.g., Kees 1928; Kaiser 1960: 132).

37   Petrie 1900–1901: pl. iiia[5–6].

38   Porter and Moss 1937: 88; Kaiser and Grossmann 1979: 159–61; Kaiser and Dreyer 1982: 213–20; Dreyer 1990: 62–64; Dreyer et al. 1996: 48–57; Dreyer et al. 1998: 138–41; Dreyer et al. 2000: 90–97.

39   Bestock 2009; 2012: 38–39.

40   Jéquier 1906: 60–62.

41   See T.A.H. Wilkinson 2000a: 92–94.

42   Concerns have been expressed at the duplication of some activities between the Palermo and Cairo fragments, some suggesting scribal error in certain cases: cf. T.A.H. Wilkinson 2000a: 187–93.

43   Taillet 2013.

44   Taillet and Laisney 2012: 387–89.

45   Now in the Sudan National Museum (Porter and Moss 1952: 140).

46   Murnane 1987.

47   Somaglino and Taillet 2015a; 2015b.

48   Porter and Moss 1937: 78–81; Dreyer 1991: 96; 2009: 165–66; 2010: 143–44; Dreyer et al. 2011: 55–62.

49   The last known examples date to the reign of Seneferu, at the Bent Pyramid at Dahshur and the pyramid of Meidum.

50   On the general question of human sacrifice in ancient Egypt, see van Dijk 2007.

51   See informal summary in Galvin 2005.

52   For such stelae from Umm el-Qaab as a whole, see Martin 2011.

53   Woolley 1934.

54   Baadsgaard et al. 2011.

55   Reisner 1923, with mistaken dating and attribution.

56   Emery 1948.

57   Porter and Moss 1974–81: 436, 437, 444.

58   Dreyer 1981.

59   Porter and Moss 1974–81: 445.

60   Petrie 1907: 2–6.

61   Porter and Moss 1937: 82–83; Dreyer 1993: 57.

62   Dreyer 1991.

63   Emery 1949–58: 3:73.

64   Eaton-Krauss 2018.

65   Roth 2001: 10–15, 18–26, 28–29, 31, 33, 273, 296, 302, 306–10, 314–15, 322, 336; Seipel 1980: 23–45; Troy 1986: 106–107, 139, 152.

66   Dreyer 1987; Kaiser 1987; she is not, however, included in the later seal of the reign of Qaa, which only included kings (Dreyer et al. 1996: 72).

67   Porter and Moss 1974–81: 444.

68   Petrie 1900–1901: 1:10–11; Porter and Moss 1937: 82.

69   See T.A.H. Wilkinson 2000a: 103–104.

70   Petrie 1900–1901: 1:pl. xi[4, 14, 15], xv[1618].

71   Dreyer 1990: 80, fig. 9, pl. 26[d].

72   Porter and Moss 1974–81: 440–42.

73   Bárta 2020: 48, 57–64.

74   Porter and Moss 1937: 83–85; Dreyer 1990: 72–79; 1993: 57–61; Dreyer et al. 1998: 141–64; 2000: 97–118; 2003: 88–107.

75   Stairways were also introduced around the same time into private tombs (e.g., Saqqara S3035, S3036, and S3506 [Porter and Moss 1974–81: 440–42, 446]); see further Clark 2016: 116–36.

76   Saqqara S2185 (Porter and Moss 1974–81: 437).

77   But see Vanhulle 2013.

78   O'Connor 1995; Ward 2000: 39–43; 2006.

79   E.g., Saqqara S3357, dating to the reign of Hor-Aha (Porter and Moss 1974–81: 444).

80   Porter and Moss 1974–81: 436.

81   Kaiser 1985; Morris 2007b: 21–28.

82   See Baka 2011, seconding Macramallah 1940; van Wetering 2017.

83   T.A.H. Wilkinson 2004: 1137.

84   T.A.H. Wilkinson 1999: 78, 79, 275.

85   Petrie 1900–1901: 1:pl. vii[6]); Quibell 1923: pl. xxxiii[5].
86   Porter and Moss 1937: 82.
87   Engel 2008.
88   Dreyer et al. 2006.
89   Darnell 2011.
90   Lacau and Lauer 1959–65: 4:12, pl. 8[41].
91   Porter and Moss 1937: 86–87; Engel 2017.
92   Porter and Moss 1974–81: 446.
93   Cf. Swelim 1974.
94   Dreyer et al. 1996: 71–72, pl. 14[a].

Notes to Chapter 2

1   Cf. Dodson 2016b.
2   Porter and Moss 1974–81: 613; Lacher 2008.
3   Reisner 1936: 138–43; Lacher 2008: 433–39.
4   Lacher 2008: 440–47.
5   See Dodson 2016b; Reader 2017: 85–87.
6   Mathieson and Tavares 1993: 27–28; Reader 2017: 77; cf. Spencer 1974: 3.
7   There are some indications on the ground that could suggest that it was actually square, but if these potential features are actually unrelated to the enclosure, one would assume a rectangular form, with roughly the proportions of the Abydos enclosures, or of the Gisr el-Mudir, discussed just below.
8   Taillet and Laisney 2012: 389.
9   Fischer 1961.
10   Porter and Moss 1974–81: 436, 437, 440.
11   Saad 1951: 17.
12   Porter and Moss 1974–81: 295.
13   The alleged First Intermediate Period "Nitokris" appears to be the result of a scribal misunderstanding (Ryholt 2000).
14   Porter and Moss 1974–81: 613; Munro 1983: 278–82; Lacher 2011; Lacher-Raschdorff 2011; 2014.
15   Lacher 2011: 222–29.
16   It should be noted, however, that it has also been suggested that the Gisr el-Mudir was unrelated to the tombs, and should be attributed to the time of Khasekhemwy, with its purpose, however, left moot (for references, see Regulski 2009: 226–27; cf., however, the discussion in Dodson 2016b).

17   Mathieson and Tavares 1993: 28–31; Mathieson et al. 1997; Reader 2017: 77–81.
18   Showing that old suggestions that the Gisr el-Mudir might be the unfinished remains of a Third Dynasty pyramid complex are impossible; in addition, the walls show no signs of the facings akin to those of the Step Pyramid enclosure wall, mentioned by some writers (cf. Mathieson and Tavares 1993: 28 n29).
19   The only exception is that the Abydos list calls the first king "Bedjau," rather than the "Netjerbau" used by the Saqqara and Turin lists.
20   Goedicke 1956a.
21   Swelim 1983: 182–83.
22   Swelim 1983: 219–20.
23   Kahl 1994: 7–10 [3332].
24   For full documentation and discussion, see Ryholt 2008.
25   Grdseloff 1944: 291.
26   Porter and Moss 1974–81: 440.
27   Lacau and Lauer 1959–65: 4:pl. vi[99–100].
28   Helck 1979: 124.
29   It has been suggested that his Horus-name might have been the "Za" mentioned on a fragment from under the Step Pyramid.
30   Porter and Moss 1974–81: 21.
31   Leclant and Clerc 1988: 330.
32   Porter and Moss 1974–81: 490; Kaiser 1991.
33   Stadelmann 1985 would prefer to attribute them to Khasekhemwy or a king ruling between him and Djoser. However,

34   See Kaiser 1969: 6–7.

35   Porter and Moss 1937: 81; Kaiser and Grossmann 1979: 161–62; Dreyer et al. 2006: 98–110; 2011: 83–90.

36   Porter and Moss 1937: 54.

37   Lacher-Raschdorff 2020.

38   BM EA35597 and Cairo JE 35261. The Seth-animals atop the serekhs have been partly erased; this could be attributed to a reaction late in the Second Dynasty, or early in the Old Kingdom. If they remained visible long enough, it is conceivable that the mutilation occurred in the Late Period, when Seth became fully diabolic, and his images removed even from the cartouches of the Nineteenth Dynasty kings Sethy I and II (cf. Te Velde 1967: 138–51).

39   Since Abydos was to become the cult center, and putative burial place, of Seth's victim, Osiris, the Seth-devotee's construction of a tomb there might seem odd in the extreme. However, Osiris's connection with the city came considerably later, perhaps as a result of the ancient kings' burial there, rather than the other way around.

40   Fairman and Blackman 1935.

41   Newberry 1922.

42   Cf. Fairman 1935: 28 n2.

43   Weigall 1925: 130–32.

44   Porter and Moss 1937: 196; Kemp 1963; Alexanian 1998; R.F. Friedman and Raue 2007; the enclosure was built over a late Predynastic cemetery (B. Adams 1987).

45   Cf. O'Connor 1989: 83–84.

46   Dreyer et al. 2011.

47   Kaplony 1981: pl. i.

48   www.hierakonpolis-online.org/index.php/explore-the-fort.

49   Kaplony 1963: 1:163.

50   Porter and Moss 1937: 175.

51   W.S. Smith 1949: 137–38.

52   Porter and Moss 1937: 196, 197; Alexanian 1998.

53   Engelbach 1934: 183–84.

54   Montet 1928: 84.

55   Kaplony 1963: 3:pl. 72[269].

56   It has been suggested that these might actually have been royal (van Wetering 2018), but the tombs are much smaller than the known kingly tombs to the north, and have not revealed any royal names, except for one occurrence of that of Khasekhemwy.

57   Second Dynasty tombs have been found to date below the sepulchers of Maya and Meryneith (Regulski 2009; 2011; 2012; Raven and van Walsem 2014: 72–74).

58   Porter and Moss 1937: 87; Dreyer et al. 1998: 164–66; 2000: 122–28; 2003: 108–24; 2006: 110–27.

59   Farag 1980.

60   Porter and Moss 1937: 52–53; M.D. Adams and O'Connor 2010.

61   A sloping feature from this phase was misidentified in O'Connor 1989: 54, 82 as part of a brick-skinned mound in the center of the enclosure. Much was subsequently made of this as a possible prototype for the placement of a pyramid in the subsequent enclosure of Djoser, and this is still sometimes repeated, although later work at the site disproved this interpretation of the feature.

Notes to Chapter 3

1   For a catalogue of much of the material from the dynasty—but with very different conclusions from those presented here—see Swelim 1983; 1992; 2014–15.

2   Helck 1956: 14; Leprohon 2013: 33 n20.

3   Dreyer 1998b; a damaged sealing of Djoser had actually been found in the tomb a century earlier (Petrie 1900–1901: 2:pl. xxiv[211]), but had been largely ignored.

4   Garstang 1903: 22–23.

5   Cf. the original excavator's belief that the tomb was actually that of Djoser himself, with the Step Pyramid a mere cenotaph (page 157, below).

6   Between his name and the notation of his reign length appears the formula "he acted in kingship," and is followed by "he lived for," which seems to have been used at the top of the original columns, the phrases being implied for entries below.

7   Although often classified as a daughter of Djoser, as well as bearing the title "King's Daughter," she was also "Great of Scepter" (wrt-ḥts), during the Old Kingdom one of the titles of a king's spouse.

8   Porter and Moss 1974–81: 407, 414; el-Aguizy 2007.

9   Porter and Moss 1974–81: 437–39.

10   Porter and Moss 1974–81: 437, 448.

11   Kaiser 1969.

12   Arnold 2020.

13   For the "dry moat" see Reader 2017: 82–83, with references to earlier discussions.

14   It is possible that this final configuration was the result of a rebuilding during the construction of the pyramid: for the debate, see Lauer 1962: 75–76; Stadelmann 1996; Kaiser 1992; Kaiser 1997.

15   Strouhal et al. 2001: 16–17.

16   In the northern entrance passage and the secondary southern access (cf. pages 130–31).

17   On these relief panels, cf. F.D. Friedman 1995.

18   Porter and Moss 1974–81: 401–405.

19   The remains of a woman in her late teens were also found somewhere in these galleries (Strouhal et al. 2001: 16–18).

20   Porter and Moss 1974–81: 415.

21   Hurry 1926; Wildung 1977a: 5–188.

22   Wildung 1977a: 34.

23   Wildung 1977a; 1977b.

24   Wildung's proposal (1977a: 30–32) that Imhotep's death under Huni was mentioned in the Turin Canon has now been shown to be incorrect (page 102, below).

25   It may be noted that Imhotep's fellow demigod, Amenhotep-son-of-Hapu, also seems to have had a wide range of responsibilities during his lifetime, few of which are made explicit by his titulary.

26   See Green 1987.

27   But cf. Swelim 1983: 219–24 for a very different view.

28   Porter and Moss 1952: 439–40 (called Semerkhet); Giveon 1974.

29   For this and all other Old Kingdom sarcophagi, see Donadoni Roveri 1969.

30   Lauer 1967: 502–505; 1969: 463.

31   Firth and Quibell 1935: 141, fig. 18.

32   For K3–K5, see Garstang 1903: pl. xxvi.

33   Contrary to the original excavator's belief that K2 was the king's actual tomb—and that K1 was the tomb of Djoser himself: see pages 157–58.

34   Garstang 1903: 13–14.

35   Porter and Moss 1974–81: 5–8.

36   Vyse 1840–42: 3:9; Palanque 1902; Macramallah 1932; Swelim 1983: 36–39; 1987: 91–95.

37   Porter and Moss 1974–81: 500.

38   Porter and Moss 1974–81: 337.

39   Porter and Moss 1974–81: 313; Lehner 1996; Dodson 2000.

40   Swelim 1983: 77.

41   For references to these and all other attestations of the king, see Rowland and Tassie 2017: 377–79.

42   Gardiner 1946; Lichtheim 1973: 59.

43   Wildung 1977a: 30–33.

44   Ryholt 1997: 20.

45   Goedicke 1956b; Meltzer 1971; Barta 1973.

46   Borchardt 1909; cf. Schäfer 1914.

47   Goedicke 1956b.

48   Kadish 1970: 99 n8; Meltzer 1971.

49   Goedicke 1956b; Kadish 1970; Barta 1973; Stadelmann 2007.

50   Bárta 2011; Jirásková 2012.

51   Porter and Moss 1974–81: 493–94.

52   T.A.H. Wilkinson 2000a: 177–78.

53   When pPrisse was written during the Middle Kingdom, the occasional inclusion of the s3-rʿ title within nomen cartouches had been known since the reign of Unas.

54   Cf. Meltzer 1971: 203; Barta 1973; Helck 1976; Dreyer and Kaiser 1980: 57–58; Kahl, Kloth, and Zimmermann 1995: 165.

55   That it came from a nearby former fortification is only an assumption (see Goedicke 1956b: 22).

56   Dreyer and Kaiser 1980.

57   Muhlestein, Pierce, and Jensen 2020: 48–92.

58   E.g., Ćwiek 1998, with references to earlier discussions.

59   E.g., Lauer 1962: 218–20.

60   Swelim 1987.

61   Although some scholars have expressed skepticism—e.g., Edwards 1997: 88; Verner 2002: 152.

62   From the reign of Djedefre onward, at least until the end of the Old Kingdom, pyramid substructures were invariably constructed from separate blocks at the bottom of an open trench in the bedrock, backfilled before the pyramid itself was completed over it. Indeed, the *only* Old Kingdom pyramids with wholly rock-cut substructures are that of Sekhemkhet, the Layer Pyramid, and the Brick Pyramid;

the first phase ("descending passage") of that of Khufu also employed this approach.

63   A similar approach was taken with the next brick pyramid to be built: Senwosret II's monument at Lahun (Porter and Moss 1934: 107–109). Consequently, this was also the first pyramid to have a wholly tunneled substructure since the early Old Kingdom.

64   Cemetery H (Bisson de la Roque 1924: 59–63).

65   Clark 2016: 61 n424.

66   Porter and Moss 1974–81: 442.

67   Porter and Moss 1974–81: 449–50.

Notes to Chapter 4

1   E.g., Strudwick 1985.

2   Milan RAN 997.02.01 (Tiradritti 2018).

3   Porter and Moss 1974–81: 52.

4   The last year recorded on any fragment is Neferirkare's eleventh (T.A.H. Wilkinson 2000a: 179–80).

5   For discussion and references, see Wilkinson 2000a: 23–28.

6   See the "Year 59" allocated to Horemheb in the legal text of Mose, compiled under Rameses II (see Dodson 2018: 129 for a discussion).

7   Although some were subject to detail "hypercorrections" to make them conform to the X-Y-Re format that had became typical of royal prenomina—the form of the name generally used in the king lists (see Ryholt 2008: 166–68).

8   Berlin ÄM7702 (Malek 1999: 3).

9   As described in the Instruction for Merykare (Lichtheim 1973: 102, 105, 109 n24.

10   For the material from here, see Simpson 1974.

11   On the development of Osiris's sacred landscape at Abydos, see Leahy 1989.

12   Probably: the names of the original dedicator of the stela have been erased, and only a few traces remain under those of its usurper, Neferhotep I (see Leahy 1989: 48–49).

13   Because the royal names and titles had been largely erased, the date of the piece was long debated, estimates varying from the Old Kingdom to the Thirtieth Dynasty. However, Anthony Leahy's re-study (1977) makes it all but certain that it was commissioned by Khendjer.

14   Louvre stelae C.11 and C.12; Garstang E.30 also belongs to the same man (Kitchen 1962).

15   The basic publication of the piece is Leahy 1977.

16   He may have been the owner of pyramid S9 (Wegner 2020).

17   The pyramid was devoid of any traces of a burial, in spite of only a tiny robber's hole in the sepulchral chamber.

18   Amélineau 1899a: pl. v; the object was sold in 1904 and its present location appears unknown.

19   Porter and Moss 1937: 79–81, 89–90.

20   Damarany and Cahail 2016.

21   Amélineau 1899a: 16–28; Vernus 1976; on the other hand, it has been suggested that the tomb might actually have been a cenotaph, on the basis of the discovery of a fragment of coffin bearing Iuput's name in the Twenty-second Dynasty priestly cemetery in the Ramesseum at Thebes (Quibell 1898: 21, pl. xxxA[2]). However, this fragment might simply represent the filiation of one of Iuput's descendants.

22   Tomb D22 (MacIver and Mace 1902: 65, 77–78, 94, pls. xxvi, xxxi, xxxix).

23   Leahy 1994: 171–92.

24   BM EA1358 (Petrie 1900–1901: 1:7, pl. xxxviii).

25   See Effland 2013.

26   Petrie 1900–1901: 1:7.

27   Arnold 2002.

28   Dodson 1988.

29   Although a Fourth Dynasty mastaba has been noted one hundred meters to the north, with later Old Kingdom tombs to the south (Arnold 2002: 107–108); indeed, Arnold wonders whether the Senwosret III complex was built on the site of an utterly destroyed Third Dynasty structure (cf. Seidlmayer 2006: 121–22). However, it seems unlikely that the destruction will have been such as to leave no other substantive traces.

30   Oppenheim 2007. The piece was found at the bottom of a Fourth Dynasty tomb shaft overbuilt by Twelfth Dynasty mastaba 18 (Nebit), and the excavators assumed that it was there as a result of having been reused in paving of the Fourth Dynasty burial chamber. However, such an early reuse of an item from the Step Pyramid complex, which in any case lay seven kilometers to the north of the tomb in question, seems unlikely. Rather, it would seem better to see it as another item brought to Senwosret III's complex for amuletic purposes, which found its way to its final resting place during the destruction of the Middle Kingdom monuments in the area.

31   A fragment of column of a kind otherwise found at the Step Pyramid was also recovered at Senwosret's complex (Arnold 2002: 100–101) and may be another item brought at the same time—unless it is an archaizing Twelfth Dynasty piece.

32   See Dodson 2016a: 45–46, with references.

33   pEbers (in Leipzig—Ebers 1875: pl. ciii, l.2).

34   pBerlin 3038 (Wreszinski 1909).

35   pBerlin 3033 (Lichtheim 1973: 215–20; Lepper 2008).

36   Tiradritti 2010: 333–35.
37   Porter and Moss 1974–81: 412–14.
38   See translations of the graffiti in Firth and Quibell 1935: 78–85.
39   See Dodson 2019: 8–12 for a summary of what is known about the dynasty's background.
40   I.e., excluding the kings from Akhenaten to Ay; the omission of Hatshepsut is more likely to be owing to her having never been an independent ruler, only ever a coregent of Thutmose III.
41   For the standard transcription into hieroglyphs, see Gardiner 1959, subject to the revisions in Ryholt 2004, which also provides an excellent discussion of issues surrounding the composition and a full bibliography of earlier works. An extremely useful website regarding the Canon is https://pharaoh.se/royal-canon-of-turin.
42   For the first two dynasties to the exact day, for the Third through Sixth Dynasties just to the year, with day-exact lengths resumed for the Seventh through Tenth Dynasties, back to years only for the Eleventh Dynasty, then back to years, months, and days for the Twelfth, and then largely years-only for the Second Intermediate Period.
43   These columns were previously known as II and III (as in Gardiner 1959 and earlier works), but Ryholt (2004) subsequently noted that what had been reconstructed as the middle part of Column IX actually joined with Column X to form the second column of the text. Following this revision, the columns of the Canon have now been renumbered with Arabic numbers to distinguish them from the "old" Roman column numbering.
44   Porter and Moss 1974–81: 666–67.
45   The Abydos lists also omit the Second Intermediate Period, although including the beginning of the First Intermediate Period.

46   Morkot 2003; Manuelian 1994; the origins of this have often been ascribed to the Nubian Twenty-fifth Dynasty, but although they were enthusiastic adopters, its origins should be placed in the north, under the last scions of the Twenty-second Dynasty.
47   Peyraudeau and Meffre 2016.
48   MMA 11.150.30; 11.150.31 (Winlock 1917) and Cairo TR 30/9/23/2 (Borchardt 1928).
49   Interestingly, the MMA example allegedly came from the Delta, fitting well with a Tanite point of origin of the whole group.
50   Von Bissing 1933–34: 35 n4 argued for direct copying of the MMA piece, an idea rejected in Bianchi 1979: 21.
51   Indeed, an early find from this latter group, lacking any cartouche, was proclaimed a "véritable portrait de Djeser" (Goyon 1987: 37); likewise the two plaques, until redated to the Twenty-sixth Dynasty by von Bissing (1933–34).
52   Jurman 2009: 129–32.
53   For which, see Dodson 2019: 113–29.
54   Cairo JE46915 (Jurman 2009: 134, figs. 3–4).
55   As suggested by Jurman 2009: 132; Morkot 2014.
56   It is interesting that the "nub" epithet is also found on the block from the tomb of Mahu (fig. 110).
57   Louvre IM.3036 (Porter and Moss 1974–81: 790); it is unclear exactly to which Apis bull's burial the stela should be assigned (cf. Jurman 2009: 131).
58   The "quote" has often been attributed to one of the relief niches under the South Tomb (e.g., Jurman 2009: 131), but there seems no evidence for eighth-century penetration below this monument; in fact, identical texts are to be found above the "gridded" reliefs under the Step Pyramid itself.

59   Often dubbed the "Saite Gallery" on the earlier assumption that "antiquarian" activity belonged primarily to the Twenty-sixth Dynasty, which ruled from Sais.

60   Vyse 1840–42: 3:44–45.

61   Lacher-Raschdorff 2011.

62   Statue Berlin ÄM14765 (Erman 1900: 115, 117). A deposit of demotic papyri found in the probable portcullis shaft of Sekhemkhet (Migahid 2003) may be connected with his late cult.

63   Sarcophagus Berlin ÄM34 (Gauthier 1907: 2).

64   Stela Louvre IM.3689, from the Serapeum (Porter and Moss 1974–81: 812).

65   Berlin ÄM8433 (Malek 1999: 1).

66   The standard edition remains Waddell 1940, with a full discussion of the origins and editorial history of the work.

67   Barguet 1953.

68   Hurry 1926; Wildung 1977a: 5–188.

69   pCarlsberg 85, from Tebtunis (Ryholt 2009).

70   M. Smith 1980; Quack 1997: 299.

Notes to Chapter 5

1   Noted by all the early researchers (see Porter and Moss 1972: 434 for references).

2   Burton 1825–28: pl. xxvii[6].

3   J.G. Wilkinson 1835: 337.

4   Vyse 1840–42; Perring 1839–42.

5   Vyse 1840–42: 1:193–94; 3:9; Perring 1839–42: 3:4.

6   Vyse 1840–42: 3:9; Perring 1839–42: 3:4.

7   Vyse 1840–42: 3:41–50.

8   Vyse 1840–42: 3:53–54.

9   It was removed by Jean-François Mimaut (1773–1837*) in 1837, and purchased by the British Museum at the sale of his collection after his death at the end of that year.

10   Cf. Ryholt 2004: 136 n7.

11   For his work in the museum, see Champollion 1824–26.

12   For which, see Renouf 1859; 1862; Dodson 2021.

13   See Seyffarth 1828.

14   Birch 1843.

15   Lepsius 1842: pls. iii–vi.

16   Hincks 1850a; 1850b.

17   Berlin ÄM1185.

18   Lepsius 1897–1913: 1:189–95.

19   Cf. Mariette 1856: 61.

20   Brugsch 1879: 59.

21   Lepsius 1849–59: 1:pl. xii; 1897–1913: 1:21–22.

22   Swelim 1987.

23   Prisse d'Avennes 1847.

24   J.G. Wilkinson 1851.

25   With more to come to light later in the nineteenth century (see Porter and Moss 1974–81: 490).

26   The papyrus was remounted and many of the mistakes in its reconstruction remedied in 1930. However, errors remained, and a further revision was put forward in Ryholt 2004, upon which the discussion in this book is based.

27   Mariette 1860: 20–23; 1864.

28   Rougé 1866.

29   T.A.H. Wilkinson 2000a: 20, 29–30.

30   Rougé 1866: 29–30.

31   Petrie 1894: 16; cf. 18–19.

32   Robert Hay had seen it and copied some of the text in the 1820s, but his material had never been published.

33   On the discovery, see https://www.brooklynmuseum.org/community/blogosphere/2010/06/24/wilbour-and-the-stela-of-the-seven-years-famine-part-i/ and https://www.brooklynmuseum.org/community/blogosphere/2010/06/29/wilbour-and-the-stela-of-the-seven-years-famine-part-ii/.

34   Brugsch 1890; 1891.

35   Steindorff 1890.

36   Bénédite 1894.

37 Wilson 1869.

38 Giveon 1974.

39 Petrie 1906; Gardiner and Peet 1917; Gardiner, Peet, and Černý 1952–55.

40 Weill 1904: 76, 95.

41 Petrie 1896b: 7–9.

42 Petrie 1896a: 59–64.

43 De Morgan 1896–97: 1:84–87.

44 De Morgan 1896–97: 2:147–212; for a summary, see Legge 1899: 189–93, which also summarizes the initial work of Amélineau at Umm el-Qaab, and highlights some of the confusions surrounding the interpretation of his discoveries.

45 Jéquier in De Morgan 1896–97: 2:229–68.

46 Borchardt 1898.

47 Garstang 1905a; 1905b.

48 Petrie 1901: 2, attributing de Morgan's dating of the El-Amrah material to "but a happy guess," based on "evidence [that] still remained against such an early dating"; on the poor relationship between de Morgan and Petrie, see Thompson 2015–18: 2:68–69.

49 Petrie 1901: 4–12; on subsequent views on Petrie's scheme, cf. Dee et al. 2014.

50 Amélineau 1899a; a useful English summary of his first season's results is Legge 1899: 183–89.

51 Sethe 1897: 2; Maspero 1895: 66.

52 Amélineau 1902.

53 Petrie 1900–1901: 2:31–32.

54 Amélineau 1899b; Amélineau 1904–1905: 149–99.

55 Amélineau maintained his belief in the ownership of the skull even after professional examination (by Dr. G. Papillaut, published in Amélineau 1904–1905: 735–36) had shown it to be small and probably that of a woman, even wondering whether sculptures might support a view that Osiris was microcephalic!

56 Drower 1985: 251, 255.

57 Amélineau 1902: ii.

58 Drower 1985: 250–59, 261–62.

59 Including the second stela of the tomb of Qaa, the first having been found by Amélineau.

60 Some had also been published by Gustave Jéquier in De Morgan 1896–97: 2:229–68 (cf. Petrie 1900–1901: 4–5).

61 Petrie 1900–1901.

62 Arthur Mace (1874–1928)*, later Howard Carter's assistant in the early stages of the excavation of the tomb of Tutankhamun.

63 Petrie 1900–1901: 2:16.

64 Petrie 1932: 188–89.

65 Bouriant 1885: 36.

66 Case and Payne 1962; Payne 1973; Kemp 1973.

67 Naville 1899.

68 Pellegrini 1895.

69 Schäfer 1902; Naville 1903.

70 Garstang 1903: 3–4, citing in particular the proposal that the "blue rooms" and their texts were intrusions (page 138).

71 Barsanti 1901.

72 Barsanti 1902.

73 Maspero 1902: 187–90.

74 Palanque 1902; the structure has been confused with the Brick Pyramid by a number of authors (cf. Swelim 1987: 91–95).

75 Ayrton, Currelly, and Weigall 1904: 2–3.

76 Petrie 1925: 2–9.

77 Published in two parallel editions, Weill 1908a and 1908b.

78 Naville 1914: 35–36.

79 In Goedicke 1956b: 22, where the author confuses Gautier with Henri *Gauthier*, thus querying why the latter failed to mention the piece in his *Livre des rois*—although as the relevant volume had been published in 1907, Gauthier could not have included it in any case!

80 Cairo JE44859 [CF1], 39735 [CF2], 39734 [CF3].
81 Cairo JE44860 [CF4].
82 Petrie UC15505 (acquired "a few years" before 1916, according to Petrie 1916: 115).
83 Cairo TR 15/1/75/2 [CF5] (Cenival 1965: 13).
84 Gauthier 1914; 1915.
85 For the majority of studies down to the end of the 1990s, see Wilkinson 2000a.
86 Firth and Quibell 1935.
87 Emery 1939; 1949–58.
88 **Kemp 1966; 1967.**
89 Although including members of the wider royal family: cf. Morris 2007a;

for arguments that the distribution of imported ceramics implies a higher status for the Umm el-Qaab burials as compared to Saqqara, see Nakano 1998.
90 Hassan 1938.
91 Swelim 1987: 95.
92 Saad 1942–43; 1947; 1951; 1969.
93 Köhler 2005–17.
94 Goneim 1956 (and various foreign-language editions); 1957.
95 Gardiner, Peet, and Černý 1952–55: 2:53, crediting William Hayes with the original observation.
96 The redating was, however, questioned by Yeivin 1968: 48–50.

BIBLIOGRAPHY

Abbreviations for Periodicals

AE — *Ancient Egypt* (London: British School of Archaeology in Egypt).

AfO — *Archiv für Orientforschung* (Berlin: Ernst F. Weidner).

ASAE — *Annales du Service des Antiquités de l'Égypte* (Cairo: Institut français d'archéologie orientale/Supreme Council of Antiquities Press).

BASOR — *Bulletin of the American Schools of Oriental Research* (Alexandria VA: American Schools of Oriental Research).

BES — *Bulletin of the Egyptological Seminar* (New York: Egyptological Seminar of New York).

BIFAO — *Bulletin de l'Institut français d'archéologie orientale du Caire* (Cairo: Institut français d'Archéologie orientale).

BMMA — *Bulletin of the Metropolitan Museum of Art* (New York: Metropolitan Museum of Art).

BSFE — *Bulletin de la Société française d'Egyptologie* (Paris: Société française d'Egyptologie).

CdE — *Chronique d'Égypte* (Brussels: Fondation égypologique Reine Élisabeth).

CRAIBL — *Comptes rendus des séances de l'Académie des Inscriptions et Belles-Lettres* (Paris: Académie des Inscriptions et Belles-Lettres).

EgArch — *Egyptian Archaeology: Bulletin of the Egypt Exploration Society* (London: Egypt Exploration Society).

GM — *Göttinger Miszellen* (Göttingen: Universität Göttingen, Ägyptologisches Seminar).

JARCE — *Journal of the American Research Center in Egypt* (New York: Eisenbraun).

JEA — *Journal of Egyptian Archaeology* (London: Egypt Exploration Fund/ Society).

JEH — *Journal of Egyptian History* (Leiden: Brill).

JNES — *Journal of Near Eastern Studies* (Chicago: Chicago University Press).

MDAIK — *Mitteilungen des Deutschen Archäologischen Instituts, Kairo* (Mainz: Philipp von Zabern).

PSBA — *Proceedings of the Society for Biblical Archaeology* (London: Society for Biblical Archaeology).

RevArch — *Revue Archéologique* (Paris: Presses Universitaires de France).

RecTrav — *Recueil de travaux relatifs à la philologie et à l'archéologie égyptiennes et assyriennes* (Paris: Librairie Edouard Champion).

SAK	*Studien zur Altägyptischen Kultur* (Hamburg: H. Buske).
TRSL	*Transactions of the Royal Society of Literature* (London: John Murray).
ZÄS	*Zeitschrift für Ägyptische Sprache*

und Altertumskunde (Leipzig: J.C. Hinrichs'sche Buchhandlung/ Berlin: Akademie Verlag).

ZPE *Zeitschrift für Papyrologie und Epigraphik* (Cologne: Universität zu Köln).

Works Cited

Adams, B. 1987. *The Fort Cemetery at Hierakonpolis (Excavated by John Garstang).* Studies in Egyptology. London: Kegan Paul International.

———. 1995. *Ancient Nekhen: Garstang in the City of Hierakonpolis.* New Malden: Sia Publishing.

Adams, M.D., and D.B. O'Connor. 2010. "The Shunet el-Zebib at Abydos: Architectural Conservation at One of Egypt's Oldest Preserved Royal Monuments." In *Offerings to the Discerning Eye: An Egyptological Medley in Honor of Jack A. Josephson,* edited by S.H. D'Auria, 1–8. Leiden: Brill.

El-Aguizy, O. 2007. "Une nouvelle stèle-borne au nom de Djoser." *BIFAO* 107: 1–4.

Alexanian, N. 1998. "Die Reliefdekoration des Chasechemui aus dem sogenannten Fort in Hierakonpolis." In *Les critères de datation stylistiques à l'Ancien Empire,* edited by N. Grimal, 1–29. Cairo: Institut français d'archéologie orientale.

Amélineau, É. 1899a. *Les nouvelles fouilles d'Abydos, 1895–1896: compte rendu in extenso des fouilles, description des monuments et objets découverts.* Paris: Ernest Leroux.

———. 1899b. *Le tombeau d'Osiris: monographie de la découverte faite en 1897–1898.* Paris: Ernest Leroux.

———. 1902. *Les nouvelles fouilles d'Abydos, 1896–1897: compte rendu in extenso des fouilles, description des monuments et objets découverts.* Paris: Ernest Leroux.

———. 1904–1905. *Les nouvelles fouilles d'Abydos, 1897–1898: compte rendu in extenso des fouilles, description des monuments et objets découverts.* 2 vols. Paris: Ernest Leroux.

Arnold, D. 2002. *The Pyramid Complex of Senwosret III at Dahshur: Architectural Studies.* New York: Metropolitan Museum of Art.

———. 2020. "Reflections on Construction Phases of the Djoser Complex at Saqqara." In *Guardian of Ancient Egypt: Studies in Honor of Zahi Hawass,* edited by J. Kamrin, M. Bárta, Salima Ikram, Mark Lehner, and Mohamed Megahed, 1:145–53. Prague: Faculty of Arts, Charles University.

Ayrton, E.R., C.T. Currelly, and A.E.P. Weigall. 1904. *Abydos,* III. London: Egypt Exploration Fund.

Baadsgaard, A., J. Monge, S. Cox, and R.L. Zettler. 2011. "Human Sacrifice and Intentional Corpse Preservation in the Royal Cemetery of Ur." *Antiquity* 85: 27–42.

Baka, C. 2011. "'Rectangle de Macramallah,' un cimetière archaïque à Saqqarah." *GM* 230: 19–28.

Barguet, P. 1953. *La stèle de la famine à Séhel.* Cairo: Institut français d'archéologie orientale.

Barich, B.E., G. Lucarini, M.A. Hamdan, and F.A. Hassan, eds. 2014. *From Lake to Sand: The Archaeology of Farafra Oasis, Western Desert, Egypt.* Florence: All'Insegna del Giglio.

Barsanti, A. 1901. "Ouverture de la pyramide de Zaouiet el-Aryan." *ASAE* 2: 92–94.

———. 1902. "Fouilles autour de la Pyramide d'Ounas." *ASAE* 3: 182–84.

Bárta, M. 2011. "An Abusir Mastaba from the Reign of Huni." In *Times, Signs and Pyramids: Studies in Honour of Miroslav Verner on the Occasion of His Seventieth Birthday*, edited by V.G. Callender, L. Bareš, M. Bárta, and J. Janák, 41–50. Prague: Faculty of Arts, Charles University in Prague.

———. 2020. *Analyzing Collapse: The Rise and Fall of the Old Kingdom*. Cairo: American University in Cairo Press.

Barta, W. 1973. "Zum altägyptischen Namen des Königs Achēs." *MDAIK* 29: 1–4.

———. 1981. "Die Chronologie der 1. bis 5. Dynastie nach den Angaben des rekonstruierten Annalensteins." *ZÄS* 108: 11–23.

Baud, M. 2002. *Djéser et la IIIe dynastie*. Paris: Pygmalion/Gérard Watelet.

Bénédite, G. 1894. "Le nom de l'épervier du roi Sozir au Sinaï." *RecTrav* 16: 104.

Bestock, L. 2009. *The Development of Royal Funerary Cult at Abydos: Two Funerary Enclosures from the Reign of Aha*. Wiesbaden: Otto Harrassowitz.

———. 2012. "Brown University Abydos Project: Preliminary Report on the First Two Seasons." *JARCE* 48: 35–79.

Bianchi, R.S. 1979. "Ex-votos of Dynasty 26." *MDAIK* 35: 15–22.

Bierbrier, M.L. 2019. *Who Was Who in Egyptology*. 5th ed. London: Egypt Exploration Society.

Birch, S. 1843. "Observations upon the Hieratical Canon of Egyptian Kings at Turin." *TRSL*, 2nd ser., 1: 203–208.

Bisson de la Roque, F. 1924. *Rapport sur les fouilles d'Abou-Roasch (1922–1923)*. Cairo: Institut français d'archéologie orientale.

Borchardt, L. 1898. "Das Grab des Menes." *ZÄS* 36: 87–105.

———. 1909. "König Huni?" *ZÄS* 46: 12–13.

———. 1917. *Die Annalen und die zeitliche Festlegung des Alten Reiches der ägyptischen Geschichte*. Berlin: Behrend.

———. 1928. "Ein Bildhauermodell aus dem frühen Alten Reich." *ASAE* 28: 43–50.

Bouriant, U. 1885. "Les tombeaux d'Hiérakonpolis." In *Études archéologiques, linguistiques et historiques: dédiées à Mr le Dr. C. Leemans à l'occasion du cinquantième anniversaire de sa nomination aux fonctions de directeur du Musée Archéologique des Pays-Bas*, edited by W. Pleyte, A.P.M. van Oordt, and F. de Stoppelaar, 35–40. Leiden: Brill.

Braun, E. 2011. "Early Interaction between Peoples of the Nile Valley and the Southern Levant." In *Before the Pyramids: The Origins of Egyptian Civilization*, edited by E. Teeter, 105–22. Chicago: Oriental Institute.

Brugsch, H. 1879. *A History of Egypt under the Pharaohs, Derived Entirely from the Monuments: To Which Is Added a Memoir on the Exodus of the Israelites and the Egyptian Monuments*. Translated by H.D. Seymour and P. Smith. 2 vols. London: John Murray.

———. 1890. "Der König 𓉟𓏏𓄿." *ZÄS* 28: 109–11.

———. 1891. *Die biblischen sieben Jahre der Hungersnoth nach dem Wortlaut einer altägyptischen Felseninschrift*. Leipzig: Hinrichs.

Burton, J. 1825–28. *Excerpta hieroglyphica: Or Exact Copies of Various Hieroglyphical Inscriptions and Sculptured Monuments Still Existing in Egypt and Nubia, and at Mount Sinai*. Cairo: privately printed.

Case, H., and J.C. Payne. 1962. "Tomb 100: The Decorated Tomb at Hierakonpolis." *JEA* 48: 5–18.

Castillos, J.J. 2002. *The Predynastic Period in Egypt*. Montevideo: Ediciones Maat.

Cenival, J.-L. de. 1965. "Un nouveau fragment de la Pierre de Palerme." *BSFE* 44: 13–17.

Champollion, J.-F. 1824–26. *Lettres à M. le duc de Blacas d'Aulps, Premier Gentilhomme de la Chambre, Pair de France, etc., relatives au Musée Royal Égyptien de Turin*. 2 vols. Paris: Didot.

Chłodnicki, M. 2014. "Tell el-Farkha: The Changes in Spatial Organisation of the Settlement—from the Predynastic to the Early Dynastic Periods." In *The Nile Delta as a Centre of Cultural Interactions between Upper Egypt and the Southern Levant in the 4th Millennium* BC, edited by A. Mączyńska, 57–72. Poznań: Poznań Archaeological Museum.

Ciałowicz, K. 2011. "The Predynastic/Early Dynastic Period at Tell el-Farkha." In *Before the Pyramids: The Origins of Egyptian Civilization*, edited by E. Teeter, 55–64. Chicago: Oriental Institute.

Clark, R. 2016. *Tomb Security in Ancient Egypt from the Predynastic to the Pyramid Age.* Oxford: Archaeopress.

Ćwiek, A. 1998. "Date and Function of the So-called Minor Step Pyramids." *GM* 162: 39–52.

Damarany, A., and K.M. Cahail. 2016. "The Sarcophagus of the High Priest of Amun, Menkheperre, from the Coptic Monastery of Apa Moses at Abydos." *MDAIK* 72: 11–30.

Daressy, G. 1916. "La pierre de Palerme et la chronologie de l'Ancien Empire." *BIFAO* 12: 161–214.

Darnell, J.C. 2011. "The Wadi of the Horus Qa-a: A Tableau of Royal Ritual Power in the Theban Western Desert." In *Egypt at Its Origins 3: Proceedings of the Third International Conference "Origin of the State: Predynastic and Early Dynastic Egypt," London, 27th July–1st August 2008*, edited by R.F. Friedman and P.N. Fiske, 1151–93. Leuven: Peeters.

Davis, W. 1992. *Masking the Blow: The Scene of Representation in Late Prehistoric Egyptian Art.* Berkeley: University of California Press.

Dee, M.W., D. Wengrow, A.J. Shortland, A. Stevenson, F. Brock, and C. Bronk Ramsey. 2014. "Radiocarbon Dating and the Naqada Relative Chronology." *Journal of Archaeological Science* 46: 319–23.

De Morgan, J. 1896–97. *Recherches sur les origines de l'Égypte.* 2 vols. Paris: Ernest Leroux.

Dodson, A. 1981. "King (𓏏𓊪)." *ZÄS* 108: 171.

———. 1988. "Egypt's First Antiquarians?" *Antiquity* 62: 413–17.

———. 2000. "The Layer Pyramid at Zawiyet el-Aryan: Its Layout and Context." *JARCE* 38: 81–90.

———. 2016a. *The Royal Tombs of Ancient Egypt.* Barnsley: Pen & Sword.

———. 2016b. "Go West: On the Ancient Means of Approach to the Saqqara Necropolis." In *Mummies, Magic and Medicine in Ancient Egypt: Multidisciplinary Essays for Rosalie David*, edited by C. Price, R. Forshaw, A. Chamberlain, and P.T. Nicholson, 3–18. Manchester: Manchester University Press.

———. 2018. *Amarna Sunset: Nefertiti, Tutankhamun, Ay, Horemheb, and the Egyptian Counter-reformation.* 2nd ed. Cairo: American University in Cairo Press.

———. 2019. *Afterglow of Empire: Egypt from the Fall of the New Kingdom to the Saite Renaissance.* 2nd ed. Cairo: American University in Cairo Press.

———. 2021. "The Last Rebel: Gustavus Seyffarth and His 'Decipherment' of the Hieroglyphs." *Kmt* 31/1: 44–50.

Donadoni Roveri, A.M. 1969. *I sarcofagi egizi dalle origine alla fine dell'Antico Regno.* Rome: Istituto di Studi del Vicino Oriente—Università.

Dreyer, G. 1981. "Ein frühdynastischen Königsfigürchen aus Elephantine." *MDAIK* 37: 123–24.

———. 1987. "Ein Siegel der frühzeitlichen Königsnekropole von Abydos." *MDAIK* 43: 33–43.

———. 1990. "Umm el-Qaab: Nachuntersuchungen im frühzeitlichen Königsfriedhof. 3./4. Vorbericht." *MDAIK* 46: 53–90.

———. 1991. "Zur Rekonstruktion der Oberbauten der Königsgräber der 1. Dynastie in Abydos." *MDAIK* 47: 93–104.

———. 1993. "Umm el-Qaab: Nachuntersuchungen im frühzeitlichen Königsfriedhof. 5./6. Vorbericht." *MDAIK* 49: 23–62.

———. 1998a. *Umm el-Qaab, I: Das prädynastische Königsgrab U-j und seine frühen Schriftzeugnisse.* Mainz: von Zabern.

———. 1998b. "Der erste König der 3. Dynastie." In *Stationen: Beiträge zur Kulturgeschichte Ägyptens, Rainer Stadelmann gewidmet*, edited by H. Guksch and D. Polz, 31–34. Mainz: Philipp von Zabern.

———. 2000. "Egypt's Earliest Historical Event." *EgArch* 16: 6–7.

———. 2009. "Report on the 21st Campaign of Reexamining the Royal Tombs of Umm el-Qaab at Abydos 2006/2007." *ASAE* 83: 165–75.

———. 2010. "Report on the 22nd Campaign of Reexamining the Royal Tombs of Umm el-Qaab at Abydos 2007/2008." *ASAE* 84: 143–56.

———. 2011. "Tomb U-J: A Royal Burial of Dynasty 0 at Abydos." In *Before the Pyramids: The Origins of Egyptian Civilization*, edited by E. Teeter, 127–36. Chicago: Oriental Institute.

Dreyer, G., A.I. Blöbaum, E.-M. Engel, H. Köpp, and V. Müller. 2011. "Umm el-Qaab: Nachuntersuchungen im frühzeitlichen Königsfriedhof. 19./20./21. Vorbericht." *MDAIK* 67: 53–92.

Dreyer, G., A. Effland, U. Effland, E.-M. Engel, R. Hartmann, U. Hartung, C. Lacher, V. Müller, and A. Pokorny. 2006. "Umm el-Qaab: Nachuntersuchungen im frühzeitlichen Königsfriedhof. 16./17./18. Vorbericht." *MDAIK* 62: 67–129.

Dreyer, G., E.M. Engel, U. Hartung, T. Hikade, E.V. Köhler, and F. Pumpenmeier. 1996. "Umm el-Qaab: Nachuntersuchungen im frühzeitlichen Königsfriedhof. 7/8. Vorbericht." *MDAIK* 52: 11–81.

Dreyer, G., R. Hartmann, U. Hartung, T. Hikade, H. Köpp, C. Lacher, V. Müller, A. Nerlich, and A. Zink. 2003. "Umm el-Qaab: Nachuntersuchungen im frühzeitlichen Königsfriedhof. 13./14./15. Vorbericht." *MDAIK* 59: 67–138.

Dreyer, G., U. Hartung, T. Hikade, E.C. Köhler, V. Müller, and F. Pumpenmeier. 1998. "Umm el-Qaab: Nachuntersuchungen im frühzeitlichen Königsfriedhof. 9./10. Vorbericht." *MDAIK* 54: 77–167.

Dreyer, G., and W. Kaiser. 1980. "Zu den kleinen Stufenpyramiden Ober- und Mittelägyptens." *MDAIK* 36: 43–59.

Dreyer, G., A. Von Den Driesch, E.-M. Engel, R. Hartmann, U. Hartung, T. Hikade, V. Müller, and J. Peters. 2000. "Umm el-Qaab: Nachuntersuchungen im frühzeitlichen Königsfriedhof. 11./12. Vorbericht." *MDAIK* 56: 43–129.

Drower, M.S. 1985. *Flinders Petrie: A Life in Archaeology*. London: Gollancz.

Eaton-Krauss, M. 2018. "The Stela of King Djet: A Masterpiece of Ancient Egyptian Art." In *Pérégrinations avec Erhart Graefe: Festschrift zu seinem 75. Geburtstag*, edited by A.L. Blöbaum, M. Eaton-Krauss, and A. Wüthrich, 119–31. Münster: Zaphon.

Ebers, G. 1875. *Das Hermetische Buch über die Arzneimittel der alten Ägypter in hieratischer Schrift*. Leipzig: Hinrichs.

Edwards, I.E.S. 1994. "Chephren's Place among the Kings of the Fourth Dynasty." In *The Unbroken Reed: Studies in the Culture and Heritage of Ancient Egypt in Honour of A.F. Shore*, edited by C. Eyre, A. Leahy, and L.M. Leahy, 97–105. London: Egypt Exploration Society.

———. 1997. "The Pyramid of Seila and Its Place in the Succession of Snofru's Pyramids." In *Chief of Seers: Egyptian Studies in Memory of Cyril Aldred*, edited by E. Goring, N. Reeves, and J. Ruffle, 88–96. London: Kegan Paul International.

Effland, A. 2013. "Der Besuch erfolgreicher Athleten beim Orakel des Bes in Abydos." In *Der gymnische Agon in der Spätantike*, edited by A. Gutsfeld and S. Lehmann, 121–41. Gutenberg: Computus Druck Satz & Verlag.

Emery, W.B. 1938. *The Tomb of Hemaka*. Cairo: Government Press.

———. 1939. *Ḥor-Aḥa*. Cairo-Bulaq: Government Press.

———. 1948. *Nubian Treasure: An Account of the Discoveries at Ballana and Qustul*. London: Methuen.

———. 1949–58. *Great Tombs of the First Dynasty*. 3 vols. Cairo: Government Press; London: Egypt Exploration Society.

Engel, E.-M. 2008. "Das Sedfest des Semerchet." In *Miscellanea in honorem Wolfhart Westendorf*, edited by C. Peust, 11–14. Göttingen: Seminar für Ägyptologie und Koptologie.

———. 2017. *Umm el-Qaab 6: Das Grab des Qa'a—Architektur und Inventar*. Wiesbaden: Harrassowitz.

Engelbach, R. 1934. "A Foundation Scene of the Second Dynasty." *JEA* 20: 183–84.

Epigraphic Survey. 1940. *Medinet Habu*, vol. 4: *Festival Scenes of Ramses III*. Chicago: University of Chicago Press.

Erman, A. 1900. "Geschichtliche Inschriften aus dem Berliner Museum." *ZÄS* 38: 112–26.

Fairman, H.W. 1935. "The Myth of Horus at Edfu." *JEA* 21: 26–36.

Farag, R.A. 1980. "A Stela of Khasekhemui from Abydos." *MDAIK* 36: 77–79.

Firth, C.M., and J.E. Quibell. 1935. *The Step Pyramid*. Cairo: Institut français d'archéologie orientale.

Fischer, H.G. 1961. "An Egyptian Royal Stela of the Second Dynasty." *Artibus Asiae* 24: 45–56.

Friedman, F.D. 1995. "The Underground Relief Panels of King Djoser at the Step Pyramid Complex." *JARCE* 32: 1–42.

Friedman, R.F., and D. Raue. 2007. "New Observations on the Fort at Hierakonpolis." In *The Archaeology and Art of Ancient Egypt: Essays in Honor of David B. O'Connor*, edited by Z.A. Hawass and J.E. Richards, 309–36. Cairo: Conseil Suprême des Antiquités de l'Egypte.

Galvin, J. 2005. "Abydos: Life and Death at the Dawn of Egyptian Civilization." *National Geographic*, April 2005: 106–21.

Gardiner, A.H. 1946. "The Instruction Addressed to Kagemni and His Brethren." *JEA* 32: 71–74.

———. 1959. *The Royal Canon of Turin*. Oxford: Griffith Institute.

Gardiner, A.H., and T.E. Peet. 1917. *The Inscriptions of Sinai*, vol. 1: *Introduction and Plates*. London: Egypt Exploration Fund.

Gardiner, A.H., T.E. Peet, and J. Černý. 1952–55. *The Inscriptions of Sinai*. 2nd ed. 2 vols. London: Egypt Exploration Society.

Garstang, J. 1903. *Maḥâsna and Bêt Khallaf*. London: Egyptian Research Account.

———. 1905a. "Note upon Excavations Made 1904–5." *Man* 5: 145–46.

———. 1905b. "The Tablet of Mena." *ZÄS* 42: 61–64.

Gauthier, H. 1906. "Notes et remarques historiques, § III–VII." *BIFAO* 5: 41–57.

———. 1907. *Livre des rois d'Égypte*, 1. Cairo: Institut français d'archéologie orientale.

———. 1914. "Quatre fragments nouveaux de la pierre de Palerme au Musée du Caire." *CRAIBL* 58: 489–96.

———. 1915. "Quatre nouveaux fragments de la pierre de Palerme." In *Le Musée Égyptien: recueil de monuments et de notices sur les fouilles d'Égypte* 3, edited by G. Maspero, 29–53. Cairo: Institut français d'archéologie orientale.

Giveon, R. 1974. "A Second Relief of Sekhemkhet in Sinai." *BASOR* 216: 17–20.

Goedicke, H. 1956a. "King *Ḥwdf3*?" *JEA* 42: 50–53.

———. 1956b. "The Pharaoh *Ny-Śwtḥ.*" *ZÄS* 81: 18–24.

Goneim, M.Z. 1956. *The Buried Pyramid.* London: Longmans, Green.

———. 1957. *Horus Sekhem-khet: The Unfinished Step Pyramid at Saqqara,* 1. Cairo: Institut français d'archéologie orientale.

Goyon, G. 1987. *La découverte des trésors de Tanis: aventures archéologiques en Egypte.* Paris: Éditions Perséa.

Grdseloff, B. 1944. "Notes d'épigraphie archaïque." *ASAE* 44: 279–310.

Green, C.I. 1987. *The Temple Furniture from the Sacred Animal Necropolis at North Saqqara 1964–1976.* London: Egypt Exploration Society.

Hartung, U. 2018. "Cemetery U at Umm el-Qaab and the Funeral Landscape of the Abydos Region in the 4th Millennium BC." In *Desert and the Nile. Prehistory of the Nile Basin and the Sahara: Papers in Honour of Fred Wendorf,* edited by J. Kabaciński, M. Chłodnicki, M. Kobusiewicz, and M. Winiarska-Kabacińska, 313–37. Posnań: Poznań Archaeological Museum.

Hartung, U., E.C. Köhler, V. Müller, and M.F. Ownby. 2015. "Imported Pottery from Abydos: A New Petrographic Perspective." *Ägypten und Levante* 25: 295–333.

Hassan, F.A. 1988. "The Predynastic of Egypt." *Journal of World Prehistory* 2: 135–85.

Hassan, F.A., G. Tassie, T.L. Tucker, J.M. Rowland, and J. van Wetering. 2003. "Social Dynamics at the Late Predynastic to Early Dynastic Site of Kafr Hassan Dawood, East Delta, Egypt." *Archéo-Nil* 13: 37–46.

Hassan, S. 1938. "Excavations at Saqqara (1937–1938)." *ASAE* 38: 503–21.

Heagy, T.C. 2014. "Who Was Menes?" *Archéo-Nil* 24: 59–92.

Helck, W. 1956. *Untersuchungen zur Manetho und den ägyptischen Köningslisten.* Berlin: Akademie-Verlag.

———. 1976. "Der Name des letzten Königs der 3. Dynastie und die Stadt Ehnas." *SAK* 4: 125–30.

———. 1979. "Die Datierung der Gefäßaufschriften aus der Djoserpyramide." *ZÄS* 106: 120–32.

———. 1987. *Untersuchungen zur Thinitenzeit.* Wiesbaden: Harrassowitz.

Hendrickx, S. 2006. "Predynastic–Early Dynastic Chronology." In *Ancient Egyptian Chronology,* edited by E. Hornung, R. Krauss, and D.A. Warburton, 55–93. Leiden: Brill.

Hendrickx, S., and E.C.M. van den Brink. 2002. "Inventory of Predynastic and Early Dynastic Cemetery and Settlement Sites in the Egyptian Nile Valley." In *Egypt and the Levant: Interrelations from the 4th through the Early 3rd Millennium BCE,* edited by E.C.M. van den Brink and T. E. Levy, 346–99. London: Leicester University Press.

Hincks, E. 1850a. "On the Portion of the Turin Book of Kings which Corresponds to the Sixth Dynasty of Manetho." *TRSL* 3: 128–38.

———. 1850b. "On the Portion of the Turin Book of Kings which Corresponds to the Twelfth Dynasty of Manetho." *TRSL* 3: 139–50.

Hurry, J.B. 1926. *Imhotep: The Vizier and Physician of King Zoser and Afterwards the Egyptian God of Medicine.* Oxford: Oxford University Press.

Jeffreys, D., and A. Tavares. 1994. "The Historic Landscape of Early Dynastic Memphis." *MDAIK* 50: 143–73.

Jéquier, G. 1906. "De l'intervalle entre deux règnes sous l'ancien empire." *BIFAO* 5: 59–62.

Jirásková, L. 2012. "Stone Vessels of AS54 at Abusir South: Preliminary Report." In *Abusir and Saqqara in the Year 2015,* edited by M. Bárta, F. Coppens, and J. Krejčí, 1–18. Prague: Faculty of Arts, Charles University.

Jurman, C. 2009. "From the Libyan Dynasties to the Kushites in Memphis: Historical Problems and Cultural Issues." *In The Libyan Period in Egypt: Historical and Cultural Studies into the 21st–24th Dynasties. Proceedings of a Conference at Leiden University, 25–27 October 2007*, edited by G.P.F. Broekman, R.J. Demarée, and O.E. Kaper, 113–38. Leiden: Nederlands Instituut voor het Nabije Oosten.

Kadish, G.E. 1970. "An Inscription from an Early Egyptian Fortress." *JNES* 29/2: 99–102.

Kahl, J. 1994. *Das System der ägyptischen Hieroglyphenschrift in der 0.–3. Dynastie*. Wiesbaden: Harrassowitz.

Kahl, J., N. Kloth, and U. Zimmermann. 1995. *Die Inschriften der 3. Dynastie: eine Bestandsaufnahme*. Wiesbaden: Harrassowitz.

Kaiser, W. 1960. "Einige Bemerkungen zur ägyptischen Frühzeit. I (Forts.)." *ZÄS* 85: 118–37.

———. 1969. "Zu den königlichen Talbezirken der 1. und 2. Dynastie in Abydos und zur Baugeschichte des Djoser-Grabmals." *MDAIK* 25: 1–21.

———. 1982. "Umm el-Qaab: Nachuntersuchungen im frühzeitlichen Königsfriedhof. 2. Vorbericht." *MDAIK* 38: 211–69.

———. 1985. "Ein Kultbezirk des Königs Den in Sakkara." *MDAIK* 41: 47–60.

———. 1987. "Zum Siegel mit frühen Königsnamen von Umm el-Qaab." *MDAIK* 43: 115–19.

———. 1990. "Zur Entstehung des gesamtägyptischen Staates." *MDAIK* 46: 287–99.

———. 1991. "Zur Nennung von Sened und Peribsen in Sakkara B 3." *GM* 122: 49–55.

———. 1992. "Zur unterirdischen Anlage der Djoserpyramide und ihrer entwicklungsgeschichtlichen Einordnung." In *Gegengabe: Festschrift für Emma Brunner-Traut*, edited by I. Gamer-Wallert and W.

Helck, 167–90. Tübingen: Attempto.

———. 1997. "Zu den Granitkammern und ihren Vorgängerbauten unter der Stufenpyramide und im Südgrab von Djoser." *MDAIK* 53: 195–207.

Kaiser, W., and P. Grossmann. 1979. "Umm el-Qaab: Nachuntersuchungen im frühzeitlichen Königsfriedhof. 1. Vorbericht." *MDAIK* 35: 155–63.

Kaplony, P. 1963. *Die Inschriften der ägyptischen Frühzeit*. 3 vols. Wiesbaden: Harrassowitz.

———. 1981. *Die Rollsiegel des Alten Reichs, 2: Katalog der Rollsiegel*. Brussels: Fondation égyptologique Reine Élisabeth.

Kees, H. 1928. "Zum Ursprung der Horusdiener." In *Nachrichten von der Gesellschaft der Wissenschaften in Göttingen: Philologische-historische Klasse aus dem Jahre 1927*, 196–207. Göttingen: Vandenhoeck & Ruprecht.

Kemp, B.J. 1963. "Excavations at Hierakonpolis Fort, 1905: A Preliminary Note." *JEA* 49: 24–28.

———. 1966. "Abydos and the Royal Tombs of the First Dynasty." *JEA* 52: 13–22.

———. 1967. "The Egyptian First Dynasty Royal Cemetery." *Antiquity* 41: 22–32.

———. 1973. "Photographs of the Decorated Tomb at Hierakonpolis." *JEA* 59: 36–43.

Kitchen, K.A. 1962. "Amenysonb in Liverpool and the Louvre." *JEA* 48: 159–60.

Köhler, E.C. 2005–17. *Helwan I–IV*. Rahden: Marie Leidorf.

———. 2014. "Of Pots and Myths: Attempting a Comparative Study of Funerary Pottery Assemblages in the Egyptian Nile Valley during the Late 4th Millennium BC." In *The Nile Delta as a Centre of Cultural Interactions between Upper Egypt and the Southern Levant in the 4th Millennium BC*, edited by A. Mączyńska, 155–80. Poznań: Poznań Archaeological Museum.

———. 2014–15. *"Auch die letzte Scherbe*: More Thoughts on the 'Naqada Culture.'" *MDAIK* 70–71: 255–64.

Kołodziejczyk, P. 2005. "Lower Egypt in Modern Research on State Formation in Egypt." *Folia Orientalia* 41: 149–57.

Krauss, R. 2006. "Egyptian Sirius/Sothic Dates, and the Question of the Sothis-based Lunar Calendar." In *Ancient Egyptian Chronology*, edited by E. Hornung, R. Krauss, and D.A. Warburton, 438–57. Leiden: Brill.

Kuper, R., and S. Kröpelin. 2006. "Climate-controlled Holocene Occupation in the Sahara: Motor of Africa's Evolution." *Science* 313/5788: 803–807.

Lacau, P., and J.-Ph. Lauer. 1959–65. *La pyramide à degrés*, 4–5: *Inscriptions à l'encre sur les vases*. Cairo: Institut français d'archéologie orientale.

Lacher, C.M. 2008. "Das Grab des Hetepsechemui/Raneb in Saqqara: Ideen zur baugeschichtlichen Entwicklung." In *Zeichen aus dem Sand: Streiflichter aus Ägyptens Geschichte zu Ehren von Günter Dreyer*, edited by E.M. Engel, V. Müller, and U. Hartung, 427–52. Wiesbaden: Harrassowitz.

———. 2011. "The Tomb of King Ninetjer at Saqqara." *In Egypt at Its Origins 3: Proceedings of the Third International Conference "Origin of the State: Predynastic and Early Dynastic Egypt," London, 27th July–1st August 2008*, edited by R.F. Friedman and P.N. Fiske, 213–31. Leuven: Peeters.

Lacher-Raschdorff, C.M. 2011. "The Tomb of King Ninetjer and Its Reuse in Later Periods." In *Abusir and Saqqara in the Year 2010*, edited by M. Bárta, F. Coppens, and J. Krejčí, 537–50. Prague: Czech Institute of Egyptology, Faculty of Arts, Charles University.

———. 2014. *Das Grab des Königs Ninetjer in Saqqara: Architektonische Entwicklung frühzeitlicher Grabanlagen in Ägypten*. Wiesbaden: Harrassowitz.

———. 2020. *Umm el-Qaab* VIII: *Das Grab der Peribsen: Archäologie und Architectur*. Wiesbaden: Harrassowitz.

Lankester, F. 2011. *Who Is King 'Scorpion'?* https://www.academia.edu/4168248/Who_is_King_Scorpion.

Lauer, J.-Ph. 1936–55. *La Pyramide à degrés*. 5 vols. Cairo: Institut français d'archéologie orientale.

———. 1962. *Histoire monumentale des pyramides d'Égypte*, 1: *Les pyramides à degrés (IIIᵉ Dynastie)*. Cairo: Institut français d'archéologie orientale.

———. 1967. "Recherches et travaux menés dans la nécropole de Saqqarah au cours de la campagne 1966–1967." *CRAIBL* [111]: 493–510.

———. 1969. "Recherches et travaux à Saqqarah (campagnes 1967–1968 et 1968–1969)." *CRAIBL* [113]: 460–79.

———. 1972. "Recherches et travaux à Saqqarah (campagnes 1970–1971 et 1971–1972)." *CRAIBL* [116]: 577–600.

Leahy, M.A. 1977. "The Osiris 'Bed' Reconsidered." *Orientalia* 46: 424–34.

———. 1989. "A Protective Measure at Abydos." *JEA* 75: 41–60.

———. 1994. "Kushite Monuments at Abydos." In *The Unbroken Reed: Studies in the Culture and Heritage of Ancient Egypt in Honour of A.F. Shore*, edited by C. Eyre, A. Leahy, and L.M. Leahy, 171–92. London: Egypt Exploration Society.

Leclant, J., and G. Clerc. 1988. "Fouilles et travaux en Égypte et au Soudan, 1986–1987." *Orientalia* 57 (1988): 330.

Legge, F. 1899. "Recent Discoveries at Abydos and Negadah." *PSBA* 29: 183–93.

Lehner, M. 1996. "Z500 and the Layer Pyramid of Zawiyet el-Aryan." In *Studies in Honor of William Kelly Simpson*, edited by P. Der Manuelian, 507–22. Boston: Museum of Fine Arts.

Leplongeon, A. 2017. "Technological Variability in the Late Palaeolithic Lithic Industries of the Egyptian Nile Valley: The Case of the Silsilian and Afian Industries." *PLOS ONE* 12(12): e0188824. https://doi.org/10.1371/journal.pone.0188824.

Lepper, V.M. 2008. *Untersuchungen zu pWestcar: eine philologische und literaturwissenschaftliche (Neu-)Analyse*. Wiesbaden: Harrassowitz.

Leprohon, R.J. 2013. *The Great Name: Ancient Egyptian Royal Titulary*. Atlanta: Society for Biblical Literature.

Lepsius, C.R. 1842. *Auswahl der wichtigsten Urkunden des aegyptischen Alterthums*. Leipzig: Georg Wigand.

———. 1849–59. *Denkmaeler aus Aegypten und Aethiopien*. 12 vols. Berlin: Nicolaische Buchhandlung.

———. 1897–1913. *Denkmäler aus Aegypten und Aethiopien: Text*. 5 vols. Edited by E. Naville and L. Borchardt. Leipzig: Hinrichs.

Lichtheim, M. 1973. *Ancient Egyptian Literature: A Book of Readings*. 1: *The Old and Middle Kingdoms*. Los Angeles: University of California Press.

MacIver, D.R., and A.C. Mace. 1902. *El Amrah and Abydos*. London: Egypt Exploration Fund.

Macramallah, R.N. 1932. "Une forteresse du Moyen Empire (?) à Abou-Rawâch." *ASAE* 32: 161–73.

———. 1940. *Un cimetière archaïque de la classe moyenne du peuple à Saqqarah*. Cairo: Imprimerie nationale.

Malek, J. 1999. *Topographical Bibliography of Ancient Egyptian Hieroglyphic Texts, Reliefs and Paintings*. 8: *Objects of Provenance Not Known*, 1. Oxford: Griffith Institute.

Manning, S.W. 2006. "Radiocarbon Dating and Egyptian Chronology." In *Ancient Egyptian Chronology*, edited by E. Hornung, R. Krauss, and D.A. Warburton, 327–55. Leiden: Brill.

Manuelian, P. Der 1994. *Living in the Past: Studies in Archaism of the Egyptian Twenty-sixth Dynasty*. London: Kegan Paul International.

Maragioglio, V., and C.A. Rinaldi. 1967. *L'Architettura delle piramidi Menfite*. VI: *La grande fossa di Zauiet el-Aryan, la piramide di Micerino, il mastabat Faraun, la tomba di Khentkaus*. Rapallo: Officine Grafiche Canessa.

Mariette, A. 1856. "Renseignements sur les soixante-quatre Apis trouvés dans les souterrains du Sérapéum: §7. XXIVᵉ Dynastie—un Apis." *Bulletin archéologique de l'Athénaeum français* 2: 52–62.

———. 1860. "Lettre de M. Aug. Mariette à M. le Vicomte de Rougé sur les résultats des fouilles entreprises par ordre du Vice-Roi d'Égypte." *RevArch* 2: 17–35.

———. 1864. "La table de Saqqarah." *RevArch* 10: 169–86.

———. 1869–80. *Abydos: description des fouilles exécutées sur l'emplacement de cette ville*. 2 vols. Paris: Librairie A. Franck/Imprimerie nationale.

Martin, G.T. 2011. *Umm el-Qaab VII: Private Stelae of the Early Dynastic Period from the Royal Cemetery at Abydos*. Wiesbaden: Harrassowitz.

Maspero, G. 1895. "Notes sur différents points de grammaire et d'histoire." *RecTrav* 17: 56–78.

———. 1902. "Note sur les objects recueillis sous la pyramide d'Ounas." *ASAE* 3: 185–90.

Mathieson, I., E. Bettles, J. Clarke, C. Duhig, S. Ikram, L. Maguire, S. Quie, and A. Tavares. 1997. "The National Museums of Scotland Saqqara Survey Project 1993–1995." *JEA* 83: 17–53.

Mathieson, I.J., and A. Tavares. 1993. "Preliminary Report of the National Museums of Scotland Saqqara Survey Project, 1990–1." *JEA* 79: 17–31.

Meltzer, E.S. 1971. "A Reconsideration of ⟨+⟩." *JEA* 57: 202–203.

Midant-Reynes, B. 2000. *The Prehistory of Egypt: From the First Egyptians to the First Pharaohs*. Oxford: Blackwell.

Migahid, A. el-G. 2003. "Aus den Denkmälern einer memphitischen Priesterfamilie (Stelenbruchstück Saqqara Sechem-Chet)." *MDAIK* 59: 305–15.

Minutoli, H. von. 1824–27. *Reise zum Tempel des Jupiter Ammon in der Libyschen Wüste und nach Ober-Aegypten in den Jahren 1820 und 1821*. Berlin: Rücker.

Montet, P. 1928. "Notes et documents pour servir à l'histoire des relations entre l'ancienne Égypte et la Syrie, 2: Nouvelles traces des Égyptiens à Byblos." *Kêmi* 1: 83–93.

Morkot, R.G. 2003. "Archaism and Innovation in Art from the New Kingdom to the Twenty-sixth Dynasty." In *"Never Had the Like Occurred": Egypt's View of Its Past*, edited by J. Tait, 79–99. London: UCL Press.

———. 2014. "All in the Detail: Some Further Observations on 'Archaism' and Style in Libyan–Kushite–Saite Egypt." In *Thebes in the First Millennium BC*, edited by E. Pischikova, J. Budka, and K. Griffin, 379–95. Newcastle-upon-Tyne: Cambridge Scholars.

Morris, E.F. 2007a. "On the Ownership of the Saqqara Mastabas and the Allotment of Political and Ideological Power at the Dawn of the State." In *The Archaeology and Art of Ancient Egypt: Essays in Honor of David B. O'Connor*, edited by Z.A. Hawass and J.E. Richards, 2:171–90. Cairo: Conseil Suprême des Antiquités de l'Egypte.

———. 2007b. "Sacrifice for the State: First Dynasty Royal Funerals and the Rites at Macramallah's Rectangle." In *Performing Death: Social Analyses of Funerary Traditions in the Ancient Near East and Mediterranean*, edited by N. Laneri, 15–37. Chicago: Oriental Institute.

Muhlestein, K., K.V.L. Pierce, and B. Jensen, eds. 2020. *Excavations at the Seila Pyramid and Fag el-Gamous Cemetery*. Leiden: Brill.

Munro, P. 1983. "Einige Bemerkungen zum Unas-Friedhof in Saqqara: 3. Vorbericht über die Arbeiten der Gruppe Hannover im Herbst 1978 und im Frühjahr 1980." *SAK* 10: 277–95.

Murnane, W.J. 1987. "The Gebel Sheikh Suleiman Monument: Epigraphic Remarks." *JNES* 46: 282–85.

Nakano, T. 1998. "Abydos Ware and the Location of the Egyptian First Dynasty Royal Tombs." *Orient* 33: 1–32.

Naville, É. 1899. "Les plus anciens monuments égyptiens." *RecTrav* 21: 105–23.

———. 1903. "La pierre de palerme." *RecTrav* 25: 64–81.

———. 1914. *The Cemeteries of Abydos*, 1. London: Egypt Exploration Fund.

Newberry, P.E. 1922. "The Set Rebellion of the IInd Dynasty." *AE* 1922: 40–46.

O'Connor, D. 1989. "New Funerary Enclosures (*Talbezirke*) of the Early Dynastic Period at Abydos." *JARCE* 26: 51–86.

———. 1995. "The Earliest Royal Boat Graves." *EgArch* 6: 3–7.

———. 2011. "The Narmer Palette: A New Interpretation." In *Before the Pyramids: The Origins of Egyptian Civilization*, edited by E. Teeter, 145–52. Chicago: Oriental Institute.

Oppenheim, A. 2007. "A New Boundary Stela of the Pharaoh Netjerikhet (Djoser) Found in the Pyramid Complex of Senwosret III, Dahshur." *BES* 17: 153–82.

Palanque, C. 1902. "Rapport sur les fouilles d'El-Deïr." *BIFAO* 2: 163–70.

Payne, J.C. 1973. "Tomb 100: The Decorated Tomb at Hierakonpolis Confirmed." *JEA* 59: 31–35.

Payraudeau, F., and R. Meffre. 2016. "Varia Tanitica 1: Vestiges royaux." *BIFAO* 116: 273–302.

Pellegrini, A. 1895. "Nota sopra un'inscrizione egizia del Museo di Palermo." *Archivo Storico Siciliano* 20: 297–316.

Perring, J.S. 1839–42. *The Pyramids of Gizeh from Actual Survey and Admeasurement*. 3 vols. London: James Fraser.

Petrie, W.M.F. 1894. *A History of Egypt from the Earliest Kings to the XVIth Dynasty*. London: Methuen.

———. 1896a. *Naqada and Ballas*. London: Bernard Quaritch.

———. 1896b. *Koptos*. London: Bernard Quaritch.

———. 1900–1901. *Royal Tombs of the First/ Earliest Dynasties*. 2 vols. London: Egypt Exploration Fund.

———. 1901. *Diospolis Parva: The Cemeteries of Abadiyeh and Hu*. London: Egypt Exploration Fund.

———. 1906. *Researches in Sinai*. New York: E.P. Dutton.

———. 1907. *Gizeh and Rifeh*. London: British School of Archaeology in Egypt.

———. 1916. "New Portions of the Annals." *AE* 1916/3: 114–20.

———. 1925. *Tombs of the Courtiers and Oxyrhynchos*. London: British School of Archaeology in Egypt.

———. 1932. *Seventy Years in Archaeology*. New York: Henry Holt.

Phillipps, R., S. Holdaway, W. Wendrich, and R. Cappers. 2012. "Mid-Holocene Occupation of Egypt and Global Climatic Change." *Quaternary International* 251: 64–76.

Porter, B., and R.L.B. Moss. 1934. *Topographical Bibliography of Ancient Egyptian Hieroglyphic Texts, Reliefs and Paintings*, 4: *Lower and Middle Egypt*. Oxford: Clarendon Press.

———. 1937. *Topographical Bibliography of Ancient Egyptian Hieroglyphic Texts, Reliefs and Paintings*, 5: *Upper Egypt: Sites*. Oxford: Clarendon Press.

———. 1939. *Topographical Bibliography of Ancient Egyptian Hieroglyphic Texts, Reliefs and Paintings*, 6: *Upper Egypt: Chief Temples (excl. Thebes)*. Oxford: Clarendon Press.

———. 1952. *Topographical Bibliography of Ancient Egyptian Hieroglyphic Texts, Reliefs and Paintings*, 7: *Nubia, Deserts, and Outside Egypt*. Oxford: Clarendon Press/Griffith Institute.

———. 1960–64. *Topographical Bibliography of Ancient Egyptian Hieroglyphic Texts, Reliefs and Paintings*, 1: *The Theban Necropolis*. 2nd ed. Oxford: Clarendon Press/Griffith Institute.

———. 1972. *Topographical Bibliography of Ancient Egyptian Hieroglyphic Texts, Reliefs and Paintings*, 2: *Theban Temples*. 2nd ed. Oxford: Griffith Institute.

———. 1974–81. *Topographical Bibliography of Ancient Egyptian Hieroglyphic Texts, Reliefs and Paintings*, 3: *Memphis*. 2nd ed. by J. Málek. Oxford: Griffith Institute.

Prisse d'Avennes, E. 1847. *Fac-simile d'un papyrus égyptien en caractères hiératiques, trouvé à Thèbes*. Paris: Imprimerie lithographique de Lemercier.

Quack, J. 1997. "Ein ägyptisches Handbuch des Tempels und seine griechische Übersetzung." *ZPE* 119: 297–300.

Quibell, J.E. 1898. *The Ramesseum*. London: Bernard Quaritch.

———. 1913. *The Tomb of Hesy*. Cairo: Institut français d'archéologie orientale.

———. 1923. *Excavations at Saqqara (1912–1914): Archaic Mastabas*. Cairo: Institut français d'archéologie orientale.

Quibell, J.E., and F.W. Green. 1900–1902. *Hierakonpolis*. 2 vols. London: Egyptian Research Account.

Raven, M.J., and R. van Walsem. 2014. *The Tomb of Meryneith at Saqqara*. Turnhout: Brepols.

Rawlins, D., and K. Pickering. 2001. "Astronomical Orientation of the Pyramids." *Nature* 412/6848: 699.

Read, F.W. 1916. "Nouvelles remarques sur la pierre de Palerme." *BIFAO* 12: 215–22.

Reader, C. 2017. "An Early Dynastic Ritual Landscape at North Saqqara: An Inheritance from Abydos?" *JEA* 103: 71–88.

Regulski, I. 2009. "Investigating a New Dynasty 2 Necropolis at South Saqqara." *British Museum Studies in Ancient Egypt and Sudan* 13: 221–37.

———. 2011. "Investigating a New Necropolis of Dynasty 2 at Saqqara." In *Egypt at Its Origins 3: Proceedings of the Third International Conference "Origin of the State: Predynastic and Early Dynastic Egypt," London, 27th July–1st August 2008*, edited by R.F. Friedman and P.N. Fiske, 293–311. Leuven: Peeters.

———. 2012. "La deuxième dynastie: oubliée et ensevelie à Saqqara." In *Ceci n'est pas une pyramide . . . Un siècle de recherche archéologique belge en Égypte,* edited by L. Bavay, M.-C. Bruwier, W. Claes, and I. De Strooper, 168–77. Leuven: Peeters.

Reisner, G.A. 1910. "A Scribe's Tablet Found by the Hearst Expedition at Giza." *ZÄS* 48: 113–14.

———. 1923. *Excavations at Kerma.* 2 vols. Cambridge, MA: Peabody Museum.

———. 1936. *The Development of the Egyptian Tomb Down to the Accession of Cheops.* Oxford: Oxford University Press; Cambridge, MA: Harvard University Press.

Renouf, P. Le P. 1859. "Seyffarth and Uhleman on Egyptian Hieroglyphics." *The Atlantis* 2/3: 74–97 = *The Life-work of Sir Peter Le Page Renouf,* edited by G. Maspero and W.H. Rylands, 1st series, 1:1–31. Paris: Leroux, 1902.

———. 1862. "Dr. Seyffarth and the Atlantis on Egyptology." *The Atlantis* 3/6: 306–38 = *The Life-work of Sir Peter Le Page Renouf,* edited by G. Maspero and W.H. Rylands, 1st series, 1:33–80. Paris: Leroux, 1902.

Ricci, S. de. 1917. "La table de Palerme." *CRAIBL* 61/2: 107–15.

Roth, S. 2001. *Die Königsmütter des Alten Ägypten von der Frühzeit bis zum Ende der 12. Dynastie.* Wiesbaden: Harrassowitz.

Rougé, E. de 1865. *Album photographique de la mission remplie en Égypte par le vte Emmanuel de Rougé, accompagné de M. le vte de Banville et de M. Jacques de Rougé, attachés à la mission, 1863–1864.* Paris: Samson.

———. 1866. *Recherches sur les monuments qu'on peut attribuer aux six premières dynasties de Manéthon.* Paris: Imprimerie impériale.

Rowland, J.M. 2013. "Problems and Possibilities for Achieving Absolute Dates from Prehistoric and Early Historical Contexts." In *Radiocarbon and the Chronologies of Ancient Egypt,* edited by A.J. Shortland and C. Bronk Ramsey, 235–49. Oxford: Oxbow Books.

Rowland, J., and G.J. Tassie. 2017. "A New Funerary Monument Dating to the Reign of Khaba: The Quesna Mastaba in the Context of the Early Dynastic–Old Kingdom Mortuary Landscape in Lower Egypt." In *Abusir and Saqqara in the Year 2015,* edited by M. Bárta, F. Coppens, and J. Krejčí, 369–89. Prague: Faculty of Arts, Charles University.

Ryholt, K.S.B. 1997. *The Political Situation in Egypt during the Second Intermediate Period c. 1800–1550 BC.* Copenhagen: Museum Tusculanum Press.

———. 2000. "The Late Old Kingdom in the Turin King-list and the Identity of Nitocris." *ZÄS* 127: 87–100.

———. 2004. "The Turin King-list." *Ägypten und Levante* 14: 135–55.

———. 2008. "King Seneferka in the King-lists and His Position in the Early Dynastic Period." *JEH* 1/1: 159–73.

———. 2009. "The Life of Imhotep (P. Carlsberg 85)." In *Actes du IXe Congrès international des études démotiques: Paris, 31 août–3 septembre 2005,* edited by G. Widmer and D. Devauchelle, 305–15. Cairo: Institut français d'archéologie orientale.

Saad, Z.Y. 1942–43. "Preliminary Report on the Royal Excavations at Helwan." *ASAE* 41: 405–409; 42: 357.

———. 1947. *Royal Excavations at Saqqara and Helwan (1941–1945).* Cairo: Institut français d'archéologie orientale.

———. 1951. *Royal Excavations at Helwan.* Cairo: Institut français d'archéologie orientale.

———. 1969. *The Excavations at Helwan: Art and Civilization in the First and Second Egyptian Dynasties.* Norman: University of Oklahoma Press.

Schäfer, H. 1902. *Ein Bruchstück altägyptischer Annalen.* Berlin: Verlag der Königliche Akademie der Wissenschaften.

———. 1914. "König Huni." *ZÄS* 52: 98–100.

Segato, G., and D. Valeriani. 1835. *Atlante del Basso e Alto Egitto*. Florence: Nello stabilimento posto nei fondacci di Santo Spirito.

Seidlmayer, S.J. 2006. "The Relative Chronology of Dynasty 3." In *Ancient Egyptian Chronology*, edited by E. Hornung, R. Krauss, and D.A. Warburton, 116–23. Leiden: Brill.

Seipel, W. 1980. *Untersuchungen zu den ägyptischen Königinnen der Frühzeit und des Alten Reiches*. Hamburg: Universität Hamburg.

Sethe, K. 1897. "Die ältesten geschichtlichen Denkmäler der Ägypter." *ZÄS* 35: 1–6.

Seyffarth, G. 1828. "Remarks upon an Egyptian History, in Egyptian Characters, in the Royal Museum at Turin." *London Literary Gazette* 600: 457–59.

Simpson, W.K. 1974. *The Terrace of the Great God at Abydos: The Offering Chapels of Dynasties 12 and 13*. New Haven: Peabody Museum; Philadelphia: University of Pennsylvania Museum of Archaeology and Anthropology.

Smith, M. 1980. "A Second Dynasty King in a Demotic Papyrus of the Roman Period." *JEA* 66: 173–74.

Smith, W.S. 1949. *A History of Egyptian Sculpture and Painting in the Old Kingdom*. London: Oxford University Press.

Somaglino, C., and P. Taillet. 2015a. "Une campagne en Nubie sous la Ire dynastie: la scène nagadienne du Gebel Sheikh Suleiman comme prototype et modèle." *NeHeT* 1: 1–46.

———. 2015b. "Gebel Sheikh Suleiman: A First Dynasty Relief after All. . . ." *Archéo-Nil* 25: 122–34.

Spence, K. 2000. "Ancient Egyptian Chronology and the Astronomical Orientation of Pyramids." *Nature* 408/6810: 320–24.

———. 2001. "Astronomical Orientation of the Pyramids." *Nature* 412/6848: 699–700.

Spencer, A.J. 1974. "Researches on the Topography of North Saqqâra." *Orientalia* 43: 1–11.

Stadelmann, R. 1985. "Der Oberbauten der Königsgräber der 2. Dynastie in Saqqara." In *Mélanges Gamal eddin Mokhtar* 2: 295–307. Cairo: Institut français d'archéologie orientale.

———. 1996. "Zur Baugeschichte des Djoserbezirks Grabschacht und Grabkammer der Stufenmastaba." *MDAIK* 52: 295–305.

———. 2007. "King Huni: His Monuments and His Place in the History of the Old Kingdom." In *The Archaeology and Art of Ancient Egypt: Essays in Honor of David B. O'Connor*, edited by Z.A. Hawass and J.E. Richards, 425–31. Cairo: Conseil Suprême des Antiquités de l'Egypte.

Steindorff, G. 1890. "Bemerkungen zu dem vorstehenden Aufsatz." *ZÄS* 28: 111–12.

Strouhal, E., L. Vyhnánek, M.F. Gaballah, S.R. Saunders, W. Woelfli, G. Bonani, and A. Němečková. 2001. "Identification of Royal Skeletal Remains from Egyptian Pyramids." *Anthropologie: International Journal of Human Diversity and Evolution* 39/1: 15–23.

Strudwick, N. 1985. *The Administration of Egypt in the Old Kingdom: The Highest Titles and Their Holders*. London: KPI.

Swelim, N.M.A. 1974. "Horus Seneferka: An Essay on the Fall of the First Dynasty." *Publications of the Archaeological Society of Alexandria, Archaeological & Historical Studies* 5: 67–77.

———. 1983. *Some Problems on the History of the Third Dynasty*. Alexandria: Archaeological Society of Alexandria.

———. 1987. *The Brick Pyramid at Abu Rowash—Number "I" by Lepsius: A Preliminary Study*. Alexandria: Archaeological Society of Alexandria.

———. 1992. "*Rollsiegel, Pierre de taille* and an Update on a King and Monument List of the Third Dynasty." *Studia Aegyptiaca* 14: 541–54.

————. 2014–15. "Reminders and Remarks on the Royal Substructures of the Third Dynasty." *MDAIK* 70–71: 431–44.

Taillet, P. 2013. "Une inscription du roi Djer au Sud-Sinaï: la première phrase écrite en hiéroglyphes?" *Abgadiyat* 8: 122–27.

Taillet, P., and D. Laisney. 2012. "Iry-Hor et Narmer au Sud-Sinaï (Ouadi 'Ameyra): Un complément à la chronologie des expéditions minières égyptiennes." *BIFAO* 112: 381–98.

Tassie, G.J. 2014. *Prehistoric Egypt: Socioeconomic Transformations in North-east Africa from the Last Glacial Maximum to the Neolithic, 24,000 to 4,000 cal BP.* London: Golden House.

Te Velde, H. 1967. *Seth, God of Confusion.* Leiden: Brill.

Thompson, J. 2015–18. *Wonderful Things: A History of Egyptology.* 3 vols. Cairo: American University in Cairo Press.

Tiradritti, F. 2010. "Luigi Vassalli and the Archaeological Season at Western Thebes (1862–3)." In *The Second Intermediate Period (Thirteenth–Seventeenth Dynasties): Current Research, Future Prospects*, edited by M. Marée, 329–42. Leuven: Peeters.

————. 2018. "Un sceau avec un cartouche de Péribsen au musée archéologique de Milan." *Égypte, Afrique & Orient* 90: 37–44.

Tristant, Y., and B. Midant-Reynes. 2011. "The Predynastic Cultures of the Nile Delta." In *Before the Pyramids: The Origins of Egyptian Civilization*, edited by E. Teeter, 45–54. Chicago: Oriental Institute.

Troy, L. 1986. *Patterns of Queenship in Ancient Egyptian Myth and History.* Stockholm: Almqvist & Wiksell International.

Valeriani, D. 1835–37. *Atlante del Basso ed Alto Egitto.* 2 vols. Florence: Stabilimento Posto nei Fondacci di S. Spirito.

van Dijk, J. 2007. "Retainer Sacrifice in Egypt and Nubia." In *The Strange World of Human Sacrifice*, edited by J.N Bremmer, 135–55. Leuven: Peeters.

Vanhulle, D. 2013. "Les stèles funéraires royales des deux premières dynasties à Abydos: à propos de la 'stèle' de Den des Musées royaux d'Art et d'Histoire de Bruxelles." *CdÉ* 88/176: 203–29.

van Wetering, J. 2012. "Relocating De Morgan's Royal Tomb at Naqada and Identifying Its Occupant." In *Prehistory of Northeastern Africa: New Ideas and Discoveries*, edited by J. Kabaciński, M. Chłodnicki, and M. Kobusiewicz, 91–124. Poznań: Poznań Archaeological Museum.

————. 2017. "The Macramallah Burials, Wadi Abusir, Saqqara." In *Abusir and Saqqara in the Year 2015*, edited by M. Bárta, F. Coppens, and J. Krejčí, 419–33. Prague: Faculty of Arts, Charles University.

————. 2018. "The Early Dynastic Royal Cemetery at Saqqara." In *"The Perfection that Endures . . .": Studies on Old Kingdom Art and Archaeology*, edited by K.O. Kuraszkiewicz, E. Kopp, and D. Takács, 367–96. Warsaw: Zakład Egiptologii, Wydział Orientalistyczny, Uniwersytet Warszawski.

Vermeersch, P., E. Paulissen, P. Van Peer, S. Stokes, C. Charlier, C. Stringer, and W. Lindsay. 1998. "A Middle Palaeolithic Burial of a Modern Human at Taramsa Hill, Egypt." *Antiquity* 72/277: 475–84.

Verner, M. 2002. *The Pyramids: The Mystery, Culture, and Science of Egypt's Great Monuments.* London: Atlantic Books.

Vernus, P. 1976. "Inscriptions de la troisième période intermédiare (II)." *BIFAO* 75: 67–72.

von Bissing, W. 1933–34. "Saitische Kopien nach Reliefs des Alten Reichs." *AfO* 9: 35–40.

Vyse, R.H. 1840–42. *Operations Carried On at the Pyramids of Gizeh in 1837: With an Account of a Voyage into Upper Egypt, and an Appendix.* 3 vols. London: James Fraser.

Waddell, W.G. 1940. *Manetho.* Cambridge, MA: Harvard University Press; London: William Heinemann.

Ward, C. 2000. *Sacred and Secular: Ancient Egyptian Ships and Boats*. Philadelphia: The University Museum, University of Pennsylvania.

————. 2006. "Boat-building and Its Social Context in Early Egypt: Interpretations from the First Dynasty Boat-grave Cemetery at Abydos." *Antiquity* 80/1: 118–29.

Wegner, J. 2020. "Two Recently Discovered Burial Chambers of the 13th Dynasty at Abydos: Evidence for Tombs of the Brother-kings Sobekhotep IV and Sahathor." In *Guardian of Ancient Egypt: Studies in Honor of Zahi Hawass*, edited by J. Kamrin, M. Bárta, S. Ikram, M. Lehner, and M. Megahed, 1665–82. Prague: Charles University, Faculty of Arts.

Weigall, A.E.P. 1925. *A History of the Pharaohs*, 1: *The First Eleven Dynasties*. London: Thornton Butterworth.

Weill, R. 1904. *Recueil des inscriptions égyptiennes du Sinaï: bibliographie, texte, traduction et commentaire, précédé de la géographie, de l'histoire et de la bibliographie des établissements égyptiens de la péninsule*. Paris: Société nouvelle de librairie et d'édition.

————. 1908a. *Des monuments et de l'histoire des IIe et IIIe dynasties égyptiennes*. Paris: Ernest Leroux.

————. 1908b. *Les origines de l'Égypte pharaonique*, 1: *La IIe et la IIIe dynasties*. Paris: Ernest Leroux.

Wendorf, F., and R. Schild, eds. 2001. *Holocene Settlement of the Egyptian Sahara*, 1: *The Archaeology of Nabta Playa*. New York: Kluwer Academic Publishers.

Wiedemann, A. 1898. "Observations on the Nagadah Period." *PSBA* 20: 107–22.

Wildung, D. 1977a. *Imhotep und Amenhotep: Gottwerdung im alten Ägypten*. Berlin: Deutscher Kunstverlag.

————. 1977b. *Egyptian Saints: Deification in Pharaonic Egypt*. New York: New York University Press.

Wilkinson, J.G. 1835. *Topography of Thebes and General View of Egypt*. London: John Murray.

————. 1851. *The Fragments of the Hieratic Papyrus at Turin*. London: Richards.

Wilkinson, T.A.H. 1999. *Early Dynastic Egypt*. London: Routledge.

————. 2000a. *Royal Annals of Ancient Egypt: The Palermo Stone and Its Associated Fragments*. London: Kegan Paul International.

————. 2000b. "Political Unification: Towards a Reconstruction." *MDAIK* 56: 377–95.

————. 2004. "Before the Pyramids: Early Developments in Egyptian Royal Funerary Ideology." In *Egypt at Its Origins [1]: Studies in Memory of Barbara Adams. Proceedings of the International Conference "Origin of the State: Predynastic and Early Dynastic Egypt," Kraków, 28th August–1st September 2002*, edited by S. Hendrickx, R.F. Friedman, K.M. Ciałowicz, and M. Chłodnicki, 1129–42. Leuven: Peeters.

Williams, B. 1988. "Narmer and the Coptos Colossi." *JARCE* 25: 35–59.

Wilson, C.W. 1869. *Ordnance Survey of the Peninsula of Sinai*. 5 vols. Southampton: Ordnance Survey.

Winlock, H.E. 1917. "Bas-reliefs from the Egyptian Delta." *BMMA* 12: 64–67.

Woolley, C.L. 1934. *The Royal Cemetery*. Ur Excavations 2. London: Trustees of the British Museum & Museum of the University of Pennsylvania.

Wreszinski, W. 1909. *Der grosse medizinische Papyrus des Berliner Museums (Pap. Berl. 3038)*. Leipzig: Hinrichs.

Yeivin, S. 1968. "Additional Notes on the Early Relations between Canaan and Egypt." *JNES* 27: 37–50.

SOURCES OF IMAGES

All images by the author, except as otherwise noted.

3   Courtesy Renée Friedman.
4   Bottom: Kemp 1973: pl. xxiv.
9   © German Archaeological Institute, Cairo.
12   Garstang 1905b: fig. 1-3.
14   Drawing Quibell and Green 1900–1902: pl. xxviB.
16   Top: © German Archaeological Institute, Cairo.
     Bottom: Dyan Hilton.
17   Inset: De Morgan 1896–97: 2:157, fig. 521.
19   © German Archaeological Institute, Cairo.
22   Reg Clark.
23   Murnane 1987: fig. 1a–b.
24   Dyan Hilton.
26   Bottom: Emery 1938: 64, fig. 26.
28   Dyan Hilton.
29   © German Archaeological Institute, Cairo.
30   © German Archaeological Institute, Cairo.
37   © German Archaeological Institute, Cairo.
40   Quibell and Green 1900–1902: pl. xxxvi.
43   Renée Friedman.
44   Quibell and Green 1900–1902: pl. lxv.
46   © German Archaeological Institute, Cairo; inset: Farag 1980: pl. 26.
49   Inset: Garstang 1903: pl. x[7].
50   Garstang 1903: pl. vii.
52   Gardiner and Peet 1917: pls. i, iv.
54   Quibell 1913: pls. v, xxix.
65   Adapted from Firth and Quibell 1935: pls. 20, 22.

66   Chris Naunton.
67   Adapted from Firth and Quibell 1935: pl. 21.
68   Top: Segato and Valeriani 1835: pl. 37D[i]; bottom: Chris Naunton.
69   Bottom left: Chris Naunton.
70   Firth and Quibell 1935: pl. 47.
71   Martin Davies.
72   Richard Sellicks.
75   Goneim 1957: pl. xiii.
77   Goneim 1957: pl. iv.
79   Goneim 1957: pls. xxx, lvii.
80   Bottom: courtesy MMA.
81   Adapted from Lauer 1972: 580, fig. 1.
82   Left: Julia Thorne, courtesy Garstang Museum; right: Garstang 1903: pl. xix[7].
84   Garstang 1903: pl. xviii.
86   Google Earth; left: Hussein Bassir.
87   Geoffrey Lenox-Smith.
88   Courtesy Museum of Fine Arts, Boston.
89   Goedicke 1956b: 22.
90   Bottom: © Charles University, Faculty of Arts, 2021.
93   a: Dennis C. Forbes; b: Reg Clark; c: Dyan Hilton.
94   Top: Tarek Swelim; middle & bottom: Lepsius 1849–59: 1:pl. 12.
97   Reisner 1910: fig. 1.
101   Mariette 1869–80: 2:pl. 28–30.
107   Adapted from pharaoh.com and Gardiner 1959: pls. i, ii.
109   Courtesy Peter Lundström.
110   Gauthier 1906: 42.
111   David Moyer.
112   Left: Mission française des fouilles de Tanis/Christelle Desbordes; right: MMA.
113   Erman 1900: 115.
114   Top: author; bottom: Lepsius 1849–59: 3:pl. 275.
116   Left: MMA.
117   Epigraphic Survey 1940: pl. 213.
118   Segato and Valeriani 1835: pl. 37B-D[ii].
120   Courtesy Peter Lundström.
121   Base photograph courtesy Peter Lundström.
122   Top: courtesy Peter Lundström; bottom Mariette 1864: pl. xvii.
123   Bottom: Mariette 1866: pl. ii*bis*.
124   Naville 1903: pl. i.
127   Amélineau 1899b: pls. ii[5], iii[13].
128   Petrie 1900–1901: 2:pl. i.
129   Quibell and Green 1900–1902: pl. xlvii.
130   Dyan Hilton.

INDEX

Kings of Egypt are given in CAPITALS.

Alphanumerics in parentheses are those of an individual's tomb.